'In this timely book, Professor Wiggins captures the intricate complexities of children's interactions with food by entering into "a world that is at once both utterly mundane and unexpectedly extraordinary". By carefully unpacking real-life occurrences of eating-in-interaction in fine detail, a fascinating world of one of the most fundamental activities we engage in from birth is brought to a contemporary context. Crossing disciplinary boundaries between anthropology, linguistics, psychology, and sociology, a rich backdrop of research on children's eating foregrounds chapters of empirical research from a multidisciplinary and 'interactional approach'. Each chapter gently guides the reader through unfolding discussions and examples of interactions to reveal carefully crafted and deeply insightful analysis of children's social eating practices as they naturally occur with others. Readers will enjoy greater insight into how children engage with milk feeding when infants, and are supported to eat independently, experience sensory tasting – including food likes and dislikes - and achieve a sense of fullness (or satiety), all as social activities. This deep dive into children's eating practices is essential reading for all those interested in children's social activities and eating interactions – two essential ingredients of life!'

Professor Amanda Bateman, *Department of Education, Birmingham City University, UK*

'Have you ever wondered about mealtime interactions between children and their families? If so, this book takes the everyday behaviour of children's social eating and provides an in-depth exploration of an apparently simple act, offering a thoughtful, multidisciplinary account of family mealtimes. Research on the language, psychology, sociology and anthropology of eating together is carefully and critically presented. Then a practical guide is offered to support future research with a plea to include greater cooperation between disciplines. So much can be learned about us as humans from the ways in which we interact during meals. Particularly given the biological imperative to eat set against the interpersonal dynamics of the family unit and the wider sociocultural, political and commercial structures underpinning the food supply. There is no other book which presents interactional research on children's mealtimes with such clarity, care and precision. Overall, a wonderful resource for placing interactional approaches at the centre of how children eat.'

Marion M. Hetherington, *BSc (Hons), DipEd, DPhil (Oxon), Professor Emerita, School of Psychology, University of Leeds, UK, Affiliate Professor, School of Nutritional Sciences, Penn State University, USA*

'This book is an innovative addition to the literature on the myriad aspects of children's eating. Not only is it a practical manual on the conduct of interactional research; it also serves as a novel basis for interdisciplinary work in a field unduly limited by disciplinary fragmentation. It is thus an invaluable landmark for researchers and students at all levels.'

Anne Murcott, *Honorary Professorial Research Associate, SOAS, University of London, Professor Emerita, London South Bank University, UK*

'Children's mealtimes are a microcosm of the social world, infused with morality, politics, power, pleasure, and negotiation as much as nutrition. In this rich and timely book, Sally Wiggins moves beyond idealised accounts of the family meal to show, with analytical precision, how eating together is collaboratively accomplished in everyday life. Drawing on ethnomethodology, conversation analysis, discursive psychology, and language socialisation, she offers both a conceptual reorientation and a practical guide to researching the intricate interplay of food, language, and bodies. This is an indispensable resource for scholars across anthropology, linguistics, psychology, and sociology, and a landmark contribution to the interactional study of children's eating.'

Alexa Hepburn, *Professor Emerita, School of Communication and Information Rutgers, the State University of New Jersey, USA, Honorary Professor, Department of Communication and Media, Loughborough University, UK*

RESEARCHING CHILDREN'S MEALTIMES

This groundbreaking interdisciplinary guide explores children's eating practices through the lens of social interaction. It moves beyond individualistic perspectives to uncover the rich, everyday dynamics of mealtimes, where children's eating is shaped by family, peers, and caregivers. Drawing on 25 years of research, the book provides a comprehensive framework for conducting interactional analyses of children's eating practices in real-life settings.

Using video-recorded examples from family homes and preschool environments, it illustrates how ethnomethodology, conversation analysis, discursive psychology, and language socialisation can uncover the intricate interplay of food, language, and social behaviour. From infants' first experiences with milk feeding to children's evolving food preferences, the book examines key topics such as weaning, sensory tasting, food likes and dislikes, hunger and satiety, and food refusals. Each chapter combines theoretical insights with practical guidance, offering a rich synthesis of literature reviews, data examples, and suggestions for future research. The book equips readers with the analytical tools to study children's eating practices and inspires interdisciplinary collaboration by bridging anthropology, psychology, linguistics, and sociology.

With its accessible yet rigorous approach, *Researching Children's Mealtimes* is an essential resource for researchers and students across the social sciences. Whether you are a novice researcher or an experienced scholar, this book offers a unique contribution to the study of children's eating practices and a vital tool for advancing research in this field.

Sally Wiggins Young is Professor of Discursive Psychology at Linköping University, Sweden. Her research focuses on examining social interaction during children's eating practices in family mealtimes and preschool lunches.

RESEARCHING CHILDREN'S MEALTIMES

A Practical Guide for Interactional Analyses of Children's Eating Practices in Everyday Settings

Sally Wiggins

Routledge
Taylor & Francis Group
LONDON AND NEW YORK

Designed cover image: Getty Image

First published 2027
by Routledge
4 Park Square, Milton Park, Abingdon, Oxon OX14 4RN

and by Routledge
605 Third Avenue, New York, NY 10158

Routledge is an imprint of the Taylor & Francis Group, an informa business

British Library Cataloguing-in-Publication Data
A catalogue record for this book is available from the British Library

ISBN: 978-1-032-86873-8 (hbk)
ISBN: 978-1-032-86850-9 (pbk)
ISBN: 978-1-003-52962-0 (ebk)

DOI: 10.4324/9781003529620

Typeset in Galliard
by Apex CoVantage, LLC

Access the Support Material: www.routledge.com/9781032868509

To Angus and Callum, who saw both sides.

To Angus and Callum, who saw both sides.

CONTENTS

LIST OF FIGURES

LIST OF BOXES

ABOUT THE AUTHOR

Sally Wiggins Young is Professor of Discursive Psychology at Linköping University, Sweden. Her research focuses on examining social interaction during children's eating practices in family mealtimes and preschool lunches, with other research topics including problem-based learning interaction. She is the author of a methods textbook (*Discursive Psychology*), three co-edited books (*Critical Bodies*, *Discursive Research in Practice*, and *Discursive Psychology and Embodiment*), and numerous book chapters and journal articles. Born in the north of England and having spent much of her life in Scotland, she now lives with her family in Sweden. She uses only the first part of her surname for publications.

PREFACE

This might be a good place to confess that I didn't start out with an interest in how children eat. I just wanted to understand why eating talk seemed to matter so much. Recording family mealtimes was the simplest solution at that time. What followed was nearly three decades of research which demonstrated, in spectacularly vibrant detail, how interesting and important children's mealtimes are. This book is an accumulation of things that I have learned along the way. It is a research manual and practical guide for all those who wish to understand how children eat in everyday settings, to unpack concepts such as hunger, taste, food likes, refusal, and satiety, as these are invoked and become consequential during mealtimes. This preface sketches out why this book is needed, who it is for, how to use it, information about the data examples used in the book, and the backstory to how the book came to be written.

Why this book is needed

Despite eating being fundamental to life and a basic form of human sociality, empirical and detailed research into how children *actually* eat, in everyday settings, is comparatively scarce. Most of the research into children's food consumption is based on parental questionnaires and interviews, experiments, and a limited number of observational studies. This is not due to a lack of interest in the sociality of eating. There is widespread scholarly consensus that being with other people matters and that the social context makes a difference. What is missing is knowledge about how this happens when children eat in everyday settings. Disciplinary nuances have led researchers along different research trajectories that often have prescribed methods and assumptions about research topics. Certain ways of doing research become normative, and these lead to constraints on the kinds of questions that can be asked.

Meanwhile, interactional approaches to research – those that have pioneered video-based analyses of the details of language and social interaction in everyday settings – have been emerging within interdisciplinary spaces for around half a century. These approaches have shown in extraordinary depth the complexity of what happens when people interact with one another, moment by moment. A substantial proportion of this domain of research is focused on family mealtimes, eating practices, and children's interaction. Research in this area is of great relevance for understanding how children eat. Perhaps because it sits in an interdisciplinary space and does not easily fit into disciplinary categories or methodological boxes, however, it has typically been overlooked, ignored, or dismissed. And so the gap between research fields and researchers widens.

This book is needed to bring together research from across a multidisciplinary landscape to advance empirical work into children's everyday eating practices. More collaboration is needed across disciplines. This book offers a unique contribution to research on children's mealtimes by traversing disciplinary boundaries and demonstrating the value and potential of interactional and interdisciplinary research. The time to do this has never been more urgent. Children's health and wellbeing is dependent on their food consumption, and environmental, economic, and political changes continue to impact on the food that is available and expectations around how to eat. Children's mealtimes are where it all starts.

Who this book is for

Given the multidisciplinary framework within which the book is situated, it is aimed at a wide audience; although it is likely to be of particular interest to those within the social sciences and cognate disciplines, such as anthropology, childhood studies, early years education, linguistics, paediatric nutrition, psychology, and sociology. There are no expectations about readership in terms of level of research expertise or experience: it should suit a student as much as a senior academic. Terminology has been explained as clearly as possible, to allow readers to become familiar with concepts used in different disciplines. Some readers may already be familiar with interactional approaches, though care has been taken to make no assumptions about this and to explain analytical principles with examples. There is a risk, of course, that addressing a broad multidisciplinary audience means that some aspects of theory or analysis are overly simplified or misrepresented. Hopefully, this risk is balanced by ensuring that the book is widely accessible. For those who have interests that do not fit neatly into one research genre or discipline, you are particularly welcome.

In this multidisciplinary landscape, it is an advantage to be able to reach across boundaries and to examine research from multiple perspectives. Explore the landscape and find your place to thrive.

How to use this book

All readers should start with the first chapter, to become familiar with the core topics discussed in the book and for a guide to subsequent chapters. For those who are entirely new to interactional approaches, it will be worth spending time on Chapters 2 and 3, to become attuned to the underlying principles of different approaches and the methods used for ensuring good-quality video-recordings for analysis. Some disciplines and approaches pull more towards theory than method, so find a way through the book that fits your own research interests and disciplinary home. Readers who are already familiar with interactional analyses might wish to go straight to the analytical chapters (Chapters 4 to 8), dipping into Chapters 2 and 3 as required.

The analytical chapters (Chapters 4 to 8) are themselves based around the core interactional projects that make up children's mealtimes – from first mouthfuls to developing tastes and establishing likes, and finally to negotiating refusals and achieving satiety. They do not, therefore, work with topics such as parental strategies or family dynamics. Instead, they begin by approaching eating from an interactional standpoint: with how things happen during mealtimes. These chapters start with an overview of literature within the focal area to help readers to navigate some of the core issues and concepts (as well as citations to assist with literature searches) within that field. The 'how to' sections that follow have been written specifically with novice researchers in mind, to guide readers through some of the basic principles of interactional research. Examples are taken from my own data collection (see the section below) to provide real-life clips that demonstrate core features of interactional analyses. These sections do not provide polished analyses; nor do they discuss everything that might be analysed in the data – that would require a book in itself. The point is instead to demonstrate routes into analyses and to inspire readers to look for similar issues in their own data.

The analytical chapters continue with an illustrated research example from published papers (there are five of these in total, each from my own publications) to provide more detail on the kinds of analyses can be done. There is then a description of interactional research that has already been conducted in the relevant area, which can be used as the foundation from which further work can be based. Finally, concrete suggestions for how interactional research might be used are provided; each of these might be a project or separate avenue of research in itself. In sum, these chapters are jam-packed with references and conceptual tools to navigate the literature and analytical examples to inspire readers to conduct their own research in this area.

Chapter 9 is a reflective chapter, summarising key issues addressed in the book while also looking ahead into new territory; it can thus be referred to when a wider perspective on the contents of the book is needed. Otherwise, each chapter is self-contained and can be read in isolation, in any order.

The data and examples used in this book

Video recordings embody the heart of the book and the examples used are taken from two large data corpora that I have collected over the last few decades.

The first corpus comprises family mealtimes, including a subset of infant meals, recorded in homes in England and Scotland between 2000 and 2014 (with one recorded in Sweden; see Extract 4.1 in Chapter 4, given with the kind permission of Emily Hofstetter). In all cases, parents used video cameras to record meals in their own homes, at their own pace, without any further researcher involvement. The recordings aimed to collect examples of 'real' everyday family mealtimes, to capture life as it happens, uncensored. No funding was received for the collection of this data, save for a small departmental fund to support a student assistant during one summer. Ethical approval was obtained from the University of Strathclyde prior to data collection and all parents gave permission for sections of anonymised transcript and images to be used in published work.

The second corpus comprises preschool lunches in Sweden, recorded between 2021 and 2022, collected for a project funded by the Swedish Research Council, with subsequent analyses funded by FORMAS and Riksbankens Jubileumsfond. Ethical approval was given by the Swedish Ethical Review Authority and written informed consent was gained from both parents/guardians for each child and for staff members to include sections of anonymised transcript and images in published work. The ages of the children shown in the extracts are given in the form (y;m) to indicate years and months (e.g. (5;6) means five years, six months), unless stated otherwise (e.g. 'five months old'; 'four years old'). The staff members had a mix of roles and levels of professional education (e.g. some were trained preschool teachers) and have been named as either teachers or caregivers throughout the book.

The mealtimes recorded in family homes were collected before screens (e.g. tablets, smartphones) became more prominent and thus reflect mealtimes where digital technologies were not explicitly present. In the preschools, such mobile devices were available but not present during mealtimes, save for the occasional moment when teachers checked something on their phones (though this was a rare occurrence). The language spoken in the family meal corpus is English, and in the preschool lunch corpus it is Swedish. No other demographic information about participants (e.g. socioeconomic status, ethnic/racial category, or dietary requirements) was collected. Most of the examples used in this book are taken from children up to the age of ten years, with several from infancy (up to two years) and at around five years old. The adults in the data clips are at times named as 'Mum'/'Dad', as 'Parent', or as 'Teacher'/'Caregiver' for the preschool examples.

The backstory of the book

This is the book that I wish had existed over 30 years ago. As a psychology graduate who loved studying and was curious about people, I gravitated towards research. Serendipity brought me to Loughborough University in England, where discursive and interactional research was burgeoning. Thanks to the nurturing guidance of Jonathan Potter, Derek Edwards, Charles Antaki, Mick Billig, and many other eminent scholars, I gradually found my feet.

The research began long before I had kids of my own. Imagine, if you can, an age before digital video cameras, smartphones, and YouTube: such was the situation in England in the late 1990s. A clunky cassette recorder was all that was available and, as a somewhat naive doctoral student, I began with family mealtimes because I thought that they were the best chance I had to capture conversations about eating. The families themselves were slightly bemused as to why their mealtimes would be of interest: surely research should be focused on more important matters than what they ate for dinner? Given that the only home videos that people were familiar with at that time were those seen on TV programmes such as *You've Been Framed* or *America's Funniest Home Videos*, their bafflement was not misplaced.

In the decades that followed, those analogue cassettes were replaced by digital video cameras and the rise of video in everyday life. Most of my research on family mealtimes was squeezed into gaps between teaching and other work commitments and repeated rejections of grant applications. Then I began raising a family of my own and suddenly the kids started to matter. While remaining in my home discipline of psychology, analyses of the video data frequently took me down rabbit-holes across and between disciplines, shattering any presumptions about language, eating, and children. Much of my work has thus been an attempt to bring together disparate fields of research, in a manner not dissimilar to introducing strangers at a party in the hope that they might find mutual areas of interest.

Moving countries and acquiring a new language have provided further depth to this sense of trying to understand something from different perspectives. Something never looks the same once you've seen it from the other side. My journey through this research landscape has thus been in parts one of curiosity, determination, good fortune, and the privilege afforded to those who are white and middle-class, with English as their first language. The structured organisation of this book is in no way a reflection of the journey that it took to get here. I went the long way round; this book is your shortcut.

ACKNOWLEDGEMENTS

This book is for the kids and all those who nourish them. Having studied children's mealtimes for a considerable part of my life, I can confirm that they really are the most incredible yet underrated area to research. Heartfelt thanks, therefore, to all the children, their parents and caregivers, and the preschool staff, for capturing the magic on film.

I would not have been able to write this book had it not been for the generous funding of Riksbankens Jubileumsfond for a sabbatical year and the time to bring together things that have been taking up considerable head space for many years. I am also indebted to the Swedish Research Council and FORMAS for funding the preschool projects. Having conducted much of my earlier work on family mealtimes in my 'spare' time, you have no idea what a difference that made. Warm gratitude to Routledge for publishing this book and to my editor, Molly Selby, for unwavering patience and enthusiastic support.

There are innumerable scholars whose work and support has guided my own research over the years, but some deserve a particular thanks here. First, to those students at Strathclyde University who helped with recording family meals and inspired future analyses. To the preschool project team who never failed to match my levels of enthusiasm about the research: Jakob Cromdal, Annerose Willemsen, and Sandra Nyberg-Akremi. To my brilliant co-authors on some of the most fun writing projects about eating in interaction: Bogdana Humă, Leelo Keevallik, Eric Laurier, and Amy Van der Heijden. I would never have got here without the scholarly inspiration and collegial support from the brilliant members of the SIS Interaction group at Linköping University and our regular data sessions. A warm thank you to Mancy Bateman, Marion Hetherington, Annemarie Mol, and Anne Murcott for encouragement at key stages in the writing process. Finally, I owe Emily Hofstetter, Eric Laurier, and Liz Stokoe a stack of tea and cakes for their invaluable feedback and support; I am especially grateful to Emily for permission to use the video clip in Chapter 4. The book is considerably better thanks to all of your suggestions. I am of course entirely responsible for any remaining errors and omissions.

This book could not have been written without sci-fi, the music of Hildur Gudnadóttir, and forests to hide in. Each of these things provided the mental and physical spaces required to do the writing. Copious amounts of Assam Hatimara CTC also helped (thanks, Liz). Our Great Dane, Björk, provided round-the-clock therapy and really does deserve more snacks. It is not without irony that the last months of writing the book had me abandon my own family mealtimes on several occasions. Final thanks, therefore, to H, Angus, and Cal, for unconditional love and support and for tolerating my singular focus on writing the book for much longer than expected.

1

ON RESEARCHING CHILDREN'S MEALTIMES

To research how children eat in social settings is to enter a world that is at once both utterly mundane and unexpectedly extraordinary. These are settings in which people can thrive or starve, experience gustatory pleasure or visceral disgust, receive encouragement or encounter threats, and be socialised into lifelong social and cultural practices – all in the space of anywhere between one minute and one hour. Few other research areas hold the potential for the diversity of topics that can be examined and analytical approaches that can be used, or indeed the variation in how the context itself can unfold. Children's mealtimes are not just about meals; they are a microcosm of everything that we think we know about eating. Eating is infused with morals, politics, knowledge, and power, as much as it is with nutrition. Children's eating practices begin at the very start of life and are essential for development into adulthood. In short, they are the basis for everything that follows. This book is a practical guide for conducting research into this microcosmic world of how children eat with other people.

The book has two core aims. The first is to create a scholarly space within a multidisciplinary landscape to encourage greater collaboration across and within disciplines. No single discipline can claim ownership of research into how children eat; nor can it provide all the answers. Fragmentation across this landscape has been a hindrance to the development of new ideas and empirical work, and much more needs to be done to capture the complexity and variety of how children eat. The second aim is to offer a practical guide to the intellectual frameworks and analytical stances of conducting interactional research on children's mealtimes. These involve detailed empirical analyses of video recordings of eating in everyday life, focusing on the intersection between food, language, and bodies within social interaction. Interactional approaches

DOI: 10.4324/9781003529620-1

to research are not tied to any specific discipline and are ideally placed to be used within this multidisciplinary landscape.

This introductory chapter sets out the main argument of the book: that – despite widespread consensus that the social context is important for how children eat – disciplinary boundaries and diverging research trajectories have meant that the details of how children 'eat together' are typically treated as analytically unavailable or reduced to individual factors. Yet work already exists that reveals the intricate details of social interaction. Interdisciplinary in their roots, interactional approaches such as ethnomethodology and conversation analysis (EMCA), discursive psychology (DP), and language socialisation (LS) provide robust and established analytical frameworks that enable researchers to empirically investigate the interactional details of children's meals while addressing fundamental questions about how children eat. This chapter lays the foundations for the rest of the book and points ahead to the remaining chapters.

Social interaction as fundamental to children's eating practices

From the very beginning of life, eating involves the participation of other people. The social dimensions of eating are so crucial, in fact, that human survival depends on them. Without the assistance of caregivers to ensure that milk and solid food are transferred into mouths, and to facilitate the process of chewing and swallowing food, infants would perish. This dependence on others is, however, not to be confused with passivity. Even in the first weeks of life, social interaction is a collaborative event in which caregiver and infant are mutually responsive to each other and in which infants actively engage with their surroundings (Trevarthen & Aitken, 2001). Newborns can turn their heads and open their mouths to receive milk, for instance, or turn away to reject it; their actions are meaningful and consequential. Children's eating practices are, from the start, an active process embedded within, and scaffolded by, social interaction. The importance of social interaction for children's food consumption has long been recognised across the social sciences, and the rest of this section discusses three core research areas in which this has been particularly notable: commensality, family meals, and social influence.

Commensality as a normative ideal

Eating together is firmly established as one of the most basic forms of human sociality. Referred to across the social sciences as 'commensality' (Fischler, 2011; Grignon, 2001; Murcott, 2019; Neuman, 2024), it has been variably defined, with a weak version denoted simply as 'eating with other people' (Sobal & Nelson, 2003: 181) and a strong version incorporating hierarchies of social relations determining who eats with whom (Bloch, 2020; Grignon,

2001). There are differing forms of commensality, some of which have particular relevance for children, such as the shared meals that take place in family homes (James et al, 2009; Persson Osowski & Mattson Sydner, 2019; Udagawa, 2022), kindergarten (O'Leary, 2022; Wergedahl, 2024), and schools (Lalli, 2017; Stone & Murakami, 2023). Eating with other people is not only central to human sociality; it is also a foundational aspect of many children's eating routines in the home and beyond.

The idea of commensality is not simply about sharing food and meals; it is also about what happens while people are eating together and the benefits that this might bring. For instance, it is considered important for maintaining social relationships (Bloch, 2020; Grignon, 2001); has been associated with positive health and wellbeing outcomes for children (e.g. Neumark-Sztainer et al, 2013; Snuggs & Harvey, 2023); and has been associated with healthier eating practices and lower rates of depressive symptoms among young people (e.g. Hammons & Fiese, 2011; Videon & Manning, 2003). The idealistic aspects of commensality are further evident in work that discusses the importance of what is sometimes called a 'positive mealtime environment', in which enjoyable eating experiences are balanced with a relaxed atmosphere, which is deemed important for developing good eating practices in children (e.g. Mita et al, 2015). Eating together is thus often considered as more than the sum of its parts: it brings added value to the otherwise individual needs of consuming food.

Commensality, however, does not automatically or necessarily result in a convivial atmosphere when people eat food together (Jönsson et al, 2021; Neuman & Jönsson, 2024). Enjoyment is not a given. Sharing a table is much more complicated than simply eating in the same physical space. Over-emphasising the idea – or the ideal – of commensality can further lead to assumptions about its benefits without examining in detail what actually happens when people gather to eat. As Murcott warns, 'reliance on the weak version risks eclipsing even asking about, let alone documenting, the extent of disharmony, exclusion, the unequal distribution of labour or of satisfaction of preferences' (2019: 47). Commensality is a valuable concept, but at times there has been an assumption that the act of eating together is by definition a Good Thing – and this is particularly the case where family meals are concerned.

The idyllic family meal?

The family meal has received considerable attention in terms of its moral status as foundational to societal values around not only food, but also families and cultural ideals (see Murcott, 1997, 2012, 2013, 2019). As a corollary, concerns have been raised, in scholarly discourse as well as public media, over the apparent 'decline' of the family meal. Eating as a family unit – and the assumed benefits that it provides – is considered to be under threat from social trends that encourage individualistic eating practices, such as grazing or snacking (Fischler, 1980), selective diets (Fischler, 2013), and an explosion of fast-food outlets and eating out (Ritzer, 2000) resulting in shorter, rushed meals eaten alone (Yates & Warde, 2017). While there may be little doubt that the abundance and wide availability of food within urban landscapes have changed eating practices, this does not necessarily correspond to how families eat together in the home. There is, more importantly, a paucity of evidence that eating together *regularly* as a family was ever so historically and culturally pervasive (Jönsson et al, 2021; Murcott, 2012, 2019; Riley & Paugh, 2018). As Murcott (2012) argues, there has been something of a moral panic around the apparently dwindling frequency of the family meal.

The status of the family meal as both a cultural ideal and a panacea for social ills has therefore been challenged as overly simplistic and moralistic (Jönsson et al, 2021; Lestar et al, 2024; Le Moal et al, 2024; Murcott, 2013; Skafida, 2013; Wilk, 2010). As Wilk argues, 'on survey form, a meal where everyone shares jokes and tells stories is the same as one where everyone stares at their plate bolting food silently under the glare of an angry father' (2010: 432). The idyllic family meal, in which everyone is happy and eats the same food without complaints, is in some situations an unrealistic ideal. Commensality research has been skewed towards emphasising the benefits of eating together while glossing over the details of what happens when people interact during shared meals. Moreover, the ideal does not take into account variations in the circumstances in which families live and eat. Eating as a family is not always considered an aspirational or moral obligation (e.g. Helton et al, 2023; Jarrett et al, 2016; Riley & Paugh, 2018; Tuomainen, 2014). The commensality literature is, moreover, based to a large extent on surveys or interviews primarily from white, heterosexual, middle-class populations within Euro-American cultures, and does not represent everyday realities for much of the world.

The truth is that very little is known about what actually transpires when children eat with others in everyday homes, in all their variations. A combination of assumptions around commensality as a normative ideal and the moral burden placed on family mealtimes has resulted in a tendency towards romanticising meals in the home (e.g. Holm & Lund, 2019). At the same time, research that aims to capture social trends about commensality and family meals has often used methods such as surveys or census data that illustrate broader societal patterns but lack detailed information about the nuances of social interaction around a table. The family mealtime is at risk of becoming a black box, of which much might be known about its surrounding environment, but whose contents are, at times, observed through a rose-tinted window.

Social influences on the individual

The third area of research that has acknowledged the importance of the social context on children's eating practices and afforded a glimpse into the black box of eating together is psychological research on social influences (e.g. Birch, 1980; Meiselman, 1992; see Cruwys et al, 2015 for an overview). Early research into social facilitation, for example, demonstrated that people typically eat more in the presence of others than they do when alone (De Castro, 1991, 1997; Herman et al, 2003; Pliner & Mann, 2004). This area of work has long recognised that eating with others has implications for adults' and children's eating practices (Birch & Fisher, 1998). In contrast to writing on commensality and family meals, this work endeavours to empirically investigate the social processes through which children's eating is influenced by others.

Psychological research in this area has generated a considerable amount of work examining the various factors that can influence how (and what) children eat in social settings, with a substantial proportion of this focusing on parental feeding styles or strategies (e.g. Schratz et al, 2023; Shloim et al, 2015a). These include behavioural styles that are labelled 'authoritarian' or 'authoritative', which translate into specific behavioural strategies such as requiring or encouraging children to eat certain foods (e.g. Ventura & Birch, 2008). This research has shown, for instance, that parental lack of responsiveness to children's satiety cues can be associated with weight gain and health issues (e.g. DiSantis et al, 2011; Lumeng et al, 2012; Redsell et al, 2021). Other research has examined the influence that adults (e.g. Addessi et al, 2005; Mitchell et al, 2013; Palfreyman et al, 2015) or peers (e.g. Farrow et al, 2011; Ragelienė & Grønhøj, 2020; Street et al, 2024) can have on children's food consumption, such as through modelling, in which children imitate or match the eating habits of their dining companions (Blissett, 2018; Cruwys et al, 2015). This expansive body of work has demonstrated not only that the social context is important for children's eating practices but also that parents (and other caregivers) and peers can have a particularly significant impact.

In summary, there is widespread agreement across these three scholarly areas that eating with other people matters. Eating together is considered a central aspect of human sociality, of being a family, and something that has consequences for what and how children eat. While this literature and empirical work have begun to examine the social factors that can impact on children's eating practices, very little of this research examines mealtimes in everyday situations. The details of *how* social influence occurs, therefore, are less well understood. It is when the disciplinary divergences of research are considered that it becomes clearer how these gaps in understanding have appeared.

The multidisciplinary research landscape of children's mealtimes

There is no shortage of academic interest in how children eat. Literature on food consumption throughout childhood can be found in disciplines such as anthropology, history, linguistics, nutrition science, philosophy, psychology, and sociology, as well as many interdisciplinary fields such as childhood studies, early years education, and paediatric nutrition. In terms of how children eat *with other people* – that is, at mealtimes and in other social settings where food is consumed – the research domain becomes a little more focused. As discussed in the previous section, there is a solid evidence base across different research areas that demonstrates the importance of social interaction for children's eating practices. Four disciplines have been particularly important for research that examines the sociality of eating: anthropology, linguistics, psychology, and sociology. This section provides a brief guide to these disciplines to help readers navigate this complex terrain. It is not possible, of course, to adequately summarise the diversity and richness of these areas, so the aim here is to point to some of the intellectual foci that have helped to shape the landscape of work on children's eating practices in social settings. Each discipline is briefly overviewed before discussing how their diverging research trajectories have pulled in somewhat opposing directions.

Anthropology

Anthropological research – particularly that situated within linguistic anthropology and social anthropology – has been pivotal in illuminating the importance of language as a medium through which children are socialised into culturally relevant ways of eating (Cavanaugh et al, 2014; Cavanaugh & Riley, 2023; Riley & Paugh, 2018). From the work of Lévi-Strauss (1966/2012) and Douglas (Douglas, 1972; Douglas & Nicod, 1974) on the structural properties of meals, the mealtime has long been a focal point for understanding how culture is woven into and through food and eating practices. Ochs' groundbreaking research on family meals was important not only for demonstrating how children are socialised into culturally appropriate eating and language practices (e.g. Ochs, Pontecorvo & Fasulo, 1996; Ochs & Shohet, 2006) but also, together with Schieffelin, for the development of LS (Schieffelin & Ochs, 1986; Ochs & Schieffelin, 1979; see Chapter 2). For collections on the anthropology of food, see Counihan and van Esterik's (1997) *Food and culture: A reader*, Riley and Paugh's (2018) *Food and language*, and Paugh and Riley's (forthcoming) *Food talk.*

Linguistics

The importance of language is, of course, familiar ground for linguistics; and work within naturally occurring language, such as that studied within the ethnography of communication and interactional sociolinguistics, has been particularly important for examining how children acquire and are socialised into language practices in everyday settings. Family mealtimes have been used as a prime data source and some of the earlier work in this area has demonstrated how children acquire and develop language skills around the dinner table (e.g. Aukrust & Snow, 1998; Beals, 1997; Beals & Snow, 1994; Forrester, 2008; Pan et al, 1999; Snow & Beals, 2006). The analytical focus on the details of everyday language practices has been pivotal in showing how language is acquired during mealtimes (e.g. in preschools; Kultti, 2014), children's natural language practices (e.g. Gardner & Forrester, 2009), and the interconnectedness between food and language (e.g. Riley & Paugh, 2018). For collections on food and linguistics, see Gerhardt, Frobenius, and Ley's (2013) *Culinary Linguistics*, Rüdiger and Mühleisen (2020) *Talking about food*, and Szatrowski's (2014) *Language and food*.

Psychology

Research into the psychological aspects of eating dates back to Clara Davis's (1939) work on children's self-selection of foods and Cannon and Washburn's experiments on gastric hunger in adults (Cannon, 1934; Cannon & Washburn, 1912). The pioneering research of Birch on children's eating practices (e.g. Birch, 1979, 1980) was particularly important for inspiring a legacy of work on children's eating practices, specifically concerning the development of food likes (see Hetherington & Chawner, 2022, for an overview). While the individual is typically the focus of study in psychological research, the social context and the influences of peers or parents have long been recognised as having an impact on children's food consumption (e.g. Higgs & Ruddock, 2020; Houldcraft et al, 2014). Parental feeding styles or strategies and their impact on children's eating practices have been a common point of interest (e.g. Blissett, 2011; Schratz et al, 2023). For collections on the psychology of eating, see Chaffee and da Silva's (2022) *A guide to the psychology of eating*, Lumeng and Fisher's (2018) *Pediatric food preferences and eating behaviors*, and Splane et al's (2024) *Psychology of eating*.

Sociology

Sociological research into societal norms and practices around eating, and work on commensality, have been essential in establishing the meal as a central focus of analysis (e.g. Simmel, 1910; Symons, 1994). Research on the sociology of food and eating has examined topics such as taste (Warde, 1997), manners (Mennell, 1996), rules (Grieshaber, 1997), eating out (Finkelstein, 1989; Warde & Martens, 2000) and the pleasures and morals of eating (Coveney, 2006). Early research on the family mealtime was particularly important for demonstrating the gendered and social class divisions of labour surrounding children's meals (Charles & Kerr, 1986; Delphy, 1980; De Vault, 1991; Murcott, 1982). Subsequent work in this area has illustrated the importance of examining children's eating practices as embedded within organisational structures of families, working life, and leisure practices (e.g. Brannen et al, 2013; Middleton et al, 2022). For collections on the sociology of food and eating, see James, Kjørholt, and Tingstad's (2009) *Children, food, and identity in everyday life*, Germov and Williams' (2017) *A sociology of food and nutrition*, and Murcott's (2019) *Introducing the sociology of food and eating.*

BOX 1.1 DEFINING MULTIDISCIPLINARITY

Research on how children eat with other people, as discussed in this chapter, is not wholly conducted within one discipline. For this reason, this book explicitly advocates drawing on multiple disciplines in order to enrich research and stimulate new developments. Using the definitions set out by Choi and Pak (2006), this could be considered akin to multidisciplinarity, where knowledge from across various disciplines is used while maintaining disciplinary distinctions and frameworks. This concept can be compared to interdisciplinarity, which seeks to synthesise disciplines into a coherent whole; and transdisciplinarity, which aims to integrate knowledge and transcend disciplinary boundaries. There is, moreover, a considerable amount of *intra*disciplinary tension: each discipline is not a coherent or homogenous domain.

Diverging research trajectories

The four disciplinary areas briefly sketched above have been of central importance for research into how children eat with other people and specifically (though not exclusively), the importance of family mealtimes. Collectively, they explicate the ways in which food and language are central to children's eating practices. However, the scholarly roots, theoretical influences, and methodological inclinations of each discipline have meant that they continue to develop along diverging research trajectories. Each discipline pulls in a different direction. Psychological research, for instance, values the importance of the social context for individuals, but this is a very different understanding of sociality from that used within sociological research. Social psychology provides a space in which these disciplines might overlap, though children's eating practices are typically studied within other areas (and not necessarily within developmental psychology, as might be expected). Anthropological work, meanwhile, has long demonstrated the importance of language but approaches this differently from linguistic research. Situated at the intersection between these disciplines, linguistic anthropology has done much to blur the boundaries between language and culture, though eating in itself has been less of a concern (though see Mol, 2021, 2024 for an alternative vision).

Disciplinary spaces provide important arenas for the emergence and development of research that contributes to understanding how children eat with others in everyday social settings. It is clear, however, that no single discipline holds all the answers. The divergent research trajectories within each discipline have meant that researchers can be entirely unaware – or at times dismissive – of work in neighbouring fields that could unlock new understandings of a research problem. Methodological preferences and theoretical assumptions have led to constraints on the kinds of research questions that can be asked and what is considered good-quality research.

What is needed is research that goes to the heart of human sociality: to examine how children eat with others without glossing over 'eating together', idealising certain kinds of mealtimes as morally superior, or reducing social interaction to individual factors – that is, to study everyday settings in a rigorous manner without losing the complex choreography that makes up the variability of daily life. This means starting from social interaction rather than from an individual or cultural level of analysis. By beginning with interaction and by working across a multidisciplinary landscape, it soon becomes clear that such research already exists. It is research that cannot be easily placed into a single disciplinary category and that takes interaction seriously, providing the rigorous set of analytical tools needed for researching how children eat in everyday settings.

Interactional and interdisciplinary research on children's eating

One distinctive area of research has examined the details of human sociality within language and social interaction in everyday life since the 1970s. Starting from a focus on social interaction in everyday settings, this collection of what is termed in this book 'interactional approaches' has gathered an enormous range of evidence of what happens when people share a social space. Much of this work has been conducted in settings that either directly correspond to children's eating practices (e.g. during family meals or meals in institutional settings) or have particularly acute relevance for mealtime practices (e.g. how children interact with parents or peers). EMCA, DP, and LS are presented in this book as three core examples of interactional approaches. Collectively, they demonstrate that commensality is not something that happens automatically but is instead an interactional achievement – that is, people interacting together can be shown to move in and out of moments of participation with each other, and these moments constitute what it means to 'be together'.

An overview of the historical roots and research foci of these approaches is presented in Chapter 2; but for now, it is worth considering how they are situated within the aforementioned multidisciplinary landscape and why they are so useful for understanding children's mealtimes. Each of the three approaches emerged within a home discipline but is closely interwoven with at least one other. Sociology is the home discipline of ethnomethodology (through the work of Harold Garfinkel and Erving Goffman) and subsequentially conversation analysis (CA) (e.g. Sacks, Schegloff, & Jefferson, 1974); while EMCA research, such as that on multisensoriality and eating (e.g. Mondada, 2018, 2021, 2023) and children's interaction in homes and institutional settings (e.g. Bateman, 2015; Kidwell, 2011, 2013; Goodwin & Cekaite, 2018), evades disciplinary categorisation and has relevance for research across sensory science and education respectively. CA research is notoriously interdisciplinary (Clift et al, 2024; Sidnell, 2016; Sidnell & Stivers, 2014) and work on family mealtime interaction is a prime example (e.g. Craven & Potter, 2010; Hepburn, 2020a,b; Hepburn & Potter, 2011). While psychology was the home discipline of DP research, work in this area – such as that on the negotiation of children's food likes during family meals (e.g. Van der Heijden et al, 2022; Wiggins, 2014a, 2023; Wiggins et al, 2001) – has a clear relevance for related research in linguistics anthropology and sociology. Anthropology is the home discipline of LS (Ochs & Schieffelin, 1979), though its foundations are also interdisciplinary and LS research – for example, that on how children are socialised into taste in institutional settings such as Japanese kindergartens (Burdelski, 2014, 2025) – has strong connections with linguistics and educational research.

The resistance of these analytical approaches to neat allocation into one or other disciplinary category means that they have at times been unseen, misunderstood, or disregarded. They do not fit into a particular theoretical or methodological box and may be excluded from standard student textbooks. They are used in research across numerous disciplines, but it is often the case that researchers working with other methodologies will be entirely unaware of their existence (Icbay, 2026). This book is an effort to break down the boundaries that have built up across this multidisciplinary landscape and explicate the ways in which interactional approaches provide rigorous analytical tools that can unpack the black box of children's mealtimes. The following sub-sections explain why these approaches are ideally placed to answer research questions about how children eat with other people in social settings.

Interactional approaches provide rigorous and transparent methods

At the core of interactional approaches such as EMCA, DP, and LS is a large corpus of video recordings from real-life settings. These recordings, and the transcripts that accompany them, become the research data that is analysed using rigorous methods that have been established and used by researchers over several decades (see Chapter 3). Much of the 'raw' data – that is, transcripts, still images from the videos, and sometimes clips from the recordings themselves – is presented alongside analyses in published work and presentations, allowing the findings and conclusions from the research to be openly scrutinised. This is what Edwards has referred to as the 'interpretative gap:' 'the distance between the object under scrutiny and, via method, data processing, and inferences, what you eventually want to say about it' (2012: 428). The audience has access to both the data (i.e. the object under scrutiny) and the analytical interpretations. The data clips used in publications also enable other researchers to compare it with their own data and build up cumulative knowledge within a research area about various features of interaction. Research on talk about children's food likes, for example, has been shown to be similar across Chinese-American (Waring, 2025), Dutch (Van der Heijden et al, 2022), and UK (Wiggins, 2014a) family mealtimes, precisely because these researchers presented sections of the (anonymised) raw data in their publications.

The use of established and rigorous methods and the inclusion of raw data in publications are vital for research that is engaged with the values of open science and associated issues of reproducibility, transparency, and integrity of research (e.g. Humă & Joyce, 2023; Stokoe et al, 2026). Interactional analyses have built up robust findings about some of the tiniest details of social interaction – such as micro-pauses, turn-taking, and non-lexical vocalisations – because of this transparency in methods and analyses. Research findings can be understood and disseminated across a wide interdisciplinary (and multidisciplinary) landscape, using examples from real-life social interaction that are more widely accessible than data that has been coded or translated into numbers or categories. This is, moreover, exactly the kind of data that non-academic audiences, such as health professionals and parents, can engage with and use to make sense of their own practices in everyday life.

Interactional approaches focus on details that are missed by other approaches

The second main reason why interactional approaches are ideally placed to facilitate an examination of children's eating practices follows directly from the first. The use of rigorous and transparent methods involves a large corpus of video recordings and close analyses of these recordings, illuminating details that are often missed by other research approaches. Data is transcribed (a written version of the speech, often with multimodal details) either in full or in part, and these transcripts allow researchers to focus on aspects such as turn-taking, pauses between speech, and features of speech delivery alongside the video recordings. Tiny details can be examined in microscopic detail, such as the synchrony between a parent's eye gaze as they produce a gustatory *mmm* (see Chapter 6) and their infant who is taking a mouthful of food (Wiggins, 2019). These details can subsequently be examined across a data corpus, ensuring that collections of instances can be interrogated thoroughly, enabling researchers to explicate patterns of interactional sequences that are evidenced across participants, settings, and circumstances.

The focus on the details of social interaction (of language and gesture) means that interactional approaches can answer questions about the specifics of what happens when children eat with others in everyday settings. What might be glossed as the 'social context' or 'environment' can be examined in a methodological manner. The black box of social interaction can be unpacked. Concepts such as social influence and what it means to eat 'together' can be analytically interrogated in situ, without recreating them in other settings or reducing them to categories or measurements. Interactional approaches focus on the intricacies of everyday language in social interaction and examine how life is accomplished through these intricate details. This means that children's eating practices can be examined as temporally unfolding sequences of social life, capturing their details without losing their complexity.

Interactional approaches study everyday life in all its complexity

The third main reason for using interactional approaches to examine children's mealtimes is because they study everyday life as it happens. Participants do not have to change their routines, eat certain foods, or eat in experimental settings; they can simply carry on as usual. A focus on everyday practices is important *because* of the ways in which interactional approaches examine social life. There is no separation of eating from other social activities. As Mondada (2009: 58) notes, 'From an interactionist perspective eating practices are considered as situated within social collective events, and as indissociable from other social activities such as dining and talking together.' Taking eating out of its usual habitat would change eating entirely. The social context is not just an additional factor; it is fundamental to what happens when children eat. Interactional approaches can study eating as it happens, in all its complexity.

A corollary of examining real-life settings, combined with the use of rigorous methods and a focus on the details of language, reveals further benefits. The variability and nuances of everyday life turn out to be not so variable after all. What may be treated by some approaches as too 'messy' for analysis is shown, through detailed transcriptions and a close examination of video recordings, to be highly organised (e.g. Sacks, 1992; Sacks et al, 1974; Schegloff, 2007). There are regularities in social interaction that cannot be reduced to individual characteristics or extrapolated to social or cultural factors. The food, the people, the situations may change, but some features of social interaction (e.g.

turn-taking and the organisation of social actions) remain disarmingly similar at a much finer-grained level of detail that might ever have been imagined.

With social interaction as the foundation not only of children's eating practices but also of the research approaches themselves, the hitherto hidden details of mealtimes can be revealed through rigorous and established methodologies that have already accumulated considerable knowledge about how children eat. Mealtimes can be recorded in situ, in everyday life, in whatever setting they take place. Data and analyses are transparent and widely accessible. The approaches themselves are theoretically grounded and robust but not tied to specific disciplines: they are interdisciplinary and can be used across a multidisciplinary landscape. The core principles and analytical concepts of these approaches are described and illustrated in Chapter 2, to provide further details about where they developed and how they can be used. What remains to be considered in this chapter is the analytical object itself.

What are children's mealtimes?

This book is about researching how children eat and, more specifically, what happens when children eat with other people in everyday settings. The focus is almost entirely restricted to the consumption of food, rather than drink (i.e. the consumption of liquids), with the exception of breastmilk and formula for infants. Some core terms are therefore used repeatedly throughout this book – namely 'eating', 'children', and 'mealtimes'. These concepts can be considered fuzzy, in that they have specific meanings but are deliberately vague in their applications. One might reasonably ask, for instance, whether there even *is* such a thing as a 'children's mealtime', since it suggests that there is a predefined eating occasion in which only children gather together to consume a particular kind of food. This section explicates some of the variation that can be considered within these core concepts and provides some inspiration for the diverse range of settings that can be studied.

On 'eating'

Eating is such a routine and fundamental activity that it is easy to overlook the myriad practices and processes that surround what is sometimes defined as 'the ingestion of food': the act of manipulating food in the mouth before it is swallowed and digested. Food, however, does not suddenly land in the mouth. There are complex interactional processes that lead up to the moment of ingestion, particularly when children are involved, and 'eating' as a term blurs the boundaries between what happens before and what happens after food enters the body. Various terms to describe these processes include 'feeding', 'ingestion', 'consumption', 'food intake', and 'dietary behaviour'; and the activity might be broken down further into specific processes (e.g. mastication) or broadened to include a situational context (e.g. family dinners). There are further situations in which food is present but never enters the body: it may be prepared and offered to children but never reach the mouth or else be put into the mouth and then forcefully ejected. Some meals, for instance, may not actually involve ingestion at all, yet they are particularly important for research that aims to understand situations in which children refuse or reject foods (see Chapter 7).

As noted at the start of this chapter, children play an active role in their eating practice from their first mouthfuls and the prevalent use of the term 'feeding' can be rather misleading. Not only is this term used primarily when discussing infant consumption, but the term 'self-feeding' is also used to refer to infants who eat independently for themselves (see Chapter 4). 'Feeding' suggests a somewhat asymmetric and one-sided process involving a person providing the food (the feeder) and a person passively receiving the food (for which there is no equivalent expression – no 'feedee'). What is demonstrated throughout this book, however, is that the interaction between child and caregiver during mealtimes is collaborative: children are actively involved in their food consumption, even in the earliest stages of life. This book is focused on how children *eat with* (not fed by) other people, from the earliest moments of life all the way through childhood. The term 'feeding' is, however, used where appropriate throughout the book, such as 'milk-feeding' to refer to both breastmilk and formula (whether consumed via breast, bottle, cup, or spoon) or 'complementary feeding' to refer to the transitionary stage to solid food.

There are also variations in eating events and their purpose: eating may be primarily in the service of hunger, but there are times when it might be done out of boredom, companionship, duty, celebration, or anguish. Eating is not always, or not only, a necessity for life. Mol (2024) has furthermore argued that the use of the English language in analytical writing has constrained our understanding of what it means to eat. Other languages have different words for eating in various forms which may not be captured or translatable into English. Mol (2024) suggests, therefore, that the academic language used to describe research is not neutral: it changes things. Consider, for instance, how the English language differentiates between the ingestion of solids ('eating') versus liquids ('drinking'). 'Eating' is therefore a rather broad concept that might be used as a shorthand to refer to a vast range of different practices and processes, and language is the medium through which research discusses and makes sense of these practices.

On 'children'

A similar complexity around terminology arises when the terms 'child' and 'children' are considered. Far from being self-evident categories, these terms are imbued with a range of associations and expectations that can differ according to the historical, social, cultural, and disciplinary context within which research is conducted (e.g. Corsaro, 2011; Prout & James 2015). While the term 'child' may refer to a person of a particular age category – often defined as between birth and puberty – the upper limits of this category can be fluid and negotiable. There is no precise moment when someone stops being a child and becomes an adult, even if there might be certain activities through which that transition is undertaken and culturally recognised as a turning point. Meanwhile, a person within the age period defined as 'puberty' is subject to variable physical, emotional, and mental changes that are not always easy to recognise, even for that person themselves. Nor is this likely to be a linear and unidirectional path: an adult might be criticised for acting childishly or engaging in childlike activities, while a child might be praised for being mature or admired for engaging in adult behaviours.

The concept of childhood itself can further be divided into smaller units, such as 'early years' and 'early childhood', some of which are used more commonly within specific disciplines. Developmental psychology, for instance, has defined 'childhood' as a series of ages and stages, such as neonate/newborn, baby, infant, toddler, preschooler, school-age, and pre-teen, or early and middle childhood and adolescence. There are notably more categories for younger children, as these developmental stages are considered to be more distinct. Other terms – such as 'teenager', 'juvenile', and 'young adult' – might be added to distinguish between persons at the boundary between childhood and adulthood; or terms such as 'minor', 'dependant', or 'paediatric' in relation to those not yet classed as adults or independent persons. These childhood terms are not simply abstract categories: they have implications in terms of psychological development, as well as in relation to educational, healthcare, and legal matters.

The category of 'child' and related terminology can also be considered to carry a vast range of culturally specific assumptions and expectations around agency, competency, and responsibility that are important not only for society but also for research on mealtimes. What is expected of eating practices can often vary according to the age category to which people are attributed. Infants and young children might be treated as needing to develop their exposure to new flavours in ways that adults are not (see Chapter 5). The ability to know when one has had enough to eat in situations where there is plentiful food is sometimes considered a skill to be learned and something which children may not always be able to judge accurately for themselves (see Chapter 8). Due to the diversity in how children's eating is researched across disciplines and the varied definitions of 'child', a range of terms are used in analysis and in empirical articles and book chapters. What some researchers might label 'child eating', others might call 'infant feeding' or 'paediatric ingestion'. An awareness of different categories of childhood and of the ways in which these are used in different research contexts not only is important for literature searches but also has analytical implications.

On 'mealtimes'

If 'childhood' can be considered a fuzzy concept, then the same can be said of the terms 'meal' and 'mealtime' (see Meiselman, 2008; Meiselman et al., 2000). These terms are often used to describe a situation in which eating together takes place. Meals, as Douglas (1972) noted, tend to have names, such as those indicating the time of day when the eating takes place ('breakfast', 'snack', 'lunch', 'dinner', 'supper'), or characterised by the occasion, such as a celebratory event, religious festival, or national holiday. This may be further complicated by regional or cultural variations regarding the names of mealtimes. The word 'mealtime' can thus be considered an umbrella term for a vast range of situations in which people eat with other people – from family dinners to school lunches, picnics in the park to celebratory feasts. It might therefore be judicious to use Douglas and Nicod's (1974: 744) term 'food event', as 'an occasion when food is eaten, without prejudice as to whether it constitutes a meal or not'. The term 'mealtime' is also, at times, used to downplay the seriousness of eating research itself (see Chapter 9 for more on the status of eating research).

If one is interested in what happens when *children* eat with other people, then the range of situations and spaces in which eating happens might vary even more. They could include when food is eaten in the presence of other people in home environments but not necessarily at a table (e.g. eating snacks on the sofa); in gatherings of young children and their caregivers in public spaces, such as play groups, soft-play centres, theme parks, museums, forests, parks, or beaches; and in transient spaces, where people are eating while on various modes of transport, such as cars, trains, planes, and ferries. As noted in the previous sub-section, sometimes the expectations and norms surrounding children's food consumption can vary considerably in relation to those defined as adults. There are countless variations of children's mealtimes in terms of their duration, location, food consumed, persons present, norms and rules, settings, and expectations. A silent night-time feed for a ten-month-old infant at home is as much a children's mealtime as a raucous ten-year-old's birthday party in a fast-food restaurant.

The collective term 'children's mealtimes' is used in this book, therefore, as shorthand to refer to any situation in which one or several children are (potentially) eating in the presence of other people, including those food events in which food is offered but not ingested (see Chapter 7). The definition of a 'child' is that up to the age of puberty; but the research presented in this book should not be considered as limited by chronological age or any other category ascriptions. While the examples used are taken primarily from family mealtimes and preschool lunches from European cultures, these are used only as illustrations of concrete interactional analyses on real data as inspiration for how to work with empirical data.

A guide through the book

This closing section provides an overview of the remaining chapters to help readers navigate the rest of the book. The book comprises nine chapters in total: the first three (including this introductory chapter) form its foundations; the subsequent five chapters provide analyses of core aspects of children's eating practices; and the final chapter concludes the book. The contents of each chapter are as follows.

Chapter 2 equips readers with the analytical sensitivities that are central to interactional approaches and outlines those showcased in this book: EMCA, DP, and LS. The chapter describes how to begin with social action as the foundational concept of interactional research and illustrates this with brief transcribed examples from video-recorded data. This chapter is essential for those new to interactional approaches to research.

Chapter 3 details the practicalities of conducting interactional research from start to finish – from ethical considerations and participant recruitment to data collection, transcription, analysis, and dissemination. This is a substantial chapter, detailing methodological steps while also explaining why things are done in a particular way. This chapter should be read in conjunction with planning research and can be used as a companion alongside the subsequent chapters to tease out the nuances of interactional analyses.

Chapters 4 to 8 comprise the analytical chapters of the book and address the core activities involved in children's eating practices (which may also be considered 'interactional projects'; see Chapter 2). They follow an identical structure for clarity and consistency:

- A brief overview, to enable readers to navigate the analytical area within a multidisciplinary landscape, highlighting key concepts and core literature,
- A section that demonstrates how to research this area using interactional approaches, presenting real-life data examples to detail specific analytical tools,
- An illustrated research example, to provide a behind-the-scenes discussion of a published piece of research,
- An overview of interactional research that has already been conducted in this area, to provide a foundation from which readers can build their own research,
- A list of suggestions regarding how interactional approaches can be used, as inspiration for future research.

These chapters do not focus on topics that other writing on children's eating typically does, such as fruit and vegetable consumption or parental strategies.

Instead, they focus on the interactional projects that underpin eating practices. They can be read in any order and their areas of focus are as follows.

Chapter 4 addresses how children start to eat, from the first mouthfuls of milk-feeding to the introduction of solid foods (complementary feeding). It focuses on the concepts of responsive feeding and hunger cues as the primary means through which eating begins. The chapter unpacks the process of assisted eating as a series of interconnected stages through which infants play an active and independent role alongside caregivers.

Chapter 5 examines the development of taste and other sensory practices in infants and older children, thus addressing an area that traverses a vast range of disciplines, from philosophy to sensory science. The chapter focuses on tasting as a social practice rather than a phenomenon and on efforts to develop or expand tastes throughout childhood. It demonstrates how tasting is 'performed' in interaction and how children might be encouraged to 'dare' to taste new foods.

Chapter 6 considers the enjoyment of food with a specific focus on the concepts of food likes and gustatory pleasures. The chapter examines how food likes are established as individual knowledge about the child, including the association with tasting practices, and how food pleasures can be invoked through non-lexical vocalisations and treated as entirely separate from a food 'like'. The chapter further demonstrates the implications of food likes in terms of changing preferences and diversifying eating practices.

Chapter 7 focuses on those instances during mealtimes when children do not or will not eat, and the practices that might be used to negotiate these food 'refusals'. It addresses a range of issues, from food avoidance and aversions to disgust and food refusals. Core concepts include resistance as a social action and children's expressions of disgust. The chapter examines the role of disgust within trajectories of eating practices and the importance of examining meals as unfolding sequences of action.

Chapter 8 explicates how meals come to an end, in terms of both having had enough to eat and closing the meal. It examines the concept of satiety alongside practices that temporally progress the meal. The chapter demonstrates how the organisation of mealtimes and meal termination is central to understanding how children stop eating – that satiety is as much a collaborative achievement as it is an individual interoceptive state.

Chapter 9 closes the book with a summary of how interactional research has addressed some of the core issues raised across the multidisciplinary landscape. It subsequently considers how interactional research can move beyond the mealtime and contribute to a wider range of research topics and areas that concern children's eating. It closes with a reflection on how research in this field could be developed to be more diverse in terms of people, languages, and eating practices.

Three appendices constitute the final material for the book, comprising a glossary of key terms, a sample consent form that can be adapted for data collection, and a list of Jeffersonian transcription notations. This transcription key will be helpful when examining the data extracts used throughout the book and is discussed in more detail in Chapter 3.

Summary

Eating together is not only one of the most basic forms of human sociality; it is also the principal arena in which children eat in their everyday lives. This chapter has introduced the central argument of the book: that social interaction is foundational to how children eat and that interactional approaches provide a rigorous and robust set of analytical tools through which to analyse eating in social interaction. The chapter has laid out the multidisciplinary landscape of research across anthropology, linguistics, psychology, and sociology, highlighting some of the ways in which these disciplines have shaped the field. Interactional approaches are woven throughout this landscape and offer the means through which to work across disciplinary boundaries. They allow researchers to investigate how children *really* eat in everyday life. How they do this, in terms of core principles and methodological practices, is considered next in Chapters 2 and 3.

2

EATING AS A SOCIAL ACTIVITY

When children eat in the presence of other people, eating is more than simply putting food into their mouths; it is an activity embedded within a specific context that involves unique constellations of food, people, and actions. The previous chapter set out some of the main reasons why interactional approaches provide a unique analytical tool for researching children's mealtimes. This chapter first explains the core principles behind these approaches, familiarising readers with the analytical sensitivities and perspectives on language and social interaction that underpin these approaches. Three interactional approaches – ethnomethodology and conversation analysis (EMCA), discursive psychology (DP) and language socialisation (LS) – are subsequently introduced as key examples of how interactional research can contribute to understanding the details of how children eat in social settings. The chapter focuses the analytical gaze on eating as a social activity and social interaction as the very foundation on which eating together is built.

Social actions as the cornerstone of social life

At the heart of interactional approaches is a focus on the social actions through which everyday interaction is accomplished. Social actions are the things that happen when people interact with other people. They are activities that involve talk, sounds, and gestures, situated and accomplished within and through the turn-by-turn organisation of human interaction (Goodwin, 2000; Raymond et al, 2024; Schegloff, 2007). In the context of shared mealtimes, examples include offering, refusing, and assessing food. Actions are distributed across various modalities (e.g. gesture, eye gaze, words and their production) and turns in talk – that is, the words and gestures in themselves are not the action. Instead,

DOI: 10.4324/9781003529620-2

social action can be said to emerge through the sequential unfolding of the interaction. Analysing social interaction from an interactional approach does not start, therefore, by coding individual behaviours but rather by examining social actions as they are produced across interlocutors' turns in interaction.

A short data clip helps to illustrate what this means in terms of analysing children's mealtimes. As noted in Chapter 1, interactional research uses transcripts from video or audio recordings to ensure that the analysis stays close to the details of language and social interaction. Extract 2.1 is an excerpt of data from a family dinner, in which two parents (Mum and Dad) are sharing a meal with their three children. Food is being served from dishes in the centre of the table and Mum is holding out a plate of salad vegetables towards her daughter, Emma (age five years). Much more is happening around the dinner table that is not included here, so the transcript is only one representation of the recording itself; this is one of the reasons why a transcript is a central part of the analytic process (see Chapter 3 for more discussion on this). There are features of the transcript that are useful to know at this point: the numbers in brackets refer to the length of silence in seconds; the question marks on lines 01 and 03 refer to questioning intonation rather than grammar; and the '*bleughh*' on line 04 is a representation of the sound of disgust that Emma makes. Extract 2.1 provides a turn-by-turn account of a few seconds of interaction between Mum and Emma. See Chapter 3 for details of how to produce a transcript as part of the analytical work and Appendix 3 for a full list of transcription symbols.

Extract 2.1

```
01 Mum   d'y'want pepper?
02       (0.4)
03 Mum   want a bit of pepper?
04 Emm   bleughh (.) nope.
05       (2.3)
06 Emm   never tasting it.
```

One way to describe this piece of social interaction is to gloss it in a way that draws on everyday concepts associated with eating: a child is offered a vegetable and shows disgust in refusing to taste it. In under ten seconds' worth of interaction, the data clip provides examples of some prototypical occurrences within children's mealtimes: a food offer, a food refusal, and an expression of disgust. If these are analysed as social actions, they can be unpacked in terms of *how* they become an offer, a refusal, and a disgust expression. For instance, Mum's turn on line 1 ('d' y' want pepper?') works as a food offer in combination with holding up the serving dish within reach of Emma, her eye gaze, the questioning intonation on the word 'pepper', and the slightly modified repeat of the question soon after. In another sequential context, with a different combination of gestures, the same phrase ('Do you want pepper?') could be seeking a clarification (about wanting this food rather than another kind of food: 'Do you want *pepper*?') or questioning the motivation of the other person (about 'wants' rather than feeling obliged to eat – for instance: 'Do you *want* pepper?'). Much depends on the intonation and emphasis in how these words are produced. Similarly, while the '*bleughh*' might be a recognisable sound of disgust (in English, at least), it is the production of it at this point in the interaction, coordinated with Mum's offer and Emma's other turns, that identifies it as disgust specifically about the possibility that Emma might taste or eat a bit of pepper.

By analysing in detail the organisation of social interaction (and the language and bodily movements therein), social actions are revealed to be subtle and finely calibrated activities produced by the coordination of people in an interactional space. They are built through collaboration between persons present and not reducible to single phrases or words, or to individual behaviours or characteristics (see Box 2.1). This is very different from other ways of interpreting talk and gesture that might examine bidirectional or transactional communication or social signals. Focusing on social actions, by contrast, enables a means through which interaction, rather than individuals, is placed at the centre of analysis. Mum's offer of food in Extract 2.1 is not just about her speech and movements, but also about how these are subsequently oriented to by Emma as an offer rather than an expectation that she must take the food. The disgust expression and the 'nope' treat Mum's offer as optional. There is no hesitation in Emma's response; no apology or indication that she might be reprimanded for turning it down. The production of the social action of a food offer is therefore contingent not only on Mum's actions but also on Emma's.

BOX 2.1 ACTIONS NOT BEHAVIOURS

Interactional approaches examine individual behaviours in terms of how they are embedded within social actions and interactional projects. This is very different from other research approaches that might interpret specific behaviours as corresponding to intentions, cognitions, or emotions. They are also distinct from behaviourist approaches in psychology which focus on behaviour and bracket off cognition as analytically unavailable. By contrast, interactional approaches examine language and gesture as part of social interaction rather than as relating only (or primarily) to an individual. There is no direct or fixed correspondence between a specific word, phrase, or gesture, for instance, and the action being performed (Heath & Luff, 2014). An infant's smile, for example, can be part of a social action relating to gustatory pleasure, satiety, or play; its meaning cannot be 'read off' without considering how it is part of the ongoing social interaction alongside other things in the interactional space. Relatedly, language is not treated as separate from behaviour because interactional approaches focus on talk (i.e. language in use) as a social practice rather than language as a theoretical model or cognitive process (Potter & Edwards, 2014). Interactional approaches such as discursive psychology (DP) examine cognitive states as produced in talk and analysable as part of social interaction (Edwards & Potter, 1992); they are not bracketed off but rather analysed as social practices. See Box 3.6 in Chapter 3 for more on the interpretation of behaviour in relation to video analysis.

Social actions can also be considered as part of longer segments of interaction called 'interactional projects' (Schegloff, 2007) or 'communicative projects' (Linell, 2009); see Levinson (2014) for further discussion on this. Interactional projects comprise 'a course of conduct being developed over a span of time' (Schegloff, 2007: 244) and multiple social actions, which might overlap with each other when there are several persons present and interacting at the same time, as often happens during a mealtime. Extract 2.1 could be considered part of an interactional project such as serving food or starting the meal, for example. The analytical chapters of this book are separated into some of the main interactional projects that take place during children's mealtimes: starting to eat (Chapter 4); developing tastes (Chapter 5); establishing likes (Chapter 6); negotiating refusals (Chapter 7); and achieving satiety (Chapter 8). What becomes evident is that one aspect of talk or gesture (e.g. a word or hand movement) can be involved in numerous social actions that can themselves be woven into various interactional projects (e.g. how food offers can be part of developing tastes as much as achieving satiety).

Talk as action

Researching social interaction in terms of social actions is based on a set of principles that is itself grounded in empirical work. One of the central principles is that talk is action – that is, talk is constitutive or constructive of, rather than reflective of, people and the world. Words *do* things. As seen in the interaction between Mum and Emma in Extract 2.1, the specific meaning of talk and gesture is constructed within a particular (micro-)interactional context. This stance is taken from the work of J.L. Austin (1962/1975) and Ludwig Wittgenstein (1953), two philosophers who made vital contributions to the scholarly work on language in everyday use. Of the many features of language that Austin and Wittgenstein discuss, it is the performative aspect of talk that is of particular importance for interactional approaches. Talk is never neutral but rather acts upon the world and becomes meaningful within social interaction. A single word or phrase – such as 'nope' – can shift in meaning depending on how it is articulated, when it is produced, and how it is situated within an unfolding turn-taking sequence. Words gain their meaning through their use within social interaction.

The upshot of treating talk as action is that: a) language is considered as primarily social rather than indicative of, or corresponding to, cognitive states; b) language is not treated as separable from other kinds of behaviour such as bodily gestures; and c) language is studied in situ (i.e. within sequential analysis). This means that while research might primarily focus on how children eat, examining language-in-use (i.e. talk, including sounds and gestures) is necessary to understand how eating happens. Language cannot be separated out as an external factor to eating, no more than the 'social environment' can be isolated (see Box 2.1) as an independent variable. Moreover, while talk might not be all there is in the world, '*it is the primary work of language to make all those "other" phenomena accountable*' (Edwards, 2006: 42, italics in original). Talk is the way in which particular understandings of eating are invoked, described, constituted, and made consequential. Different words (or sounds) construct eating as being a different kind of thing – as about a visceral reaction, for instance, or a physiological preference. In Extract 2.1, for example, the '*bleurgh*' sound formulated a disgust response at a particular moment in time to decline the food offer. It constructed the refusal as based on a visceral response rather than, for instance, a food dislike (c.f. if Emma had said, 'I don't like it'). These constructions in talk have implications for how eating – and particularly children's eating – becomes managed in certain ways (see Chapter 7 on how disgust becomes invoked during mealtimes). By viewing language through a performative rather than a representative lens, interactional approaches examine how and when different concepts or psychological states are expressed within social interaction and the social actions within which they are involved.

Situated social actions

A focus on social actions and the use of video data mean that interactional research can examine how everyday practices such as eating unfold temporally and progressively. What is important is not just *what* happens, but also *how* things happen in a particular temporal and sequential order. Life, and eating, are not static: they progress within a specific situational context. Examining behaviour as part of a food offer, for instance, involves a consideration of *when* as well as *how* the offer is produced, and this situatedness is the key to examining social life. Interactional research provides a methodological tool to examine this temporality in a rigorous manner. Sequential analysis is used – that is, analysing the sequence of how social interaction unfolds, turn by turn – to understand what happens as and when it happens. This means that social actions are examined within their sequential context, and that turn-taking is not just a trivial concern but fundamental to examining how eating practices take place within a temporal context. This is particularly important when considering infant interaction, in which the interpretation of bodily movements and positions is vital to understanding how social actions are built collaboratively (e.g. Kidwell, 2013).

This focus on sequential order is a very different kind of orderliness from that used in research that seeks to establish causal relations between factors or variables. As Edwards (2012: 432) notes, 'rather than conceiving of people's thoughts and actions as resulting from the interplay of a range of causal variables, DP approaches them as things done and understood with regard to an empirically and conceptually tractable normative order' That is, people are not passive objects that respond automatically to one another as if following a cause-and-effect model; rather, the orderliness of social life is continually attended to, resisted, managed, and upheld through the various moments of social interaction. There may be social norms that guide behaviour and sanction deviations from this, but such norms cannot be used to predict what will happen or explain the nuances of how people speak, move, and otherwise interact with each other in a particular interactional context.

Returning to Extract 2.1 and adding more details to the transcript can enable a closer illustration of how actions are built within the unfolding sequence of interaction. Extract 2.2 provides a more detailed transcript of Extract 2.1 and includes some of the multimodal features of eye gaze, hand, and head movements as these overlap with features of speech (see Chapter 3 for more on multimodal transcription). The addition of these details is integral to understanding how the social interaction is not just about voices but about embodied persons interacting in a physical space. This is not about 'body language' (an individualistic interpretation that treats behaviour as correlating with cognitive states; see Box 2.1) but rather an examination of social interaction in multimodal detail.

Extract 2.2

```
01 Mum   ^&d'y'want pepper?
   mum   ^holds veg dish in front of Emma
   emm    &gaze to veg dish

02           (0.4)
03 Mum   &want a bit of pepper?
   emm   &gaze to own plate
```

```
04 Emm   &ble&^ughh          no^pe& hh
   emm   &head shake
   emm       &gaze to veg          &gaze to mum
   mum        ^withdraws veg  ^starts to lift in chair

05       ^&(2.3)
   mum   ^places veg dish in centre of table
   emm    &gaze to own plate

06 Emm   never tasting it.
```

This transcript reveals features that were not apparent in the previous version (see also Chapter 7 for further analyses of this clip and other disgust sounds). Emma's vocal expression of disgust on line 3 is now visible in relation to her head shake and eye gaze towards the food. It is produced not on the first offer (line 01) but on the repeated offer (line 03) and after Emma has brought her gaze back to her own plate. In other words, there is slight delay between her gaze on the food and the production of the sound. The disgust expression is sequentially positioned after the food offer, with Emma's gaze back to her own food, and before her answer to Mum's question (the 'nope' on line 04). Mum's actions can also be observed in relation to how they unfold alongside Emma's turns. While the dish of vegetables is held out towards Emma during the offer, Mum starts to withdraw it before the 'nope' is produced. In fact, the withdrawal begins around halfway through the disgust expression (line 03). Even before Emma explicitly declines the offer, therefore, Mum's movements demonstrate her understanding that the food will not be taken. The timing here is finely tuned: Emma has only just begun to shake her head and make the sound when Mum's hand begins to retract the dish.

A sequential analysis of this section of social interaction enables these features of verbal and embodied behaviour to be analysed alongside one another, turn by turn, and within turns. Features of the organisation of interaction can be revealed in extraordinary detail – the example above only begins to sketch out some features that might be analysed – demonstrating an orderliness to social life that is often missed by other methods. The beauty of video recordings is that these sequential and embodied features of interaction can be analysed in slow motion, millisecond by millisecond, to understand how interaction around eating practices takes place in everyday settings.

Three interactional approaches for researching children's mealtimes

The principles set out in the previous section are grounded in microanalyses of language and social interaction within everyday settings that have been accumulating since the early 1970s. This section describes three of these approaches that have been particularly important for research into children's mealtimes: EMCA, DP, and LS. There are other discursive and interactional approaches that have not been included here, such as discourse analysis, linguistic ethnography, and interactional sociolinguistics. While these are also important for research into eating practices, the three approaches that have been chosen are essential for analysing the nuances of children's eating and language in everyday settings. The resources on the EMCA wiki site (emcawiki.net) can be used as a guide for exploring the broader landscape of discursive and interactional research.

This section provides an overview of the historical depth and analytical nuances of EMCA, DP, and LS. Each of these interactional approaches has its own complex background and the summaries below offer just a glimpse into each approach (see Mondada, 2009, for further discussion of these three areas). They interweave the disciplinary areas discussed in Chapter 1 – anthropology, linguistics, psychology, and sociology – though they are not confined to particular disciplines. They are presented here to introduce readers to the depth and breadth of work that is loosely encapsulated under the term 'interactional approaches' as used in this book, and to provide inspiration for readers to follow their own research interests along different paths. Further guidance has been provided throughout this book to key readings and methodological tools for these approaches that can be consulted when conducting research in these areas.

Extract 2.3 provides a concrete example to illuminate how the three approaches can be distinguished from each other in terms of analytical focus. The extract is taken from a preschool lunch in Sweden, in which the children are eating potatoes, fish, and vegetables. Three children – Maria (5;1), Emil (4;5), and Emma (5;7) – are eating with their teacher ('Tea'). Emil has just commented how the potatoes are very soft, to which the teacher responds in lines 01 and 02, in overlap with Maria, who has begun to move her food around the plate in what might be characterised as a playful stance. A longer extract has been used here to illustrate the sequential unfolding of the interaction involving Maria and her eating practices.

Extract 2.3

```
01 Tea   de här e ju kokt potatis,
         this is of course cooked potato
02       då blir den lite mjuk [för att man har kokat den
         then it'll be a bit soft because it's been cooked
03 Mar                         [kolla den kan inte-  (.)
                                look it can't-
04       dom kan inte gå nån stans (.) ärtorna
         they can't go anywhere        the peas
05 Tea   nhhähej  dom e fasth!
         no way they're stuck!
```

```
06        (1.0)
07 mar    m:hhehe! Heh
08        (1.0)
09 Tea    potatismur
          potato wall
((20 lines missing during which the other children join in))
29 Tea    hur ska dom komma loss då?
          how will they get out then?
30 Mar    nu gick alla ut (prt) [trt trt trt trt [trt ((enacts flicking
          peas))
          now they all got out
31 Tea                          [oj               [Maria kan du
                                 aw                Maria can you
32        sätta dej på rumpan
          sit on your bottom
33 Mar    ohhh sätter mej på £rump(h)an£=
          (sighs) sitting on my bott(h)om
34 Emm    Emil du mä får sätta dej på rumpan, inte på knäna.
          Emil you too must sit on your bottom not your knees
35 Mar    kolla här! (0.2) .hh dom gick ut nu
          look here!          they got out now
36 Tea    åh (.) du rädda dom!
          oh!  you're saving them!
```

EMCA

EMCA is the study of the social order of interaction and the intelligibility of social life, often referred to as the study of people's methods of making sense of interaction (Garfinkel, 1967). Ethnomethodology aims to understand the everyday practices through which people cooperatively make sense of their social worlds, such as how social norms and 'common sense' are produced in social interaction and become the way in which social life is constituted. Conversation analysis (CA) is focused in particular on examining the structural and organisational detail of talk-in-interaction (Maynard & Gill, 2024). Some of the earliest EMCA work used dinnertime conversations as a data source (Goodwin, 1979) and there is a wealth of CA literature on young children in interaction (e.g. Danby & Baker, 1998; Kidwell, 2005, 2009; Kidwell & Zimmerman, 2007; M.H. Goodwin, 1980; Lerner, Zimmerman & Kidwell, 2011) and language acquisition (e.g. Gardner & Forrester, 2009; Tarplee, 1996; Wootton, 1994). CA research has also examined the use of directives (Craven & Potter, 2010; Kent, 2012), threats (Hepburn & Potter, 2011), admonishments (Hepburn, 2020a), and rule invocations (Küttner et al, 2022) during family mealtimes. An emerging area of EMCA is research on tasting and sensory practices, which has already done much to illuminate the intricacy of adults' (Fele & Liberman, 2021; Hänggi & Mondada, 2025; Mondada, 2018, 2020b, 2023; Svensson, 2024, 2025) and children's (Wiggins, Cromdal & Willemsen, 2024) tasting practices (see also Hoey, 2018; Laurier, 2008, on drinking practices).

The scholarly roots of EMCA can be traced back to the work of Harold Garfinkel on ethnomethodology (Garfinkel, 1967) and Harvey Sacks on CA (Sacks, 1992; Sacks et al, 1974), as well as to the parent discipline of sociology (Jenkings et al, 2025). Garfinkel argued that people produce social order locally, within and through social interaction. In other words, there is no 'time out' from social interaction with other people; everything done in social settings is accountable for its presence. CA was itself a development of the work of Sacks, along with Emmanuel Schegloff and Gail Jefferson (Sacks et al, 1974), who were inspired not only by Garfinkel's ethnomethodological work (see Heritage, 1984) but also by the microsociological work of Erving Goffman (1961, 1963 1981) and his conceptualisation of social interaction (see Mondada & Peräkylä, 2023). Notably, it was Jefferson who developed the transcription system that is used throughout the field to this day (see Chapter 3). The overlapping nature of much of ethnomethodology and CA has meant that the abbreviation EMCA (alternatively, 'ethnomethodological conversation analysis') is typically used to refer to a range of research within this approach. Comprehensive examples of CA methods books include Robinson et al's (2024) *Cambridge handbook of methods in conversation analysis* and Sidnell and Stivers' (2014) *The handbook of conversation analysis*. Ethnomethodology is not, despite its name, a methodology; Carlin et al's (2025) *Routledge international handbook of ethnomethodology* is an excellent starting point.

In considering Extract 2.3, EMCA could be used to analyse several aspects of the interaction, from the way in which it is sequentially structured to the multimodal organisation of how the 'playful' stance of child and teacher temporally unfolds. For instance, Maria uses an announcement ('look', line 03) to establish joint attention with the teacher (Kidwell & Zimmerman, 2007) into what becomes play signalling (Bateson, 1976). She uses her fork and eye gaze to draw the teacher's and Emil's attention to the food. The malleability and the texture of material objects (e.g. the food) also provide for affordances of play while maintaining rule-based mealtime interactions (e.g. Zotevska & Martín-Bylund, 2022). CA in particular could be used to examine the directives (c.f. Craven & Potter, 2010) used by both the teacher and Emma to tell another to sit in a certain manner (lines 31–32, 34) and how these are positioned in relation to the play sequence. A focus on the 'trt' vocalisations on lines 30 could illustrate how they ventriloquise (Bateman, 2018) the action of the peas being 'saved' and thus involved in the playful transformation of the food into another kind of object (see Ogden & Keevallik, 2020, for other work on non-lexical vocalisations). EMCA could be used to explicate the detailed social organisation of this section of interaction and demonstrate how it is that the playful stance around food was not only produced but maintained and transformed by the other persons around the table. EMCA's explicit focus on how everyday interaction is organised – whether focused specifically on talk

(CA) or on the spatial and multimodal organisation of the setting – makes it a perfect choice for examining features of children's mealtimes that draw on a range of embodied and verbal resources.

DP

The primary focus of DP is to examine how and when psychological matters and concepts are discursively constructed and used in the service of social actions in everyday interaction (Edwards, 2012). DP is concerned with how psychological matters – such as those related to eating practices (e.g. food likes, hunger, appetite, satiety) – become interactional objects and become consequential within, and for, social interaction. An interest in the ways in which psychological objects such as attitudes (Potter, 1998), categories (Edwards, 1991), and emotions (Edwards, 1999) can be reconceptualised as live, interactional processes rather than cognitive states lends itself particularly well to issues that are relevant for children's mealtimes. For instance, DP has developed a rich seam of work examining how various psychological matters are constructed and handled during eating practices, such as food likes (Van der Heijden et al, 2022; Waring, 2025; Wiggins, 2014a, 2023; Wiggins & Potter, 2003), wants (Childs, 2012), disgust (Wiggins, 2013, 2014b) and gustatory pleasure (Wiggins, 2002, 2019; Wiggins & Keevallik, 2021a). DP research into how persuasion and resistance can be re-specified as interactional practices has also begun to reap rewards (Humă & Stokoe, 2023; Humă et al, 2023; Wiggins & Humă, 2026a). Other research on DP and eating in adult settings has further extended knowledge of how identities as particular kinds of eaters become manifest in social interaction (Sneijder & te Molder, 2004, 2006, 2009; Seymour-Smith et al, 2020).

The emergence of DP can be traced to psychology in the 1980s through the work of Derek Edwards, Jonathan Potter, and Margaret Wetherell (Potter & Wetherell, 1987; Edwards & Potter, 1992). In a similar manner to ethnomethodology's rejection of much of the orthodoxy of its parental discipline of sociology, DP can also be distinguished from its parental discipline of psychology. Matters of cognition – treated by many psychologists as being the foundations on which analysis is based – are turned on their heads by DP to be the topic, rather than the foundations, of analysis (Humă & Potter, 2023). Mental states are examined in terms of how they are invoked and managed in everyday talk and text. The scholarly roots of this approach echo the concerns of EMCA, though DP was also influenced by the work of language philosophers John Austin (1962/1975) and Ludwig Wittgenstein (1953), post-structuralism, and the sociology of scientific knowledge (e.g. Gilbert & Mulkay, 1984). The constructive nature of language is therefore a fundamental principle of DP. At the heart of this approach is a concern to understand how certain versions of realities are constructed and made real through discourse (Potter, 1996) – that words work to produce social realities which have consequences for issues such as how embodiment is understood (Edwards & Potter, 2020). DP's roots within EMCA mean that the aforementioned CA methods books are excellent reading material. For a DP methods book, see Wiggins' (2017) *Discursive psychology: Theory, method, and applications.*

A DP approach could be used to examine Extract 2.3 in terms of how psychological aspects of eating practices are constructed and become embedded within social actions. DP focuses on discursive constructions such as categories, pronouns, and verbs which become part of the social actions through which mental states are embedded (Edwards, 1991). Maria's reference to the peas as 'they' (line 04, 30, 35), for instance, constructs the peas as more than simply inanimate objects – as objects defined in relation to the agency of other objects (the potatoes): the peas are stuck (line 05) and then are saved (line 36; see Wiggins et al, 2001, for DP research on how food can be constructed as different kinds of objects). Both Maria and the teacher engage in a play narrative in which Maria is not simply eating peas but saving them. There is no talk about 'playing' with the food and no admonishments for her behaviour; the language constructs her as someone helping those in need (albeit peas). Pronouns ('they') and verbs ('can't go', line 04; 'stuck', line 05; 'get out', lines 29, 30, 35) are used to enact a scenario in which food could potentially have agency and in which the peas are not 'Maria's food' but rather items to be rescued. While there is limited mental state talk in this sequence, there is nevertheless the construction of food as being a particular category. The softness of the potatoes is attributed to being cooked (lines 01–02) and as a quality of the potato itself (i.e. the food), rather than to Emil's individual experience of the food in his mouth. That is, texture is constructed as an object-side reality, not a subject-side reality (Edwards & Potter, 2017). The use of different verbs to manage Maria's and Emil's bodily positions ('can you', line 31; 'you must', line 34) also makes relevant the rights of one person (i.e. a teacher or peer) to request that another person perform a particular action. DP's focus on the constructive nature of talk can thereby be used to examine how word use (e.g. categories, verbs, pronouns, but also mental state talk) constructs a particular version of reality about this setting; about how eating talk is formulated in different ways and used within different social actions. This makes it ideally suited to examining the details of language within children's mealtimes and the implications for how eating practices are understood.

LS

LS examines how children and other novices within a culture are socialised into cultural knowledge, identities, and social norms through and within the use of language in everyday settings. This approach examines culture as a living thing that is visible in everyday interactional processes, in that 'language both reflects and creates context' (Burdelski, 2025: 2). Children are socialised, within social interaction, not only into language practices but also into 'socio-culturally meaningful realities' (ibid: 2) such as those related to appetite and taste. LS research has been a particularly rich source of understanding about how children eat and how various cultural practices around food (or 'foodways') are embedded within social interaction. Much of Ochs' early work in this area examined how children are socialised into cultural and moral orders around food during family mealtimes (Ochs et al, 1996). Since then, research has examined how children are socialised not only into culturally appropriate foods and ways of tasting and eating (Burdelski, 2025; Karrabæk, 2012, 2013; Kremer-Sadlik & Morgenstern, 2022, Kremer-Sadlik et al, 2015) – including those related to table manners or politeness (Blum-Kulka, 1990, 2012; Ochs & Shohet, 2006) – but also into how their bodies should be positioned and managed while eating (e.g. Caronia & Colla, 2024).

The founding scholars of LS are Elinor Ochs and Bambi Schieffelin, including their work in the 1980s on Samoan (Ochs, 1982, 1988), Papua New Guinean (Schieffelin, 1990), and US families (Schieffelin & Ochs, 1986). The roots can be traced further back, however, to Dell Hymes (1964) and John Gumperz (1962) and their work within linguistic anthropology on the ethnography of communication; and to the anthropological work of Margaret Mead (1961) on the enculturation practices through which children become members of a culture. The approach is further rooted in developmental psychology and psycholinguistics, and specifically language acquisition research. Ochs and Schieffelin argued that children learn to become not only linguistically but also culturally competent through various socialisation practices (see Duranti et al, 2011, for further reading). The use of observational methods and video recordings is the signature tool of anthropological research (Cavanaugh & Riley, 2017) and a heritage of using ethnographic approaches means that this area of work is neatly aligned with research on examining children's eating practices in everyday settings. It can be particularly useful when considering longitudinal data collection in which a small group of children might be recorded over an extended period of time. For a guide to LS, see Duranti et al's (2011) *The handbook of language socialization*.

In analysing Extract 2.3, LS could be used to examine the way in which the children are socialised into culturally appropriate ways of eating and what is acceptable in terms of bodily behaviour such as 'playing' with food using hands or cutlery (e.g. Blum-Kulka, 1990; Caronia & Colla, 2024). What occurs in a Swedish preschool might be entirely different from what is seen in a Japanese kindergarten (cf Burdelski, 2025). This can be evidenced in the transcript through the teacher's response to Maria's initial announcement about the peas (lines 03–04). The teacher does not reprimand Maria but rather goes along with the narrative and adds further contributions: the peas are stuck (line 05) in a potato wall (line 09) and will need to be saved (lines 29 and 36). The teacher's role is thus supportive rather than corrective of Maria's behaviour. While not explicitly expressed as 'play' by any of the participants, the interaction here demonstrates how food might be oriented to something other than food (e.g. pretend play) and how language plays a crucial role in socialising children into *how* playing with food might unfold. The teacher nevertheless orients to specific ways of sitting at the table (lines 31–32) while this narrative is unfolding and illustrates how some forms of bodily comportment are acceptable while others are not. That the children are socialised into sitting in a certain manner is further evidenced by another child (Emma) telling Emil that he also needs to sit on his bottom (line 34). The focus of LS on the intersection of language and culture can be used to draw out elements of children's mealtimes that are focused more on cultural practices than on the turn-taking organisation of social interaction. Examining how children are socialised into cultural practices makes this an ideal perspective for understanding children's eating practices across different institutional and cultural settings.

Comparison of the three approaches

The three analytical approaches described above – EMCA, DP, and LS – offer distinct but complementary ways of researching the interactional features of children's eating practices in everyday settings. While they are all focused on language and social interaction, they can be distinguished as having unique areas of interest:

- EMCA is particularly useful for research that seeks to explore the organisational and sequential aspects of social interaction, even in situations that might be primarily embodied rather than verbal. It can explicate the details around tasting practices (Mondada, 2018) and the corporeal arrangements involved in milk-feeding infants (Bateman et al, 2025). A concern with the organisation of interaction and the turn-taking structures in talk renders it especially amenable to examining procedures and processes in eating practices, where temporality or progressivity is important.
- DP is particularly useful for examining how psychological aspects of eating are discursively embedded within social actions, through mental state (or bodily state) talk, and the use of categories (of people, food, or objects) to manage children's eating practices. It can examine issues such as establishing food likes as knowledge about infants (Wiggins, 2023) or negotiations around eating (Wiggins & Humă, 2026a). A focus on the constructive nature of language makes this a powerful tool for investigating how talk shapes eating practices and has consequences for how children eat.

- LS is particularly useful for explicating the various ways in which eating becomes a cultural practice and the routes through which children are socialised into these normative behaviours, though it is less focused on the structural organisation of talk. It is helpful when examining the specific language practices that socialise children into how and what should be eaten as part of one's cultural identity (Kremer-Sadlik et al, 2015), as well as those interactional practices that are used to socialise children into table manners and bodily comportment (Caronia & Colla, 2024).

Research from these three approaches is discussed in those sections of Chapters 4 to 8 which consider what interactional research has already been conducted in particular research areas. Those sections provide guidance for readers who want to explore specific approaches in more detail and to examine how each might be used to address different kinds of research questions.

Summary

Taking an interactional approach to researching children's mealtimes involves a set of principles that puts social action at the core of understanding what happens when we eat together. This chapter has presented the analytical sensitivities at the core of interactional approaches: on situated social actions as being at the heart of social life, and on talk (as language-in-use) as action and constructive of the world. Interactional approaches offer something unique to research into children's mealtimes by starting with social interaction and examining how this unfolds, turn by turn, in sequential contexts. Three core interactional approaches – EMCA, DP, and LS – were introduced as useful lenses through which the details of social interaction can be analysed. Their scholarly backgrounds and analytical nuances were presented and compared briefly. The chapter has therefore provided a starting point for familiarising the reader with the investigative scope of interactional research; the methodological principles through which this can be conducted are discussed in the next chapter.

3

CAPTURING EATING AS IT HAPPENS

To research how children eat in social settings is to capture eating as it happens. Using high-quality video to record the minutiae of the interactional spaces in which eating occurs, it is nothing short of holding time still. This chapter is a guide through the methodological stages of conducting interactional research, from research questions and ethics to the practicalities of recording, storing, and analysing video data. The most substantial sections are those which deal with ethical considerations, data collection, and transcription – the foundations upon which interactional approaches are based. As a book set within a multidisciplinary landscape, the aim is to open rather than close avenues for research. Not all interactional approaches follow a prescriptive set of methods, with ethnomethodology being a case in point. The chapter therefore provides guidelines that can be adjusted according to the specific requirements of individual projects and particular interactional approaches.

Aims and research questions

The goal of interactional approaches is to uncover the ways in which social life works, such as how children eat with other people, and to reveal these everyday practices in terms of their processes, practices, and patterns. Interactional approaches examine the social actions that underpin everyday life and begin with video recordings rather than hypotheses or theories: analysis is guided by the data (i.e. the recordings and transcripts). Before data can be collected, however, aims and research questions are used to initiate and guide the research. An interest in young children's eating practices in institutions, for instance, might lead to recording preschool or kindergarten lunches. An interest in eating outside of the home in later childhood might lead to the collection

DOI: 10.4324/9781003529620-3

of data from a variety of settings, such as takeaway venues and street food vendors. Research begins with identifying the interactional spaces in which eating might occur, rather than with individuals and their motivations, or social or cultural norms. Research questions evolve as the analysis develops and include questions such as how, when, and what happens when children eat. Since interactional research does not work with causal models of behaviour, there are no 'why' questions. It does not involve assigning people into categories such as those based on gender, age, social class, or culture; it is rather focused on social actions, not individuals or social structures. The most important thing is to clarify the aims of the project and focus on collecting good-quality data; a research question will soon follow.

Ethics

Researching children's mealtimes involves conducting research in situations that commonly take place behind closed doors, and which require sensitivity to the unpredictability of people's lives and the intimacy of private spaces. The moral issues of conducting research with children mean that ethics are of the utmost importance throughout the research process. To conduct research on everyday eating practices is to seek permission to look behind the scenes into some of the most personal areas of people's lives. Respect and consideration for those involved in the research are crucial. It is a privilege to be able to research this central aspect of people's lives in such a detailed manner. Ethics is not a stage to work through but rather a set of principles and practices that should guide the research throughout.

The core ethical issues to be considered are those that apply to all research involving human participants: obtaining informed consent; maintaining the confidentiality and/or anonymity of participants; and preserving the right to withdraw from the research. The difference for research using video recordings of children is that some aspects, such as obtaining consent, require more detailed consideration. There may also be national or institutional variations in how ethical issues might be interpreted or applied (e.g. what constitutes 'consent'), and it is essential that the research adheres to the practices appropriate to the research establishment and the specific institutional or cultural context within which the research is based. These might include, for instance, obtaining ethical approval from a national organisation, following General Data Protection Regulation provisions on the handling of personal data, and adhering to the United Nations Convention on the Rights of the Child (see www.unicef.org.uk/crc). In some countries, formal permission from authorities might be required to gain access to settings such as early years childcare.

Many of these ethical considerations have implications for data collection, analysis, and presentation, and should therefore be considered carefully in advance. They also have implications for the principles of open science and ensuring that research is accessible, transparent, and reproducible where possible. A special issue of *Research on language and Social Interaction* (Antaki et al, 2025) provides a particularly useful discussion of ethical concerns that relate to interactional research; and Hoey and Webb (2024) can be consulted on the practicalities of ethics in relation to data collection.

Informed consent

The first ethical principle is informed consent. As a fundamental tenet of scientific research on human participants, this refers to the process of providing sufficient and accessible information so that people can make an informed judgement about participation. In most cases, written consent is required, though in some situations verbal assent or consent (i.e. people agreeing to record by verbally stating this in a video recording) may suffice. When children are the participants, ethical guidelines often require the written permission of parents/guardians to provide consent on their behalf, while also ensuring that even young children are comfortable with the recording process.

Obtaining consent is not only an ethical priority; it is also a very practical issue. The nature of interactional research means that it is essential to use video recordings of mealtimes in as much of their entirety as possible. Other methods – such as note-taking, observational field notes, or partial recordings from a distance – will not provide the necessary detail. There are various considerations to bear in mind when obtaining consent, including the following:

- Consent must be obtained before data collection and only those who have consented should be recorded. Obtaining consent can be an ongoing process, such as when children join an early years childcare setting after data collection has begun.
- Consent is needed for all those being recorded. This may have implications for seating arrangements in institutions where children typically sit in regular formations, for instance, and caregivers should be involved in the process to assist with these arrangements.
- Consent requires knowing how, when, and where recording will take place, and what will happen to the recordings afterwards. Ensure that participants know where cameras will be placed and how this might impact on children who may be curious about, or want to touch, the recording equipment.
- Other people or features of the environment may be inadvertently visible on cameras or audible on the sound recordings, such as through windows or in open spaces. Consider the placement of equipment carefully to avoid this possibility.
- If someone has been recorded without their consent, that section of the video recording (or, if necessary, the whole recording) will need to be destroyed as soon as possible. One fewer recording will not ruin the research project, but unethical data will.

Discussing and planning the logistics of data collection are closely intertwined with consent issues, and it is vital to involve caregivers in this process to ensure not only a respectful research environment but also that the data will be of sufficiently high quality. See Appendix 2 for a sample consent form.

Anonymity and confidentiality

Another core ethical principle concerns anonymity and confidentiality. 'Anonymity' means ensuring that no information relating to the real identities of persons or institutions will be collected by researchers; whereas 'confidentiality' means that participant information will be known but not shared beyond the research team. Given the importance of recordings for interactional analyses, there is no avoiding the fact that people's faces and voices will be recorded. This means that while confidentiality can be maintained, anonymity cannot be guaranteed. Some details about participants that could be determined by their physical appearance will be visible from the video recordings alone and any talk about specific dietary requirements may then suggest other details related to medical, cultural, or religious factors. Beyond what will be captured through video and audio, care should be taken in terms of how much personal information is required for the research and how this will be used; record only those details that are necessary.

In terms of ensuring confidentiality, there are practical implications that can be implemented during the early stages of data collection. Pseudonyms (false names) should be used as soon as any details about individual participants, institutions, or locations are written in research files or used to label recordings themselves. It can be helpful to choose pseudonyms that match the number of syllables of the original name or which might have a long/short version that can affect how it features on the transcript. For instance, a child named 'Jennifer' might sometimes be referred to as 'Jen' or 'Jenny'; thus, something like 'Rebecca/Bec/Becky' would make a suitable substitute. Names are never neutral: they can provide indicators of culture, nationality, and even historical trends. All stages of labelling and handling data that are required for ethics thus involve decisions that have implications for analytical conclusions.

Participant recruitment

An essential stage of most research is participant recruitment, or what is referred to as gaining and maintaining access to a research site or set of participants. The first step is to identify possible gatekeepers: those 'knowledgeable insiders' (Hoey & Webb, 2024) who can grant (or withhold) access to a specific setting. These might be parents, caregivers, teachers, or other professionals who are responsible for children's eating, though they may not necessarily be the people who will be recorded. Establishing a professional relationship with these gatekeepers, and subsequently with other adults and children who will be involved in the research takes time, but it is fundamental to ensuring ethically secured data. Always provide clear and concise information about what is involved and whether participation will require any extra time or effort. It is important that participants understand the purpose of the research and are reassured that they are not being judged or assessed (see Shaw, 2024, for more advice on this).

Staff in institutional settings may act as mediators in distributing and collecting consent forms from parents and guardians. They may even have procedures that could help with recruitment, such as through the ways in which they communicate with parents and guardians of children in their care. As much as possible, ensure that research involves no changes to working routines. Note that in some cases, a gatekeeper may switch jobs or move to a different working role and those who take their place may not be similarly enthusiastic about participation in the research. This is why it is not just about 'gaining' access but also about maintaining it, and why sensitivity to the dynamics and conditions of the setting is required. In institutional settings, for instance, the priority for staff members is caring for children and the research should never get in the way of this work.

In terms of recompense for helping out with research, be clear about why people are being asked to participate and whether they will receive any compensation. Payment is usually not appropriate for research, since it might be construed as bribery, but there are alternative ways to compensate participants for their involvement. For families, for instance, a copy of some or all of the recordings might be offered; or institutions may be interested in brief reports, training materials, or workshops that could contribute to staff development. Showing brief examples of published research – particularly that in which images are anonymised – can help to reassure participants of not only what will happen to the video recordings, but also what kind of analysis will be conducted. This can help to allay fears or misconceptions about the research. Above all, be nice to people. You need them more than they need you.

Data collection

The cornerstone of interactional research is the data: a corpus of video recordings of naturally occurring social interaction and the subsequent transcripts. A focus on the organisation and sense-making practices of everyday eating practices means that the rich detail of video (or, at the very least, audio) is required; these are the best methods currently available for capturing social life. The use of video recordings as research data has emerged and expanded alongside the technological development of the video camera, from the pioneering ethnographic work of Margaret Mead and Gregory Bateson (Mead & Bateson, 1977) to advances in multimodal analysis and the complexity of interaction (Broth, Laurier, & Mondada, 2014; Haddington et al, 2023; Heath et al, 2009). Good-quality recordings are vital, where 'good' relates both to ethically obtained recordings and to clarity in the visual and auditory details – that is, all participants can be seen and heard clearly – and a recording that is carried out in a way that maintains the integrity of the setting (i.e. eating in everyday life). Plan this stage carefully and allow time for deviations from the plan, which will invariably occur. This includes ensuring that ethical concerns remain a higher priority than data collection, particularly when infants are concerned (see Box 4.1 in Chapter 4 for specific advice on this).

Recording children's eating where and when it occurs means that there will be considerable variation in terms of what is required. At its most basic, recording equipment will be needed to capture visual (i.e. faces, bodies, food, immediate surroundings) and auditory details (i.e. sufficiently clear to distinguish separate voices and other sounds), over the duration of the mealtime (see Box 3.1 for equipment suggestions). Recording will take place over a period that could range from several minutes to a few hours. The rest of this section considers the practicalities of recording children's eating within social settings alongside the analytical rationale for various decisions that need to be made. For excellent guides on data collection for ethnomethodology and conversation analysis (EMCA) and related research, see Heath et al (2009), Mondada (2014a, 2014b), and Robinson et al (2024).

BOX 3.1 EQUIPMENT

Recording children's mealtimes will require some essential pieces of equipment, which can be adapted if the recording takes place in a mobile environment rather than a static location:

- Two video cameras to capture multiple angles and allow for unexpected technical faults or batteries running out; more can be helpful, as back-up,
- Mounting brackets or mini-tripods for the video cameras,
- One or two external microphones with a separate voice recorder, as an optional extra,
- Power cables, spare batteries, and/or battery packs for charging the cameras in situ,
- Memory cards for the cameras (choose reputable brands with high-speed processing and large storage capacity),
- Strong adhesive tape for securing cables and cameras,
- A bag or case to carry everything safely and securely.

> Mobile phones should not be used for recording research data except as a last resort, since the security of the recording cannot be assured if the phone is connected to the internet or if other applications on the device may have access to the recordings (see the 'Data storage' section below).

Setting up equipment

All data collection is by default selective; not everything can be captured on camera. Decisions need to be made about how to position the equipment in a way that is not intrusive or disruptive to usual routines, without compromising on the quality of the recording. When using equipment for the first time or in a new setting, it is preferable to test it in advance to become familiar with aspects such as camera positioning, battery longevity, and the potential impact of the equipment on the eating environment. In some settings, there may be routines regarding how food is prepared and served to children, and familiarity with these routines can reduce any possible disruption. Static or fixed cameras are preferable, since they allow researchers to set up and switch on the equipment and leave the room before eating commences. Some settings may require the researcher to be physically present, with either a static or moving camera, which can follow the participants if they are moving around in a larger space (e.g. in outside settings, such as parks or fairgrounds).

Video cameras should be securely placed using small tripods or mounting brackets. Use furniture and fixtures (e.g. windowsills or bookshelves) to mount the equipment where necessary. At least two cameras are optimal to capture different visual angles of the participants – ideally opposite each other – to ensure that all faces are visible. Placing cameras near head height (i.e. at the level of participants' gaze) will provide better visuals of faces, though be aware that other people's bodies might block the view depending on where the camera is placed. At least one camera should cover the whole area of participation to be filmed (e.g. the dinner table or setting in which people are eating), so that the full setting can be seen in one camera. Additional cameras can be used to obtain closer angles of specific features. Do not use the zoom function, since this could reduce the quality of the recording. A separate microphone or several (capturing directional rather than ambient sound) can be very useful in busy settings; good-quality audio is essential for transcription. For more discussion on camera placement, see Broth et al (2014) and Mondada (2014b).

When participants set up the equipment

In most situations, it is preferable for the researchers themselves to set up the equipment, not only to reduce the burden on participants but also to ensure that the recordings will be of sufficiently good quality. There will be situations, though, where it is more feasible or appropriate to allow participants themselves to set up and switch on equipment, such as during milk-feeding or infant mealtimes in the home. In such cases, the priority is to make everything as easy as possible: reduce the amount of equipment and choose cameras that are simple to use and that can be left in place. Provide the equipment in advance so that those who will be responsible for the recordings have time to familiarise themselves with it. Consider how the cameras will be charged and how data storage will be handled so that multiple mealtimes can be recorded without requiring researcher assistance. It is possible that the recordings may begin or end abruptly because someone forgot to switch the equipment on, someone sits in front of the camera, or the camera is knocked over by children or pets. Or there may be no data at all. Plan for these kinds of eventualities and move on; there will always be another meal.

On 'reactivity' to being recorded

One of the reasons that some researchers give for not using video data is that they think that participants will not give permission to be recorded or will react differently once the cameras are rolling. The experience of researchers who have worked with video recording for many years is that this is rarely the case (see Heath et al, 2009, for discussion about this). Many participants are curious to learn what the research will discover, while others do not mind at all; some are just happy to know that they are contributing to research, while others actively want to be recorded. Some of the children in the preschool lunch research, for instance, were very keen to be on 'film'. There can be all sorts of reasons why people might not want to be recorded and many of their concerns are unlikely to be the same as those that are important to researchers.

On a related topic, researchers may have concerns that video recording will change the research object itself and that people's behaviour will no longer be natural. Here are some key points that can help to allay such concerns:

- Almost all empirical research introduces something new to people's lives; video recording is much more sympathetic to everyday realities than other methods that impose restrictions on behaviour, and which therefore require a level of reactivity, such as interviews, questionnaires, and experiments.
- Digital video recordings are a large part of contemporary life in many countries and even young children are accustomed to the presence of cameras (e.g. those on mobile phones); they have become mainstream.
- The longer participants are recorded, the more they become acclimatised to the cameras (Potter & Shaw, 2018). The equipment soon becomes part of the furniture and other concerns (e.g. children's needs) usually take priority.

- The camera might be permanently present during the interaction, but it is not omni-relevant for participants (Mondada, 2014b): for most of the time, it is not likely to be acknowledged or oriented to.
- Even for those moments where there is an explicit orientation to the cameras, these can be analysable moments in themselves (see Heath, 1986: 176; Laurier & Philo, 2006: 185–186), in terms of how the camera becomes an 'additional participant' that can observe and listen in to the conversation.
- While some people might behave slightly differently when on camera, it is almost impossible to change all aspects of the situation that are of analytical interest, such as short pauses and gestures.

It should go without saying that where a participant reacts very strongly to being recorded or appears to be very uncomfortable, particularly with children, the recording should cease immediately. Ethical considerations take precedence over everything else.

On sample sizes and the data corpus

Before data collection commences, it is important to have a plan about how much data to collect, whether that relates to hours of recording or number of mealtimes. This is important when planning not only data storage and management, but also the time required for analysis and dissemination. Interactional research can be used with variable data corpus sizes; it depends on the aim of the research, the setting, and the analytical phenomena to be examined. Some topics or interactional phenomena, for instance, may be more likely to arise in settings with several children versus one child, or with younger versus older children. What is important is to ensure that sufficient data is collected that will enable the analysis to identify robust patterns (features that are recurrent throughout the data corpus), as well as variability (with regard to things such as food eaten, time of day, participants, or setting). No mealtime is the same as any other; the task of the research is to explicate those features of eating practices that can be specific to single instances or otherwise sufficiently generic to be relatable to other contexts.

On using existing datasets

There may be some situations in which video data from mealtimes has been collected from a previous project or by another researcher. This can provide a useful avenue into research, particularly for those starting out; and it can also be a very effective way of combining or comparing data across different settings for more extensive analyses of interactional phenomena. The details of ethical agreements (i.e. what the participants consented to with regard to use of the data) and the quality of the recording (in terms of clarity in the auditory and visual details) should be checked carefully in these situations. Ensure that there are clear expectations between those who have provided the data and those who are collaborating in the analysis, to avoid any issues around authorship on publications and ownership or future use of the dataset. Also consider how data will be shared (e.g. via a secure cloud service or external hard drives) between researchers working in geographically separate locations so as to maintain the security of the data. The quality of the recordings will need to be checked, in terms of recording 'naturalistic' settings, the entirety of the meal wherever possible, and whether the participants were attuned to any specific research aims or questions.

Collecting other information

In addition to the recordings, other information may be beneficial for the analysis, such as the names and ages of children present, a description of the food served, and any allergies or dietary restrictions of the children. In institutional settings, there might be information about how and where food is prepared and cooked, whether children and staff bring their own food, and how eating arrangements are organised in terms of seating and timing. Keep notes about such information where possible. It can be useful to take photos of the eating environment when no one is present, for instance, which can later be useful when analysing the data or presenting findings. As always, collect what data is necessary without breaching ethical considerations or accumulating unnecessary material.

Data storage

The process of storing video data begins immediately after data collection. Having a clear and organised system is important not only for current analyses, but also for the archiving of the data for any future projects (see Albert & Hofstetter, 2024; Corti et al, 2019). Ensure that data notes are clear and comprehensible so that they can be used as a future resource; include any 'keys' to abbreviations or codes and make detailed notes about things that might seem obvious. Start taking notes as soon as possible after the first video recording is complete and keep meticulous records thereafter. Three main things need to be stored, as follows.

Video (and/or audio) recordings

Transfer the original video files onto external hard drives as soon as possible after the recording takes place and create a back-up copy of these recordings on a second hard drive. These separate hard drives should be kept in separate and secure locations, in case of technical failure or damage. The use of encryption (including password-protected hard drives) is recommended as additional security. Give each file a codename to identify it (see the notes on code names below). Keep in mind that high-resolution digital video data can take up considerable storage space and should be compressed only if this will not reduce the quality of the sound and visuals. Invest in an ample supply of good-quality hard drives. Secure copies of good-quality data are irreplaceable.

Consent forms and sensitive data

All signed consent forms and other sensitive or personal data about participants or locations should be securely stored in a separate location from the recordings and any other information about the data. This is an important ethical procedure to ensure that, in the nightmare scenario that the recordings are lost or damaged, there is no way to connect these to specific individuals or institutions. Included in this kind of data is likely to be a 'key' to the participant pseudonyms. One way to increase security is to use paper-only versions of particularly sensitive material, such as the pseudonym key for identifying individual children, and to store copies of these in secure, separate locations. This avoids the possibility of sensitive information been inadvertently shared or 'lost' in computer storage folders.

Metadata and anonymised material

The metadata of a project comprises information about the project and recordings, such as the date and time when the recording took place, anonymised information about the location (e.g. 'school A', 'Class 1'), and any other details that might be needed (e.g. food served, number of persons present). It can be helpful to use a spreadsheet or similar software to provide an overview of the metadata. Allocate each 'meal' or recording a code name that will help to identify it immediately. For instance, the preschool lunch data has code names such as 'MSL2_X_08': 'M' refers to 'mealtime', 'SL' to 'Sandlådan' (meaning 'the sandpit' – the pseudonym for that preschool), '2' denotes the second round of data collection, 'X' specifies Room X, and '08' indicates the eighth meal recorded in that location. The code names can then be used to label the video recordings as well as in a spreadsheet or other software. Any anonymised transcripts can also be stored in a similar location. Develop a system that will be easy to navigate in future projects.

Data management and cataloguing

A corpus of video recordings is the foundation of interactional research, but it can also be overwhelming: even just a few hours of recordings capture thousands of features that could be analysed. What is needed is a system that allows this complexity to be organised without oversimplifying or obscuring the details. A vital step is to catalogue the data. 'Cataloguing' refers to the process in which a description of each video recording (or eating event) is produced – a written reference guide that can become a searchable resource (see Albert & Hofstetter, 2024; Heath et al, 2009).

There are various ways in which a catalogue can be developed. The simplest is to create a separate document (e.g. a Word file or Excel sheet) for each recording, including a description of the event and any notes about topics discussed, people present, food eaten, etc. More information will make it easier to search the catalogue for instances of analytical foci later on. For instance, include a note about the timing of particular topics on the video so that they can be located in the future and pick out key words that will be searchable (e.g. using the 'find' function). Box 3.2 shows a brief example of an entry in the data catalogue for the preschool lunch project; 'food waste' and 'disgust' were noted due to an interest in these topics. Sometimes, of course, what is 'interesting' about the data might not become clear until later in the analysis. The catalogued files can therefore be updated as a living document throughout the course of the project. In addition to creating Word documents as catalogue entries, software such as DOTEbase (McIlvenny et al, 2022; see https://www.dote.aau.dk/) can help with organising video files as well as creating more advanced systems of cataloguing data and organising data into collections (see the next section).

BOX 3.2 EXCERPT FROM A DATA CATALOGUE ENTRY

Codename: MSL2_X_08 (Sandlådan, 2nd data collection round, Room X, meal 8)
Recorded: 22 February 2022
Time: 00:43:59 on audio file
Duration of meal: Circa 38 minutes
Teacher: Saga
Children: Valdemar (6y1m), Johan (5y7m), Hanna (5y7m), Peter (4y6m)
Food served: Sausage casserole, rice, sweetcorn, broccoli, beans

Notes (video timings from Camera A)

00:00:45–00:02:05 Saga checks to see who is table monitor and they all look at the board on the wall. Opening routines. Valdemar chooses the song, then they sing it (it is mostly Saga singing).

00:02:05 Start of serving sequence: the children serve themselves and the rice goes first to Valdemar, the casserole to Peter, and vegetables to Hanna. Saga offers milk or water to all the children.

00:03:00–00:03:20 As Peter is serving himself rice and about to take a third scoop, Saga says something about not taking too much food and is looking at Peter as she says this. Johan joins in with a comment about the food ending up in the waste and being disgusting. Relevant for food waste and disgust.

Transcription

If video recordings enable researchers to hold time still, then transcription is the means through which those moments are rendered visible and analysable on the page. At its simplest, 'transcription' is the process of converting talk, sound, and gestures into a text document, referred to as the 'transcript'. It is also an essential part of the analysis and a technical skill that requires training and a rigorous approach to detail. This is not something to be delegated to automated tools such as AI (see Box 3.4); it is a foundational analytical step. It requires a sensitivity to the nuances of talk and gesture as performing social actions, not simply as the production of sound and words. As noted in Chapter 2, a word or gesture in itself does not denote a social action or meaning.

Transcripts are also living documents; they evolve as analyses develop. Even a detailed transcript is only a partial representation of the recording. Choices will need to be made in terms of which features of the interaction are included in order to examine how social actions are accomplished. The details matter: this is not just about capturing what is said but also *how* it is said. Features of speech delivery such as the timing and sequentiality of interaction and intonation, emphases, and overlapping speech are important for producing social actions. Take Extract 3.1, for example, in which Dad is spoon-feeding his five-month-old daughter, Daisy. The transcript is taken from a moment when Dad is putting the spoon into Daisy's mouth.

Extract 3.1

```
01 Dad   this look oh mm
```

If the analysis were based solely on this transcript, it might seem as if Dad has begun to say something and then abandoned his turn. The 'oh *mm*' might even suggest that something has gone wrong with the spoon-feeding; Dad almost sounds disappointed. By adding more details of the speech delivery, however, a different interpretation can be made, even without the video recording – see Extract 3.2:

Extract 3.2

```
01 Dad   this look- ((Dad takes spoon))
02       (1.4)
03 Dad   o::aah ((spoon toward mouth))
04       (3.8) ((spoon into and out of mouth)
05 Dad   mmmm:
```

This version of the transcript includes features of speech delivery such as the development of the 'oh' (line 03) into a more open-mouthed and longer '*o::aah*' sound, and the emphasis (indicated by the underline) and extension of the '*mm*' into an '*mmmm*' sound (line 05). This last sound, in particular, is known as a gustatory *mmm*, used to orient to, or reference, food pleasure (Wiggins, 2002; see also Chapter 6); it is distinguishable in large part because of its extended and emphasised form, in comparison to a more conversational *mm* that might be used in other types of conversation (Gardner, 1997). Without these features of delivery in the transcript, it would not have been possible to identify this as a gustatory *mmm* or to distinguish the 'oh' as more of an '*oaah*' sound.

The silences and the gestural details noted in parentheses provide further information about what is going on here. Dad's talk can now be analysed as part of the interaction with Daisy: his talk and vocalisations are produced as Daisy opens her mouth (his '*oaah*' allows his mouth to mirror the same movements), and he sounds gustatory pleasure on her behalf as her mouth closes around the food. He is not disappointed after all, but is rather scaffolding – through talk, sounds, and gesture – the early eating practices of his infant daughter. This is an example of how prosody matters and why it is important to capture details in a transcript: the way in which words and sounds are uttered can change the social action entirely. In tonal languages, a change in prosody can further change the entire meaning of a word or phrase. Transcripts are not merely using 'quotes' from people but are essential for capturing the consequential details of everyday interaction.

Transcription as capturing social action

Transcription is an analytical tool used across the social sciences, though the styles presented in this book are specific to interactional approaches that focus on talk as social action. The details of speech delivery are crucial for analysing how talk *does* things rather than is simply a medium for communication.

A standard transcription system is used by interactional researchers, referred to as the 'Jeffersonian transcription system' (Jefferson, 2008; Sacks et al, 1974; see Appendix 3), named after its developer, Gail Jefferson (see Chapter 2). By using a standard transcription system, researchers ensure consistency and transparency across published research, providing access to the 'raw' data and enabling analytic claims to be accessible for other researchers, as discussed in Chapter 1.

A Jefferson transcript is more detailed than orthographic or verbatim transcripts and focuses on social action rather than phonetic and phonemic details of speech as captured in the International Phonetic Alphabet. Note that a simpler orthographic transcript is not more 'neutral'; it conceals features of delivery that are crucial for understanding how talk is produced (as evidenced in Extracts 3.1 and 3.2). Two things are invaluable for Jeffersonian transcription: a good set of headphones and a copy of Hepburn and Bolden's (2017) *Transcribing for Social Research* (see the companion website https://study.sagepub.com/hepburnandbolden). For those who will be doing a lot of transcription, software such as DOTE (see dote.au.dk) or Elan (see https://archive.mpi.nl/tla/elan) will help with creating and organising transcripts alongside video and audio files.

Creating a standard Jeffersonian transcript

The first thing to note is that, unless there is only a small amount of data (i.e. a few hours' worth), it is unlikely that it will all need to be transcribed. The cataloguing and note-taking systems discussed earlier can be used to identify sections of the recordings that could be transcribed. An orthographic transcript can be used as a starting point to begin examining the data, which can then be developed to include various details of speech delivery and timing as the analysis develops. Creating a transcript from scratch involves writing down everything that was said, by whom, and in what order. The transcript should include *exactly* what was said, without tidying up or correcting talk. A header or code name for each transcript should be used to ensure that it can be easily located within the data corpus. Line numbers are also essential so that sections of the transcript can be easily identified in the analysis.

Three columns provide the format of the transcript: the first for line numbers, the second for speaker identification, and the third for the talk and any other features (including silences and gestures). A couple of spaces between columns one and two, and around five spaces between columns two and three (see Extract 3.1 for an example), help to present the text clearly. Speaker identification is often presented as the first three letters or a shortened version of the anonymised name or their role in the interaction (e.g. 'Rob' for Robert or 'Mum' for mother). Other common features of Jeffersonian transcripts are to use Courier or Courier New font (size 10). These are fixed-width or non-proportional fonts, meaning that each character takes up the same space on the line, making them easy to read and clearly demarcating alignment between overlapping talk and gestures. Extract 3.3 is another example of an orthographic transcript from a family meal in which Dad is talking to his five-year-old son, Magnus, about the food that remains on Magnus's plate. Also present is two-year-old Robert, sitting nearby.

Extract 3.3

```
01 Dad   do you going to do you want have you
02       had enough fish finger or do you want more fish
```

As noted earlier, an orthographic transcript can provide a simplified version, though it can miss essential features of speech delivery and timings that are necessary to make sense of the talk. Dad's turn on line 01, in this example, is almost entirely incomprehensible. The addition of some basic details is needed. There is no particular order in which details of speech delivery can be added (though see Hepburn & Bolden, 2017, for a detailed guided tour); but it can be helpful to begin with aspects such as silences, the pace and production of words, and any overlapping talk. Punctuation marks are used to indicate pitch contours, for instance, and silences are measured in fractions of seconds; see Appendix 3 for a full list of transcription features that can be added. Extract 3.4 illustrates a developed version of Extract 3.3.

Extract 3.4

```
01 Dad   do- >y'going to- d'y' [want

02 Rob                         [ay::

03       (0.4)

04 Dad   have you had enough (0.2) fish finger or

05       d'y'want more fish.
```

These features of speech delivery were identified by repeatedly listening to and watching the recording. Audio editing software (e.g. Audacity; see https://www.audacityteam.org/) can slow down the playback speed or reduce background noise, to enable a sharper audible version of the recording and measure the length of silences. In this version of the transcript, Dad's talk is now more intelligible and observable as a series of what are called 'repairs' (Schegloff, 2007) in which different formulations are abruptly abandoned before re-starting the turn on lines 04–05. The overlap with Robert is also visible on line 02, and a brief silence between the abandoned turn in line 01 and that in line 04. Developing the transcript to include features of delivery can stimulate as well as support analyses (see Chapter 8 for further analysis of this transcript).

Additional aspects of transcription are important for conversation analysis (CA) in particular, which involve identifying what are known as 'turn construction units' (TCUs) (Sacks et al, 1974), defined as the words or phrases that comprise a complete action in talk. These TCUs have relevance not only for transcription (see Hepburn & Bolden, 2017) but also to understand where turn-taking might occur, since they project where there might be a 'transition relevant place' (Sacks et al, 1974) in which another speaker might take their turn in talk. A long silence after a TCU (i.e. a gap) where a response is due from another speaker can indicate a dispreferred response (Pomerantz, 1984a; Schegloff, 2007). Extract 3.5 illustrates an example of this, taken from a different family meal where Dad asks his seven-year-old son Samuel to eat up his green beans.

Extract 3.5

01 Dad >m'eat yer beans up< (.) mhh
02 (1.8) *((Samuel's hand moves towards the bread))*
03 Dad no (0.2) no (0.2) >no no ↓no< (0.4) beans.

Dad's turn on line 01 is an example of a TCU – specifically in the form of a directive that requires Samuel to comply with the action (i.e. to eat the beans). In line 02, there is a fairly long silence of 1.8 seconds, in which Samuel does not say anything or eat his beans, but rather moves his hand towards the bread in the centre of the table. Dad treats this as transgression and continues with his pursuit of the need to eat up the beans (line 03; see Wiggins & Humă, 2026a, and Chapter 7 for further analysis of this extract).

Although the use of the Jefferson transcription is standard across much interactional research, there are variations in how transcripts are presented in published work, according to the analytical focus, the specific approach used, and the publication outlet. What is important is that the transcript retains the verbal, vocal, or visual details necessary to evidence the analysis and presents this in a manner that is most accessible (see the section on 'Communication and dissemination' towards the end of this chapter).

BOX 3.3 TRANSCRIBING YOUNG CHILDREN'S SPEECH AND VOCALISATIONS

When young children or those acquiring competence in language are being recorded, some vocalisations may be unclearly articulated words or include sounds that do not relate to any known lexical system. Crying is a case in point. The use of non-lexical vocalisations is also prevalent throughout adult speech (Ogden & Keevallik, 2020). The most common approach to transcribing speech and sounds of this kind is to use a modified orthography – that is, to try to capture the sounds phonetically and, in some cases, include a candidate hearing (i.e. a best guess at what the word might be) in brackets following the phonetic representation. In some cases, a description of the sound might be provided in brackets instead. Visual images (i.e. grab frames from the video recordings) are even more important in infant mealtimes, when much of the social interaction takes place without words. Useful resources are Hepburn's (2004; Hepburn & Potter, 2007) transcription and analytic work on adult crying and Kidwell's (2011, 2013) analyses of children's interaction and vocalisations.

Transcribing languages other than English

Although the common academic language is English, many researchers work in settings where other languages are used, meaning that additional work is required to translate the original language into English for presentations and publications. While the analysis should be based on the *original* language, the transcripts used to present the work will often need to include both the original and the English translation. Given the importance of language for understanding social interaction, care must be taken to ensure that the subtle features of the original language are not lost. This is important not only for reasons for transparency and rigour in the analysis, but also for expanding knowledge of eating practices within various languages other than English.

The decisions made when transcribing and translating from languages other than English will depend on features such as whether the language uses an alphabet such as the Cyrillic, Greek, or Latin alphabet, a logographic system, or other writing systems such as abjads and abugidas. There are also many tonal languages (e.g. Lao and Thai), in which pitch contours change the entire meaning of a word or phrase. Since the Jefferson system of representing speech is based on the English language, there are no standard methods for representing these tonal changes and some researchers have developed their own systems to effectively illustrate core features of the language (see Enfield, 2007, for Lao; Moerman, 1988, for Thai).

The presentation of transcripts with languages other than English typically follows a three-line format: the first line is for the original language, the second for the morpheme-by-morpheme English gloss, and the third line for the idiomatic translation into English. This second line can be important for attuning English-speaking audiences to where features of speech delivery are located in the original language, such as pauses, emphases, or pitch contours. For languages where the word order is similar to English, the morpheme gloss might not be necessary and a two-line version can be used. In interaction where more than one language is used, the same rules apply: provide a translation for those languages in the line underneath. Extract 3.6 shows an example of a translation from Swedish (which uses an adapted form of the Latin alphabet and follows a similar word order to English):

Extract 3.6

01 Tea nu ta vi så pass mycket som vi tro att vi or::kar,
now we're taking as much as we think we can manage to eat
02 (0.6)
03 Tea för att (.) annars så:: (0.4) >får vi ju< kasta mat°et°
because (.) otherwise so: (0.4) >we have to of course< throw out the food

Note how the original language is in regular font and the translation in **bold**: this is a stylistic decision, and alternatives would be to use italicised font for the original or the English translation. What is important is that it should be easy to distinguish between the original language and the translated text. This example raises an issue that is essential for understanding eating practices: some words are not directly translatable into the English language. In Extract 3.6, these words are '*orkar*' (line 01) and '*ju*' (line 03). The word '*orkar*' is the present tense of the Swedish verb '*orka*', which is roughly translated as being able to manage, handle, or undertake a task that requires effort as well as ability. In the case of eating, therefore, it is not only about how much food someone might be able to eat, but also about whether they have the capacity – in terms of both appetite and energy or willingness – to do so (see Wiggins et al, 2026). As a verb, it is incredibly useful in terms of offering a way of understanding eating practices; but it is not easy to unpack this in English or to explain on a single line of transcript. Meanings are, to some extent, lost in translation.

The word '*ju*' is similarly tricky to translate simply into English. It can be translated in many ways, such as 'of course'/'obviously'/'as you know'/'as I've said', depending on the context. In this example, it refers to a modal particle that relates to shared knowledge or something that has already been said or which the recipient should already know (Aijmer, 2004). A sensitivity to variations across languages is an essential part of understanding how children eat in different cultural and social contexts and English may at times be a hindrance in understanding children's eating practices in other languages (see Mol, 2024, and Chapter 9 of this book, for more on this topic). For a full discussion on how to transcribe and translate various languages, see Hepburn and Bolden (2017) and Egbert et al (2016).

Transcribing multimodal details

Most of the features of a Jeffersonian transcript focus on vocal delivery and extra details need to be added to capture visual conduct. During children's mealtimes, some of the most salient features include eye gaze (towards other people or objects), facial expression (especially during or after consumption), hand movements (regarding manipulation of food or utensils), or bodily position (in relation to other people and objects). There is no single best way to do this; the aim should instead be to produce a '*serviceable* transcript of visible conduct' (Hepburn & Bolden, 2017: 101). It is impossible to describe everything that is going on; selectivity is unavoidable.

The main challenges with transcribing multimodal details are ensuring precision in terms of where these occur in overlap with vocal details (without it become incomprehensibly complicated) and avoiding descriptions or linguistic glosses that imply specific interpretations (e.g. 'looks accusingly'). Begin with a standard Jeffersonian transcript so that the vocal conduct is already transcribed, then layer on different multimodal details, focusing on either one person or one kind of conduct (e.g. eye gaze) as analysis develops. There are three main techniques for incorporating multimodal details into a transcript, ordered here according to the level of skill required.

Technique 1

Use comments to provide a written description of visual conduct and insert this in the relevant place in the transcript, using double brackets and italics; an example can be seen in Extract 3.5. This will necessarily be a gloss of what is happening and it can be difficult to locate exactly where it begins and ends. It is useful, therefore, when the transcript needs to be readable and when visible conduct is important; but its exact placement is not essential for the analysis. A further example is shown in Extract 3.7.

Extract 3.7

```
01 Dad    [do- >y'going to- d'y'[want
          [((Dad gaze to Magnus' plate, Magnus gaze to Dad))
02 Rob                          [ay::
```

Technique 2

Use visual images (i.e. frame grabs or line drawings) to supplement the textual transcript as separate figures that are positioned at key points in the transcript. These can provide a more holistic representation and can be particularly useful for understanding the position of people in relation to one another (as in Extract 3.8), eye gaze, facial expressions, or hand gestures. These visual images can also be arranged in a comic-book style, sometimes referred to as 'graphic transcripts' (Laurier, 2014; see also Extracts 4.3–4.5 in Chapter 4) to capture the sequentiality of a particular feature. Video and photo editing software can be used to anonymise images, whether by applying filters or by using drawing techniques to provide an overlay of the image.

Extract 3.8

```
01 Dad    do- >#y'going to- d'y'[want
   fig          #fig 1
02 Rob                             [ay::
```

FIGURE 3.1 You going to?

Technique 3

Use a specialised notation system, such as that developed by Charles Goodwin (1981) or Lorenza Mondada (2011), which details the precise coordination of vocal and visual conduct as it temporally unfolds within a section of interaction. These offer a much more accurate way of pinpointing where different features (e.g. eye gaze or pointing) occur in the interactional sequence and can be particularly useful when precision in placement is crucial. Note that an extra line can be placed between the multimodal line and the next interactional turn, to clearly present the transcript on the page. The use of specialised notation systems can also be combined with visual images. Extract 3.9 provides an example of a multimodal transcript.

Extract 3.9

```
01 Dad    &%do-        &>y'going to- d'y'[want
   dad    &head turn &gz to plate------>
   mag     %gz to Dad------------------->
02 Rob                                   [ay::
```

For other examples of transcripts that capture features such as eye gaze, body torque, and gestures in addition to those mentioned above, see Reynolds (2021), Rossano (2014), and Streeck et al (2011). Different variations of transcripts have been used in Chapters 4 to 8 to illustrate how and when multimodal features might be emphasised to clarify analytical points.

Analysis

As a book set within a multidisciplinary landscape and in which a plurality of interactional approaches is advocated, it would be inappropriate – if not impossible – to set out a series of analytical steps to be followed beyond those which have already been noted on recording and transcribing data. What is provided here is a guide to four analytical focal points for interactional research: data sessions, analytic focus, collections or single cases, and evidencing analyses. Specific analytical examples are detailed in Chapters 4 to 8, which should be considered as the main source of guidance on getting started with interactional analyses. See also Chapter 2 for recommendations of features of analysis using EMCA, discursive psychology (DP), and language socialisation.

Data sessions

A central feature of interactional research is the use of data sessions: gatherings of researchers to collectively scrutinise a small section of data (video and/or audio data, with transcripts) to make observations, develop analytical suggestions, and enable the interrogation of specific ideas about data. Not only are these important for developing analytical skills; they are also an integral part of the research process (Betz, 2024; Stevanovic & Weiste, 2017). The collaborative nature of data sessions means that any analytical observations should be evidenced and justified. They provide a scholarly space in which arguments can be refined and developed. The presentation of raw video data (with participant consent) within these spaces provides a level of transparency that is rarely seen in other research approaches. The format and style of data sessions can vary significantly: many are hybrid or entirely online; they might be based in certain institutions or international networks focused on specific research interests. Online resources and information about data sessions for social interactional research include a list of data sessions worldwide (rolsi.net/data-sessions/), a blog post on data sessions (saulalbert.net/blog/the-data-session/), and a website providing a recorded example of a data session (learninghowtolookandlisten.com).

Defining an analytic focus

Towards the start of the chapter, it was noted that research questions typically develop once data has been collected and the analysis is underway. It is through the process of cataloguing and transcribing some of the data that potential areas of analytical foci can be identified. In CA research, this is known as 'unmotivated inquiry': preliminary observations or noticings about the data that inform but do not determine the analysis (see Clayman, 2024). The analytical focus should be guided by the data rather than by theories, hypotheses, or expectations prior to examining the data. Time should be spent becoming familiar with the data, reviewing the recordings, searching the corpus, and making detailed notes. This is another reason why attempting to shortcut or abbreviate the analytical stages using automated software is counterproductive, since an essential aspect of analysis is a close engagement with the data at a fine-grained level. The development of analytical skills is something that requires effort, practice, and focus. The core analytical work should not be delegated to automated processes which cannot deal with the intricacies of social actions (see also Box 3.4).

The process of defining an analytic focus is likely to occur in a cyclical manner, moving between searching the recordings, identifying 'candidate' instances of a phenomenon (see Clift & Mandelbaum, 2024), and transcribing these to examine the recording in more detail. This is a further example of how transcription is an integral part of the analytical process and can be invaluable in terms of determining which aspects of interaction might become a central focus. It is therefore important to begin transcribing as a means of moving from cataloguing and searching the data to identifying an analytical focus that can then be developed more substantially. At the centre of this process are analyses of social actions (see Chapter 2) embedded within specific situational contexts.

BOX 3.4 ON WHEN (NOT) TO USE ARTIFICIAL INTELLIGENCE

The development of artificial intelligence (AI) has had an unprecedented impact on academic work and its uses as a tool at various stages of research are considerable. Caution should be exercised, however, particularly when researching video material involving children. It was noted earlier that AI is not necessarily beneficial for transcription due to its inability to capture the subtle distinction between a behaviour and a social action. A similar argument can be made against the use of AI for video analyses when an interactional approach is used. There are strong ethical reasons not to do so: uploading confidential data to AI software breaches consent, since once data is uploaded, there is no control over how or where it is used. That aside, the analysis would be of an entirely different nature. AI typically analyses work by interpreting specific facial expressions, words, or gestures as indicative of, or corresponding to, a specific cognitive, emotional, or physiological state: that a particular cry means hunger (see Chapter 4) or a smile while chewing means gustatory pleasure (see Chapter 6). As discussed in Chapter 2, however, interactional research examines social actions, not individual behaviours. A cry or a smile does not 'mean' a specific, individual thing any more than saying 'I don't like' has a simple interpretation. Social interaction is not about individuals expressing intentions; it is about how people create understandings together. AI, as yet, cannot analyse video in this way.

Building collections versus single case analysis

Assembling a collection of instances of a phenomenon is a method used predominantly in EMCA and DP research, in which multiple instances of specific discursive and interactional practices are examined across the data corpus. A collection allows research to focus on the intricate details of individual extracts while also identifying patterns that can span a much larger scale, sometimes involving hundreds of cases. In essence, a collection is the gathering together of instances of a particular phenomenon so that these can be analysed in more detail. These instances (also called 'cases' or 'candidate examples') are sections of data collated in such a way that they can be searched and analysed further. Collections should be as inclusive as possible and should include any borderline cases to avoid missing core analytical nuances. A collection can be built around a specific word or phrase (e.g. 'Have you had enough?'), a gesture (e.g. pointing to food), or an action (e.g. a food offer); see Hofstetter and Albert (2024) for guidance on building collections.

In contrast to developing a collection, single case analyses can be used where a longer section of data offers analytical insight that would not be possible with shorter segments, and which also contributes something distinct to the research literature (see Nishizaka, 2024). An example in relation to children's eating practices is the analysis of a segment of a family mealtime in which there is negotiation over one child's consumption of green beans (see Extract 3.5; Wiggins & Humă, 2026a; see also Chapter 7). The analysis demonstrates how the interaction evolves over the course of around two and a half minutes, including directives, food likes, disgust, and what we term 'reluctant compliance'. The illustrated research example in Chapter 8 provides another example of a single case analysis. Single case analyses can provide depth and detail on a specific issue, though the compromise is that they cannot capture the breadth or variability demonstrated in analyses of collections.

BOX 3.5 HOW ARE INTERACTIONAL ANALYSES DIFFERENT FROM OBSERVATIONAL METHODS?

Video recordings have been used as a tool for many other research methods and observational research in particular is often associated with this form of data collection. There are, however, important distinctions to be made between observational methods and interactional analyses.

Observation *as a research method* is the process through which coding is conducted on video recordings or in-situ observations within a specific timeframe, such as parent-infant dyads during feeding (for examples of coding schemes related to children's eating, see Haycraft & Blissett, 2008; Palfreyman et al, 2014). This is sometimes referred to as 'structured observation', in which behaviours are systematically coded according to predefined criteria over a fixed period. Discrete units of behaviour (e.g. a 'verbal offer') are coded to analyse the frequency and duration of certain behaviours in relation to other variables. For instance, parts of Extract 2.1 might have been coded as a 'verbal offer' and a 'verbal refusal'; these could then be counted alongside how often these occurred to understand more about parental feeding strategies and fussy eating in children. These coding systems typically focus on individual behaviours as separate units of analysis.

By contrast, interactional research is more akin to observation *as a methodology*: a broader framework of examining everyday settings, like ethnography. Individual behaviours are not isolated and measured but are examined in terms of their co-production and function within the overall situational context. Interactional perspectives are different from structured observational studies in that (a) behaviour is examined in terms of collaborative social actions rather than individual characteristics (see Box 2.1), and (b) the interactional context is as important as the social action: it matters where things happen and how they are involved in sequences of social actions. Interactional research examines how behaviour unfolds over time, examining social actions within their situational context and the consequences of these in the here-and-now of the current setting.

Evidencing the analysis

As in other areas of research, there are important debates about what constitutes appropriate data and adequate methods. Being accountable to standards of good quality, ethical research is an essential aspect of much academic work. Unfortunately, such debates can often rely on erroneous understandings of different approaches. As noted in Chapter 1, the interdisciplinary nature of interactional research means that it is often misunderstood or placed into a category in which it does not fit. For several decades, there has been considerable debate, for instance, about the apparent distinction between 'hard' quantitative and 'soft' qualitative data (Stokoe et al, 2026), in which methods involving numbers, measurements, and statistics are treated as more robust than those which involve words, interpretations, and qualitative analyses. This has implications not only for how research is assessed but also for publication review and funding proposals (see Clift et al, 2024, and Chapter 9 for more on this). Interactional approaches do not, however, fit neatly into either a qualitative or a quantitative category (Stokoe et al, 2026). They are very different from interview-based studies that endeavour to access people's cognitions and experiences. Neither are they quantitative – not because numbers are eschewed *per se*, but rather due to the way in which language (and other features of social interaction) are interpreted as social actions rather than something that might be measured or quantified (see Robinson, 2007, on the role of numbers in CA).

Ensuring quality throughout the research process for interactional approaches requires a sensitivity not only to what is primarily the analysis of words and gestures, but also to the epistemological and analytical principles that underlie these approaches. This quality assurance has been referred to as 'research trustworthiness' (Williamson et al, 2025) or rigour of analysis through clarity, coherence, and corroboration (Wiggins & Humă, 2026b; see also Antaki et al, 2003, for advice on DP analyses). While there is some variation in how different interactional approaches address issues of quality, trustworthiness, or rigour, the following techniques are commonly used.

Transparency

Each stage of the research process should be clearly documented in some form, from decisions made regarding recruitment to the procedures that are followed in analysis. Transparency involves making visible the research process so that it can be scrutinised by various audiences. The use of detailed transcripts and, where possible, anonymised video clips is a central example of this transparency. By presenting raw data as much as possible (video clips and transcripts), researchers can ensure that analytical claims can be interrogated thoroughly by others and enable the analysis to contribute to existing research literature. There are also moves to make some data openly available to make CA research more accessible to other researchers (see Albert et al, 2025).

Participant orientation (aka 'next turn proof' procedure)

Analytical claims must be evidenced in terms of demonstrating participants' orientations or displayed understanding (Raymond & Robinson, 2024). This does not mean trying to find out what participants think or feel, but rather how 'understanding' is something that can be empirically evidenced within the turn-by-turn unfolding of a conversation – that is, 'their being aware of, understanding, and perhaps taking-for-granted a particular sense of the matter in question' (Pomerantz, 2024: 356). Extract 4.3 in Chapter 4 provides a clear example, in which an infant points to her food and says 'mix', which ambiguously could refer to a past event (that it has been mixed) or as a request for help (that it should be mixed). What happens in the ***next turn*** in the interaction is that the caregiver requests a clarification and therefore displays the ambiguity of the prior turn. The work of analysts, therefore, is to examine how ***participants themselves*** make relevant their interpretations of what is going on.

Deviant cases

Analysis works on the basis of identifying interactional practices, often in the form of patterns or regularities (e.g. the organisation of turn-taking or the formulation of psychological states). There are often, however, outlying instances: exceptions or deviations which may not fit the analytical interpretation that is being developed. These can be incredibly useful (in some cases, essential) to demonstrating the robustness of a pattern. For instance, a delayed or mistimed gustatory *mmm* demonstrates the importance of the immediacy of these sound objects in relation to their sequential placement (Wiggins, 2002, 2019; see also Chapter 6). Deviant cases are important for interrogating and validating analytical claims and should be embraced, rather than discarded as outliers.

Communication and dissemination

The final stage of research involves communicating and disseminating the analysis through oral presentations, written publications, and other outreach activities. While much scholarly research communication is centred on academic conferences and publications in journals, there is more that can be done to ensure that research reaches a wide audience. This section offers specific suggestions about the presentation of video clips and transcripts, as well as a consideration of how to publish across disciplines and communication and dissemination of research beyond academia.

Presenting video clips

One of the most engaging aspects of interactional research on children's eating practices is the possibility of using short video clips to animate research findings. Of utmost importance here is ensuring that consent has been obtained from participants to present images or video, either anonymised (i.e. using audio and visual filters to mask faces and voices) or unfiltered. When presenting video, use short clips and focus on core analytical points. Video clips should be used to demonstrate the analysis, not as a gimmick or distraction. Techniques for masking audio and video are constantly improving and there are several forms of editing software, many of which are freely available online. Audio editing software can be used to mask voices, such as raising or lowering the pitch or replacing a name with a 'beep' or short silence. Video editing software often includes ready-made filters that can be quickly applied or manual tools that can disguise identities while preserving gestures and movements. Different filters and software can be tested with different data, since the quality of the recordings will determine what will work best. Be cautious, as always, in terms of where video clips are being uploaded for anonymisation; the security and anonymity of the video data are paramount.

Presenting transcripts

Transcripts are a mainstay of most presentations and publications of interactional research, used to demonstrate the interactional phenomenon and explicate details of the analysis. As noted earlier, however, transcripts are only ever a partial representation of the recording and are rarely finished. This means that the version which is used for a presentation or publication (the 'presentation transcript') may not be the same as that which was used in the analysis (the 'working transcript'). A compromise is required between being sufficiently detailed to illustrate the nuances of talk and gesture and not so detailed that the transcript becomes incomprehensible. In presentations, for instance, it may be appropriate for certain sections of the transcript to be more detailed than others, or to use visual aids to highlight or animate certain features. In publications, readers will have more time (compared to oral presentations) to inspect the transcript; though the focus should be on the interactional features that are salient for the analysis, as well as for the audience of the outlet. The graphic transcript in Chapter 4, for instance, captures many gestures but omits other details of the interaction (e.g. precise timing and overlap of actions). As discussed in the transcription section, the use of annotated or graphic transcripts can be a valuable means of capturing multi-modal details and the same applies for presentations and publications.

Publishing across disciplines

The interdisciplinary nature of interactional research means that in many situations, academic work is likely to be published not only within one's home discipline, but also within and across other disciplines. As discussed in Chapter 1, there is no shortage of scholarly interest in how children eat with other people. The trick, however, is to find the right audience for the specific focus or argument of the study that is being published. This may mean using terminology that is familiar to the target audience (see Clift et al, 2024, for further discussion on publishing CA work across disciplines). There may also be different assumptions about sample sizes, though consideration must be given to what is being measured here: instances of a phenomenon, hours of data, number of meals, or participants. Some disciplines are familiar with the use of video recordings, but many are not: reassurances may need to be given about 'reactivity' to the camera (see 'On "reactivity" to being recorded' above). The quantitative bias of much individual-focused eating research – such as that conducted within paediatric nutrition, psychology, or medical studies – also presents challenges. Transcripts are a particular concern: there are many fields in which such examples of 'raw data' are considered unnecessary or even undesirable. Compromises are likely to be made in terms of the number, length, formatting, and detail of the transcripts included, depending on the publication requirements and the expected audience.

Communicating and disseminating research beyond academia

The importance of communicating and disseminating research to users beyond the scope of academic research is especially relevant in relation to children's eating practices. A distinction can be made here between 'communication' and 'dissemination'. 'Communication' of research is the sharing or presentation of findings to a wide audience, without necessarily determining where it goes or how it is used. Social media and professional networking sites such as LinkedIn are examples of channels through which research can be quickly shared with a non-expert audience in ways that are more accessible or palatable. Researchers may also develop their own websites, blogs, or vlogs, depending on their level of expertise and comfort with these formats. Specific organisations or groups may also be targeted, with networks, websites, podcasts, events, and newsletters that could be used to spread information about the research. What is needed are the skills to describe the research in ways that are accessible and meaningful to the specific audience; this is where practice is essential.

'Dissemination' of research findings involves a more tailored approach, in which research is translated into a more specific and useable format for specific audiences – not just sharing results but developing ways in which they can be used. Dissemination can be more demanding in terms of incorporating input from potential user groups at earlier stages in the research, developing training resources and workshops, and identifying needs and possible outcomes. Work closely with stakeholders and other professionals to ensure that the tension between expert status is carefully managed, regarding 'who knows best' (Shaw, 2024: 929; see also Barnes, 2024). As Hepburn et al (2014: 244) note, the researcher's 'role is not to know better . . . but rather to explicate participants' own practices and displayed understandings and use these as a basis for high-level discussions about what works and the implications of different practices in different environments'. It requires a more substantial body of research and time to develop effectively, but the payoffs are substantial in terms of ensuring that findings can be used within society and, potentially, stimulating further research.

BOX 3.6 EXAMPLES OF DISSEMINATION BEYOND ACADEMIA

There are a growing number of examples of academic work whose findings have been disseminated beyond academia, such as through public science events or within professional sectors. The 'conversation analytic role-play method' approach to communication skills training (https://nest.carmtraining.org/) developed by Elizabeth Stokoe (Stokoe, 2014) is a prime example of how the findings from CA research can be disseminated in an engaging manner and used for professional training workshops. On a related theme, Saul Albert and colleagues demonstrate a novel methodology for engaging the general public in CA and what it reveals about social interaction (see Albert et al, 2018). The Child Feeding Guide (https://www.childfeedingguide.co.uk/) offers an app and online training courses, developed by Emma Haycraft, Gemma Witcomb, and Claire Farrow, and provides practical support for parents and healthcare professionals. While it does not use interactional approaches, it is an excellent example of how research into children's eating, in particular, can be used to provide evidence-based support. Other useful resources on applying interactional approaches or disseminating more widely include Antaki (2011), Lester and O'Reilly (2018) and Richards and Seedhouse (2016).

Summary

A data corpus of good-quality and ethically grounded video recordings is the foundation on which all interactional research is built. It can capture some of the most unexpectedly extraordinary moments in exquisite detail. This chapter has described the methodological steps of conducting interactional research on children's eating practices, from the conception of ideas to the dissemination of findings. Each stage illustrates a rigorous approach to transparency and consistency across the working practices of interactional approaches. Video recordings are carefully collected in ethically sensitive ways and procedures for data management, including creating collections and transcripts, are integral to the analytical process. These methodological skills form the basis for good-quality interactional research and are worth the time and effort invested. The ways in which these methods can be used to address specific social actions and aspects of children's everyday eating practices are unpacked in the analytical chapters that follow (Chapters 4 to 8).

4

STARTING TO EAT

Children do not begin life as fully fledged eaters; they need to learn to eat. The practices through which infants start to eat are crucial not only for survival but also for the establishment of eating routines throughout childhood. This field provides an opportunity to examine some of the most exciting and essential aspects of children's eating practices. Research in this area encompasses milk-feeding and the consumption of solid foods, covering approximately the first two years of infancy. The concepts of hunger cues and responsive feeding demonstrate the importance of the interplay between infant and caregiver in determining hunger states and readiness to eat.

This chapter begins with an overview of different aspects of research on milk-feeding and complementary feeding (the transition to solid foods), to orient readers to some of the central conceptual and methodological challenges within this field. The subsequent section uses data examples from family homes to demonstrate how responsiveness can be examined in terms of participation frameworks and social actions. An illustrated research example from published work details the stages of assisted eating (or 'spoon-feeding') within a preschool setting, providing a further example of how interaction can be broken down into sequential stages. The chapter closes with an overview of some of the interactional research that has already been conducted in this area before considering concrete research ideas for future projects. The chapter aims to equip readers with the intellectual and analytical tools needed to get started with research into early infant mealtimes.

DOI: 10.4324/9781003529620-4

Navigating the multidisciplinary landscape on early infant meals

The first years of life are of scholarly interest for a broad span of disciplines and research areas, and early eating practices are no exception. It is possible, for instance, to determine processes of lactation and complementary feeding from skeletal remains within bioarchaeological research (e.g. Halcrow et al, 2021), or to use historical analyses to chart changing societal associations between breastfeeding and female sexuality (e.g. Treckel, 1989). Breastfeeding, in particular, has received considerable academic and public attention, with heated debates involving cultural, social, gendered, and moral issues (e.g. Dettwyler, 2017; Locke, 2009; Maher, 2024). The transition to solid food has also been the focus of cultural and societal debates around nutrition and moral values (e.g. Palmer, 2011; Sellen, 2007; Van Esterik, 2002; Van Esterik & O'Connor, 2017). Navigating this landscape can involve a range of complex issues that extend far beyond the individual infant and the food that they eat. Quite simply, this area of children's eating practices is saturated with intellectual debate and public opinion.

It is within cognate and medical disciplines such as developmental medicine, paediatric nutrition, and psychology that empirical work on early eating practices is typically situated, and the field has developed along research trajectories that are important for these disciplines. Core concepts include hunger cues (cries or behaviours that indicate hunger, such as opening the mouth and sticking out the tongue or bringing hands to mouth) and responsive feeding, with caregiver-infant interaction being paramount in establishing an independent eater (e.g. DiSantis et al, 2011). These two concepts are closely connected, since responsiveness begins with the infant's hunger cry (Gilbert & Robb, 1996; Müller et al, 1974) and the caregiver's interpretation of this cry plays a crucial role (Zeskind et al, 1985). Hence, it is the *interplay* between infant and caregiver that is of crucial importance for understanding early infant eating practices (Acebo & Thoman, 1995).

Research into the processes of milk-feeding has examined the dynamics between caregiver and infant, such as how responsiveness may vary according to the use of breastmilk or formula (e.g. Whitfield & Ventura, 2019; Ventura, 2022) or the mode of delivery (breast alone or bottle with formula or expressed breastmilk; e.g. Brown & Arnott, 2014; Shloim et al, 2015b, 2017). An interest in parental influences on milk-feeding has also led to studies investigating, for example, how parents might pressure infants to take milk if they are perceived to be underweight (Fildes et al, 2015), or how mothers may be distracted while feeding their infants (Golen & Ventura, 2015). Since much of the research on the parent-infant dynamics of milk-feeding is situated within psychological literature, the concept of responsiveness has often been examined within frameworks of social influence and the impact of parents on infant feeding behaviours.

Following milk-feeding, the next stage in starting to eat is the transition to solid food, known as 'complementary feeding' or 'weaning'. This includes variations in the mode of food delivery, such as spoon-feeding (beginning with puréed or mashed foods before gradually progressing to more solid foods) or baby-led weaning, in which infants are encouraged to self-feed (i.e. eat independently) straight away, using small pieces of solid food (e.g. Brown et al, 2017). The concept of responsive feeding remains central to research here, too (e.g. DiSantis et al, 2011; Harbron & Booley, 2013; Hetherington, 2020; Hodges et al, 2013; McNally, 2020; Perez-Escamilla et al, 2012). This work has shown, among other things, the risks of being unresponsive (or non-responsive; Black & Aboud, 2011) to infant cues in relation to children's nutrition and weight status (e.g. Ventura & Birch, 2008). There has also been considerable research on parental feeding practices and strategies: the methods used by parents to manage their children's food consumption, ranging from individual behaviours such as praising children to broader strategies such as being 'authoritative' (e.g. Graf et al, 2022; Haycraft & Blissett, 2012; see Nicklaus, 2016b, and Shloim et al, 2015b, for reviews). This extensive body of psychological research on responsive feeding and parental feeding strategies highlights the challenges faced by caregivers in terms of knowing how and when to respond to hunger cues and negotiating the balance between controlling and permissive behaviour (e.g. Blissett & Farrow, 2007; McNally et al, 2020; Stevenson et al, 2024).

Conducting researching within this area is fraught with methodological challenges, since it involves interpreting extremely subtle indicators of hunger in infants. Parental reports are a common mode of data collection (e.g. Farrow & Blissett, 2006), though a concern with the reliability of self-reports has meant that observational research is becoming a more prominent feature of research designs (e.g. Farrow et al, 2025; Hetherington, 2017; McNally et al, 2016). Coding scales such as the Responsiveness to Child Feeding Cues Scales (Hodges et al, 2013), and the Feeding Infants: Behaviour and Facial Expression Coding System (Hetherington et al, 2016) have been developed to conduct structured observations. What remains a challenge is that while specific behaviours such as eye gaze might indicate hunger (McNally et al, 2019), hunger cues can vary according to individual infants and can change over time (Hetherington, 2017, 2020). The coding scales rely on a behaviour corresponding to a particular internal sensation or state and on the validity of accurately attributing an infant's body movements to specific individual experiences (see Box 3.6 in Chapter 3 for an explanation of how these observational studies differ from interactional approaches; similar scales are discussed in Chapter 8 on satiety cues).

Other observational research has examined the ways in which infant and caregiver become increasingly synchronised in their movements, coordinating hands and faces to guide food into the mouth (Costantini et al, 2018; Negayama, 1993; Toyama, 2013, 2014; Vacaru et al, 2022; van Dijk et al, 2022). As feeding becomes more routine, infants may even open their mouths *before* the spoon approaches their face (Toyama, 2014; van Dijk et al, 2022); and there have also been observations of caregivers opening their mouths in synchrony with the infant's mouth (Negayama, 1993; Toyama, 2013; Vacaru et al, 2022). In summary, the interplay between caregivers and infants has been shown to be an essential aspect of responsive feeding and early infant eating practices, and what is needed are analytical approaches that can examine this interplay in detail. As Costantini et al (2018: 290) note, 'there is no dearth of recommendations about *how* to feed infants'; what is lacking are studies of how feeding occurs in everyday settings (see also McNally et al, 2016).

How to research the start of infant eating using interactional approaches

The dynamic interaction between caregiver and infant that is so crucial during early mealtimes is something that interactional approaches are particularly well placed to examine, since it is precisely language and social interaction in everyday settings that are of analytical interest. This section demonstrates how to begin analysing the start of infant eating using data examples from recorded mealtimes in family homes. In particular, the focus is on milk-feeding and complementary feeding and how the concepts of hunger cues and responsive feeding can be analysed in terms of participation frameworks and social actions. In so doing, the analysis offers insights into a crucial stage of children's eating practices.

On responding to hunger cues during milk-feeding

One of the first things to consider when researching responsivity during milk-feeding is that it can happen quite spontaneously. When an infant stomach can only hold a small amount of milk, feeding may happen every two to three hours on a 24-hour cycle. Caring for an infant is a time-consuming activity and responding to hunger cues is only one of numerous other activities in which caregivers are engaged. Being responsive to hunger cues therefore means first *disengaging* from currently ongoing activities. Simply put, hunger cues do not occur in a social vacuum but are situated within an endless sequence of social interaction (c.f. the idea of there being no 'time out' from interaction, as discussed in Chapter 2). Interactional research provides a way to examine how this responsiveness unfolds within social settings.

A data example can be used to demonstrate how this works. Extract 4.1 is taken from a corpus of video recordings of infant caregiving and breastfeeding at home and includes Mum and infant Eleanor (five months). Immediately prior to this clip, Mum had been baking in the kitchen, with Eleanor lying in a baby basket close by. The transcript begins as Mum is clearing away the kitchen equipment and eating some of the residual cake mix from the mixing bowl. The transcript illustrates how the sequence unfolds in relation to the interaction between parent and infant.

Extract 4.1

```
01        (2.0) ((Mum puts spoon into her mouth, turns to infant))
02        (3.0) ((infant gazes to Mum, licks lips, kicks legs))
03 Mum    mm-hmm:,
04        (3.0) ((Mum continues to lick spoon))
05 Mum    not fair is it (0.2) °Mummy° eating you're not
06        (19.0) ((Mum turns back to bowl and continues scraping))
07 Mum    °mhm°
08        (5.0) ((Mum moves further away with back to infant))
09 Ele    ehHHH (.) eh ((infant hands in mouth))
10 Mum    I'm just movin' stuff >out of the way kiddo<
11        (3.0) ((Mum continues to tidy up))
12 Ele    ehHH eHH-eHH (.) °huh° (0.2) ngHH HHUH[HHH
13 Mum                                          [>yeh<
14        ((unclear))
15        (1.0)
16 Mum    you and I can go and sit
17        (2.0)
18 Ele    heh hehhh >huh heh<
19        (2.0) ((Mum makes preparations for feeding))
```

The transcript provides written notes about some of the infant and parent gestures, as well as the parental talk and infant vocalisations. While the opening lines are conducted almost entirely in silence, several things are already happening in this sequence. While turning towards Eleanor (line 01), Mum begins to gaze towards her while holding a spoon in her own mouth. Eleanor, meanwhile, gazes back at Mum and starts moving her legs more rapidly (line 02). In just a few simple movements, therefore, parent and infant have shifted from being engaged in separate activities (baking a cake, lying in a basket) into an interactional context in which they are mutually focused on each other. This positioning of participants in social interaction is referred to as a 'participation framework' (Goffman, 1981) or 'interactional space' (Mondada, 2013), in which people who were previously co-present but not interacting with each other have now started to establish joint attention. In other words, somewhere between lines 02 and 04, Mum and infant are no longer separate individuals in the physical space but are engaged in social interaction and, it might be said, mutually responsive to each other.

It is within this interactional space that something resembling responsive feeding can be identified, as Mum begins to turn towards the infant. In doing so, it becomes evident that it is not merely Mum who is responding to the infant but also the infant who is responding to Mum. For instance, it is at the point at which Mum turns and gazes towards her that Eleanor starts to move more energetically. Whether or not this bodily movement is deliberate, Mum's confirmatory '*mm hm*' on line 03 treats Eleanor's bodily movements as intentional – as if Eleanor were taking a turn in the conversation. That is, the infant's movements become part of the unfolding social action. Mum follows up with a comment about who is eating and who is not, which also orients to, or constructs, the infant's movements as if they were a response (a protest, perhaps?) to Mum's licking of the spoon. It is not straightforward, therefore, to be able to distinguish between what is the initiating turn and what is the response.

The answer to this analytical conundrum lies in considering how social interaction is structured and organised in particular ways, even with very young children. Even the most subtle of physical movements from infants can be understood in terms of how they are embedded within social actions (e.g. Kidwell, 2009). Interactional approaches examine features of social interaction not as indexing internal states but in terms of (a) how they are part of social actions and (b) how the participants themselves make visible and analytically available their interpretation of the social action through their own verbal, vocal, or bodily turns (see Box 2.1 in Chapter 2). In Extract 4.1, for instance, Mum's formulations oriented to Eleanor's bodily movements as meaningful – specifically, as being unfair that Mum is eating while Eleanor is not (line 05).

A similar analytic approach can be used when considering the next turns in the data clip, with the infant's vocalisations. There are lengthy silences on lines 06 and 08 as Mum resumes cleaning up and disengages from the previously established participation framework. It is following this sequence that Eleanor starts to vocalise (lines 09 and 12). The capital letters in the transcript indicate a louder volume, so the vocalisations start to increase in volume over these two turns. Note that these have not been labelled as hunger cries but rather vocalisations. It is what happens next that is important. Mum orients (on line 10) to these sounds as meaningful in demanding her immediate attention in some way: holding Mum to account for what she is doing ('I'm just moving stuff'). That is, the vocalisation is oriented to as a particular ***kind*** of sound that demands a response. It is during the longer and louder vocalisation on line 12 that Mum overlaps with a 'yeh' (line 13). The overlapping talk in itself orients to the cries as being something more urgent, that the cry is not part of the usual turn-taking of interaction but requires a prompt response. Soon after, Mum turns towards Eleanor and begins to prepare for a breastfeeding session.

By considering a sequence of everyday social interaction occurring ***before*** an apparent hunger cry, therefore, interactional analyses can unpack the ways in which responsiveness takes place as an interplay between caregiver and infant. For instance, Eleanor's leg kicks and lip-licking begin at the point at which Mum turns towards her and are in turn treated by Mum as expressing unfairness (line 05) about who gets to eat. The cries begin to escalate in volume and intensity around 20–30 seconds later, when Mum resumes the clearing up and moves a little further away from the infant. In every instance, these are not isolated individual behaviours: they are contingent on the other person and part of the unfolding social action. It is not necessary to know whether Eleanor's vocalisations are genuine hunger cries. What becomes evident is how Mum visibly demonstrates her recognition of them as being indicative of something that demands a response and making a feed the next relevant thing to do.

Establishing readiness to eat solid food

The same focus on examining the interaction between infant and caregiver in terms of unfolding social actions can be used to examine what happens during complementary feeding, when infants are being introduced to solid foods. This analytical stance can be used to consider, for instance, how establishing 'readiness to eat' is determined through a sequence of social actions. Extract 4.2 is taken from an infant's (Daisy, five months) first introduction to solid food, at home with her mum. Daisy is perched upright on a sofa and Mum offers her a strawberry to see whether she might be interested in eating it. The transcript includes some simple details to specify where hand movements and eye gaze are integrated with Mum's talk.

Extract 4.2

```
01 Mum   ↑what's °↑this° (0.6) Daisy- (0.2) °what is that°
02       (1.0) ((Mum holds up food near Daisy's face, Daisy
               gazes at strawberry and moves hands))
03 Mum   you want tha',
04       (1.8) ((Daisy gazes at food, eyebrows wrinkle))
05 Mum   d'y'want to try it
06       (0.8)
07 Mum   °here- >take this away<°
08       (3.0) ((Mum removes something from Daisy's hands))
09 Mum   °want to try that° ((food held close to face & hands))
10       (3.0) ((Daisy gazes at the food))
11 Mum   can you hold it yourse:lf,
12       (8.0) ((Mum holds food close to Daisy's hands))
13 Mum   yeah:: °come on°
14       (1.4) ((Mum tries to put food into Daisy's hand))
15 Mum   °there you go°
16       (2.0)((Daisy gazes at the food))
17 Mum   what do you think that is?
18       (0.8)
19 Mum   is that a strawberry?
20       (3.0)
21 Mum   do you not want to put it in your mouth? (.)
22       you not- interested in that
```

The transcript highlights some of the resources that parents might use to determine whether their infant is ready to progress to eating solid food: verbal questions, eye gaze, and holding food close to the infant's hands and face. What can also be seen in the transcript is how Mum's investigation of Daisy's potential interest in the food is conducted in coordination with the infant's own movements and progresses in a way that allows Mum to test out different resources. That is, it unfolds sequentially and each movement can be interpreted within this temporal framework. The food is introduced as a new and potentially interesting object (lines 01–02) and something that Daisy might want to try (lines 03–07). When there is no immediate reaching out from Daisy, Mum moves to a more explicit question about whether Daisy would like to hold the strawberry (lines 06–10). There is a shift from asking Daisy whether she wants to try it to a modified and simple offer of holding it; the demands on the infant are lowered. Mum does some work to scaffold Daisy's motor coordination (lines 07–10) and make it easier for her to hold the food, before clarifying the status of the object (line 12) and resuming the check about whether there is interest in the food (lines 13–15). Through focusing on parent and infant behaviours in terms of how they unfold within a sequence of social interaction, rather than as separable behaviours, analysis can begin to elucidate how recognition of an infant's interest in food is sequentially organised within a stretch of everyday social interaction.

Just as the parental interpretation of Eleanor's bodily movements demonstrated how establishing 'ready for a feed' was accomplished in Extract 4.1, so too can Daisy's shifting eye gaze and hand movements be examined in terms of Mum's interpretations in Extract 4.2. In fact, it might be possible to track how Mum puts into practice the various criteria of checking for an infant's readiness to eat (cf World Health Organization and United Nations Children's Fund, 2023), such as being able to coordinate their eye gaze and hold food. For instance, Mum moves the food towards Daisy and guides her hands to the food to help her to grasp it. When there is no immediate grasping of the food, Mum pursues further to establish whether a physical challenge is hindering Daisy or a lack of willingness to eat. Tracking through the transcript and recording enables an analysis of not only *what* can be done to facilitate infant eating but also *how* this unfolds sequentially.

Recording parents and infants in their home offers unique opportunities to capture some of the interactional details that are essential for understanding how young infants start to eat, whether milk or solid foods. Understanding what it means to be ready to eat, for instance, requires a close examination of the ways in which parents and infants interact with one another and how they use various resources to check out the alternative interpretations of each other's behaviour. Interactional approaches provide a means of analysing parental and infant behaviour as organised within unfolding sequences of social interaction. Eleanor's vocalisations and Daisy's eye gaze were not in themselves analysed as indicators of internal hunger states but rather as meaningful through parental orientation to them at specific moments during the interaction. Hunger cues and responsive feeding can be examined as themselves collaborative achievements, with the establishment of a participation framework and the co-construction of social actions being essential for understanding how responsiveness is accomplished. Having demonstrated how interactional approaches might be used to examine the start of eating, the next section illustrates this in more detail with a focus on sequences of assisted eating (aka 'spoon-feeding').

BOX 4.1 CAPTURING THE VERY START OF EATING

Researching very early mealtimes – that is, those involving babies and infants – demands that particular attention be paid to the ethical and practical implications of these situations, in addition to those discussed in Chapter 3. The following checklist can be used to navigate some of issues that may arise.

- Trust and respect are essential during the sensitive and exhausting period of milk-feeding; these take priority over everything else.
- Recruiting participants before birth might be advantageous so that recording can begin in the first few days of feeding, but circumstances can change postpartum and the process of securing consent to participate should be navigated cautiously.
- Ensure that there is someone else to take care of the recording process while the caregiver takes care of the infant during feeding sessions.
- Consider the possibility of asking caregivers to prepare a milk feeding area within their home, where recording equipment can be left in place (and fully charged), ready to press 'record' when the opportunity arises.
- Decide how the recording equipment (cameras, etc) will be managed in advance, including how (and when) the data will be returned to the researcher.
- Allow for caregivers to review recordings before the data/equipment is returned, as a second chance to decide whether they are happy for the recordings to become research data.

Capturing the earliest stages of complementary feeding requires a similar amount of preparatory work to that needed for researching milk-feeding, since the exact timing of the first foods might not be known precisely in advance. This is where it will be necessary to recruit potential participants in the early months of milk-feeding, so that they are prepared to record at the time when their infants show readiness to eat solid foods. The care of the infant (and the caregiver) must always take priority. If recording is likely to disrupt the feeding, it should wait for another day. One of the good things about researching eating is that it happens on a *very* regular basis; there is always another meal.

Illustrated Research Example #1: Assisted eating of infants during preschool lunches

Having demonstrated how interactional approaches might be used to research the start of infant eating, this section illustrates analyses in more depth by explicating the findings from a published journal article. The article is by Wiggins, Majlesi, Ekström, Hydén, and Cekaite (2024), entitled 'How assisted eating becomes a caring practice in institutional settings: Embodied gestures and stages of assisted eating', and was published in the journal *Appetite*. Using ethnomethodology and conversation analysis (EMCA), the study aimed to examine the organisation of sequences of assisted eating. The settings included were preschool lunches (with one to three-year-olds) and meals in care homes for older adults with dementia, both in Sweden; only the infants are in focus here. The data corpus of 97 preschool lunches was searched manually and 37 instances of assisted eating (i.e. where a teacher was actively involved in a child's ingestion of food, using utensils) were identified. Building on the discussion from the previous section, the analysis here demonstrates the importance of examining the sequence or progressivity of eating – that is, that social actions unfold in a temporal order.

The main findings from the article were that the process of assisting infants to eat can be broken down into a series of interactional stages, of which the first stage is crucial for ensuring that the infant is actively involved in the process. The stages are as follows: a) establishing joint attention on the food; b) offering the food; and c) transferring food into the mouth. Each stage is established through the coordination of social actions by both participants, in which the infant can play an independent and active role. It is the caregiver's orientation to the infant as an active participant – rather than a passive recipient – that is crucial to the accomplishment of eating as a caring practice.

Stage 1: Establishing joint attention

The analytical work that went into this paper focused initially on identifying those moments during mealtimes immediately prior to food entering the mouth – that is, before the start of ingestion. As soon as the meal was considered in terms of shorter sequences of interaction, it was possible to see how each sequence could be broken down into a set of social actions that enabled participants to move from one action to another. In the first instance, for example, it was the transition between 'doing something else' to 'identifying eating' as the next thing to happen (in a similar manner to Mum and Eleanor's interaction earlier in the chapter). What was observed in the data corpus of 37 instances of assisted eating was that a subtle blend of multimodal features could be used to establish joint attention between the caregiver and the eater. Previous research on participation frameworks guided the analysis towards examining the way in which participants shift from engaging in separate, independent activities towards establishing a mutually shared focus of attention (e.g. Goffman, 1961, 1981; see also Kidwell & Zimmerman, 2007; Lerner et al, 2011, for examples with young infants). This kind of preparatory work turned out to be essential for accomplishing eating as involving *both* participants equally, rather than being the actions of one person on a passive other. Extract 4.3 illustrates how this shared attention might be achieved in practice. As an example of a graphic transcript (cf Laurier, 2014; see also Chapter 3), it focuses on the visual details of the interaction as Stella (1;7) turns towards her caregiver in a sequence in which they establish joint attention on Stella's food.

Extract 4.3

FIGURE 4.1 Extract 4.3: Have you mixed?

The different panels of the extract illustrate not only how the caregiver and Stella coordinate their bodies to establish joint attention, but also how this occurs in a sequential and time-dependent arrangement. In Panel 1, for instance, both are engaged in other activities: the caregiver is adjusting her sleeve while Stella has her hand in her mouth and is gazing the other way. As she removes her hand, Stella turns to the caregiver while saying 'mix' ('*blanda*', in Swedish; Panel 2) and moving her finger in a circular motion (Panel 3). Various multimodal resources are used simultaneously to gain the caregiver's attention: bodily torque, eye gaze, voice, and a hand gesture. These bodily behaviours become meaningful through being combined in a specific way within a particular sequential environment and alongside the caregiver's own movements. Mutual eye gaze is established and held for a micro-pause of 0.7 seconds (Panel 4), following which the caregiver pursues clarification of the ambiguous verbal request ('mix' could refer to either what *had* been done or what *should* be done; Panel 5). As discussed in Chapter 3, the ambiguity of Stella's turn is revealed in the next turn – that is, in the caregiver's response.

Breaking down the sequence of social interaction immediately preceding the moment in which food is placed in the mouth illustrates the complexity of how co-present persons establish the food as *to be eaten* and the child as *ready to eat* in a specific moment in time. Moreover, the establishment of joint attention ensures that both the person assisting and the person eating are constructed as active participants, each with a different role. This is a further illustration of how responsive feeding can be analytically unpacked in terms of the collaborative actions of caregiver and infant, in which the unfolding sequence of action is as important as the behaviours themselves.

Stage 2: Offering food

The analysis of the next sequence of assisted eating demonstrates a similar process through which an offer of food is established sequentially as a social action. What constitutes a food offer is not simply about an individual behaviour, but rather about how participants' movements are mutually interpreted and unfold temporally within the interaction (as seen in Extract 4.2). In the assisted eating analysis, what becomes central to the establishment of the behaviours as an 'offer' is the *pacing* of the movement. A spoon brought swiftly towards an infant's closed mouth, for example, is not the same as one held within the infant's line of sight for a micro-pause to establish eye gaze before moving it towards an open mouth. Extract 4.4 provides an illustration of the latter case. Dennis (2;6) has already requested help from his caregiver to eat his spaghetti and the transcript is taken from the point at which the spaghetti is being twirled on the fork.

Extract 4.4

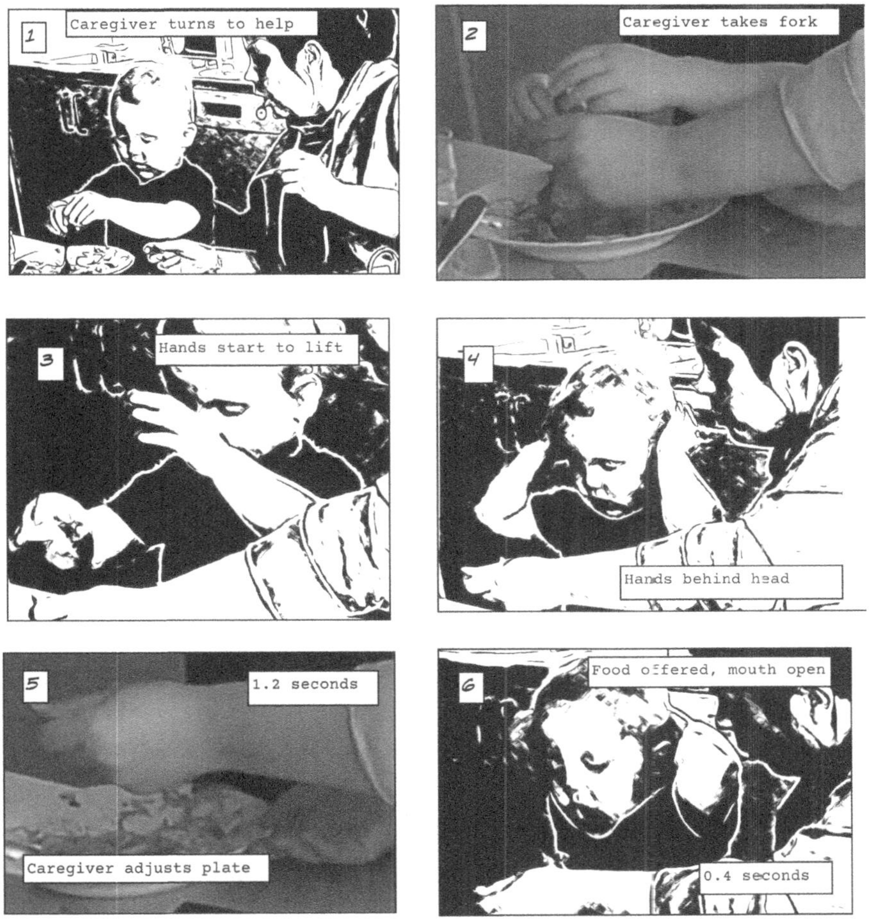

FIGURE 4.2 Extract 4.4: Twirling the spaghetti

Two aspects of this extract are worth highlighting here. First, it is clear that Dennis's eye gaze is on the food for the duration of this sequence (see Panels 1, 3, 4, and 6). Caregiver and infant have therefore already established joint attention on the food and on eating as the next relevant action (as in Stage 1), and this is essential to how the rest of the sequence proceeds. Had Dennis become distracted partway through the sequence, for instance, the offer of food might be inappropriate or premature. The establishment of joint attention is therefore not just a singular event but rather takes place over a stretch of interaction. This is a small but essential point: establishing children's readiness and/or willingness to eat is essential if they are to be independent and active participants in their own eating practices (c.f. research into willingness to try foods in Chapter 5). Interactional research can provide insights into how this readiness or willingness is accomplished on a recurring basis, second by second, as mealtimes unfold within social interaction.

The second aspect to be highlighted here is the issue of pacing, or timing, of the embodied movements of both infant and caregiver. As the caregiver takes the fork (Panel 2), Dennis begins to raise his hands out of the way, which he then holds behind his head (Panels 3 and 4) as the caregiver twirls the spaghetti on the fork. There follows a 1.2 second gap between preparing the food on the fork and raising it towards Dennis's mouth; the fork is raised while the plate is adjusted to be closer to Dennis (Panel 5). Thereafter, the food is brought up towards Dennis's open mouth as he leans forward to take the forkful (Panel 6). Not only is Dennis's visual and embodied attention fully on the food, but the caregiver paces her own movements in a way that allows her to monitor Dennis's behaviour while also getting the food ready for consumption. The analysis of the sequential organisation of the meal, and the ability to slow down and watch the video recording frame by frame, revealed just how closely coordinated the infant and caregivers actions were and how this was essential for establishing an offer of food that incorporated the infant as an active part in this process.

Stage 3: Transferring food into the mouth

The final stage of transferring food into the mouth was analysed in a similar way, detailing how the active and independent involvement of the infant could be maintained throughout. This stage can be analysed by examining the multimodal resources used by infant and caregiver to achieve the physical transfer of food: using hands to grasp food or utensils, body movements (e.g. leaning towards food), eye gaze on the food to follow its trajectory, alongside any talking or sounds made by either participant. Again, the pacing and sequentiality of this sequence were crucial. The final extract (Extract 4.5) returns to Stella in a sequence taken soon after Extract 4.3.

Extract 4.5

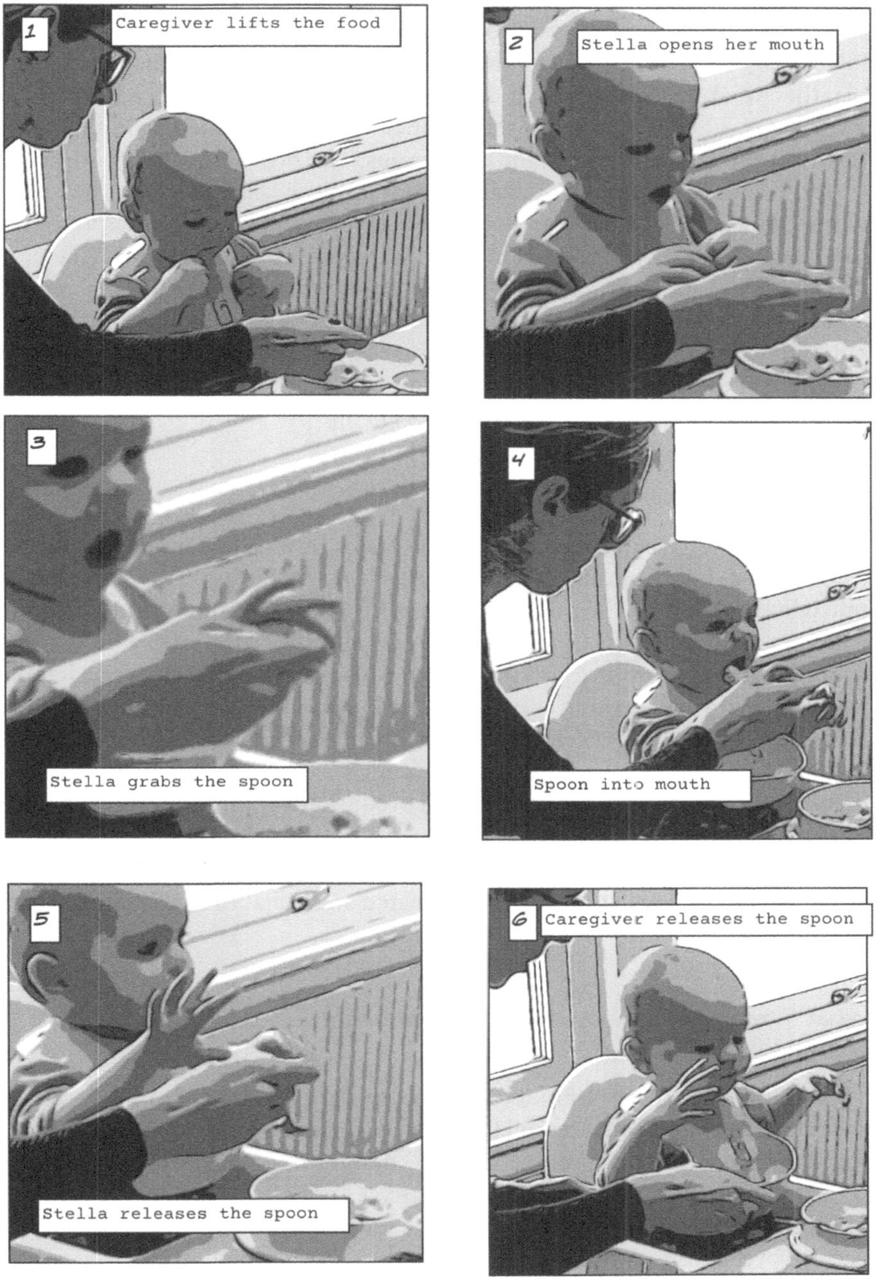

FIGURE 4.3 Extract 4.5: Stella takes a spoonful

The various images in Panels 1 to 6 show a similar pattern to that in Extract 4.5, in which Dennis eats spaghetti: Stella's eye gaze is focused on the food throughout and the caregiver lifts the spoon and lifts it up to Stella's mouth at a pace in keeping with the opening of the mouth (Panels 1 and 2). Much of the preparatory work has already been done, of course; some of that can be seen in Extract 4.3, in that both caregiver and infant have established a joint focus on the food and are coordinated in their actions. The process of transferring food into the mouth is similarly collaboratively achieved. Stella grabs the spoon beside the caregiver's hand and is actively involved in moving the spoon into her mouth. Once the spoon is in her mouth, she releases her grip (Panel 5) and by that point her eye gaze is already shifting back to the food (Panel 6). The transfer of food into mouth is a finely coordinated and mutually dependent embodied process. It is by examining the caregiver's behaviour alongside (not separate from) the infant's behaviour within the unfolding sequence of social interaction that such details are revealed.

Concluding comments

This illustrated research example demonstrates how interactional approaches (in this case, EMCA) can be used to analyse a specific aspect of early eating practices in infancy. It highlights the importance of examining social actions within a sequence or as unfolding temporally over the course of interaction. In doing so, it begins to open the black box of mealtimes, demonstrating how what is often glossed as 'spoon-feeding' can be broken down into observable stages of actions in which the active role of the infant can be encouraged. The various bodily movements of the participants were not merely physical gestures but action oriented; they required the participation of the other person to achieve their goals. The research paper highlights the importance of examining a meal or even the ingestion of food not as a single event but rather as a series of interconnected and collaboratively coordinated sequences.

What interactional research has already been conducted in this area?

This chapter has so far considered contemporary research into infant eating and illustrated how interactional approaches can be used to develop analyses of issues such as responsive feeding, hunger cues, and the processes involved in assisted eating. There is, to date, a limited amount of interactional research that focuses specifically on the eating practices of infants within the first two years of life, though there is a much broader range of interactional research on young children's interactions that offers a strong foundation on which to build new research. This section provides a summary of work from across EMCA, DP, and language socialisation (LS), to help readers navigate existing research in this area.

EMCA research has provided some early findings into parent-infant interactions during milk-feeding in everyday situations and contributes unique insights into what has rarely been studied in situ (Bateman et al, 2025; de León, 2021). Bateman, Katila, and Hofstetter's (2025) study examines the establishment of a feeding session while mother and infant are attending a routine healthcare visit in Finland and illustrates how responding to hunger cries is managed alongside other social actions. The analysis explicates the turn-by-turn details of how an emerging feeding sequence unfolds while maintaining an ongoing interaction between mother and nurse; it therefore demonstrates how 'responsive feeding' can be examined in social interaction with others present. De León's (2021) ethnographic study uses both EMCA and LS to examine milk-feeding with Mayan mothers and infants in their homes. The analysis illustrates not only how mothers and infants move through the interactional trajectory of infant crying to consolation through breastfeeding (the 'soothing nursing niche'), but also how infants are socialised into cultural practices. Drawing on what have been termed 'corporeal arrangements' (de León, 2021), 'tactile arrangements' (Katila, 2018), or 'haptic formations' (Cekaite & Kvist Holm, 2017) – that is, how bodies are positioned and move in the interactional space – de León illustrates the uniquely embodied configuration of breastfeeding interaction.

EMCA research within early childcare education and care settings has also examined how infants eating solid food use various embodied resources (e.g. eye gaze and gestures) to recruit help from caregivers during mealtimes (Bateman, 2024), and how the process of spoon-feeding is accomplished in a collaborative manner (Wiggins, Majlesi, et al, 2024; see illustrated research example). EMCA work on infant eating in family homes has examined the use of non-lexical vocalisations to scaffold mealtime processes, from lip-smacks to encourage mouth movements (Wiggins & Keevallik, 2021b) to gustatory *mmms* to construct the enjoyment of food through their placement at specific moments during infant mealtimes (Keevallik et al, 2024; Wiggins, 2019; Wiggins & Keevallik, 2021a; this work also makes use of DP – see below).

A wider range of CA research has examined early childhood interaction (e.g. Sidnell, 2016), which could be used to offer inspiration for and help develop the field of early eating interactions with infants and young children. Some of this work, for instance, focuses on peer interaction between infants, such as Kidwell and Zimmerman's (2007) study of how one to two-year-olds demonstrate joint attention with other people and their understanding of the observability of their actions. Given the heavy reliance on embodied movements in infant eating practices, Kidwell's (2005, 2009) work on young infants' displayed understandings of caregivers' eye gaze, and on crying (Kidwell, 2013), is also highly relevant for research into infant eating.

DP analyses into eating practices involving infants have begun to examine the ways in which psychological aspects of eating, such as food likes and pleasures, are embedded within social actions (Wiggins, 2019, 2023; Wiggins & Keevallik, 2021a). This work has shown, for instance, the ways in which the first moments of eating are implicated in establishing knowledge about infant food likes (Wiggins, 2023; see the illustrated example in Chapter 6) and the implications of this for negotiating dislikes in later childhood (Wiggins, 2025). Related discursive work provides other routes into this research area. Discursive constructions of breastfeeding, for instance, have made important contributions to understanding how morality and conceptions of parenthood are implicated in talk around breastmilk and the implications of these for choices around feeding approaches (Burns et al, 2012; Callaghan & Lazard, 2012; Kent et al, 2025; Locke, 2009; Taormina et al, 2021).

Work using LS includes much that relates to how children learn cultural eating practices at home. While this work to date has typically focused on school-aged children rather than infants, it nevertheless provides a foundation for work that investigates the socialisation practices through which children acquire competency in eating in situated settings (e.g. Blum-Kulka, 2008; Kremer-Sadlik & Morgenstern, 2022; Pontecorvo et al, 2001). There are also studies that focus specifically on younger infants, such as Quay's (2008) study into a trilingual two-year-old's use of different languages during a family dinner. Research focusing on early LS skills can be used to provide a route into examining how talk is embedded within the start of infant eating.

How can interactional approaches be used to research starting to eat?

This section provides suggestions for how interactional approaches can be used to investigate other issues within the expansive area of early infant eating. It should be clear by now that (excuse the pun) milk-feeding is a largely untapped empirical resource when it comes to interactional research on the earliest months of children's eating. As one of the most foundational eating practices, it is vital that more research goes into how this is accomplished.

The hunger cry within interaction

The analyses in this chapter demonstrate how hunger cues occur within an interactional context and are embedded within social activities. Interactional research on crying (Hepburn 2004; Hepburn & Potter, 2007, 2012; Kidwell, 2011, 2013; Waring & Yu, 2017) has shown how other types of crying can be analysed in terms of how they are embedded within, and consequential for, the social interaction. This body of work could provide a natural starting point for examining infant hunger cries in a similar manner. This would offer important insights for understanding responsive feeding on a more nuanced level.

Milk-feeding stages

The beginnings of milk-feeding involve a range of processes or stages beyond hunger cues and responsive feeding, such as how infants latch (and re-latch) onto the breast or bottle. Interactional research could be used to explicate how these stages are accomplished within different social contexts, taking into account the haptic formations (Cekaite & Kvist Holm, 2017, de León, 2021) of parent and infant, as well as other persons present in the interactional space. Such analyses could be useful for the work of healthcare professionals in assisting new parents in the early weeks of breastfeeding.

Transitioning to solid food

The social and cultural values that surround milk-feeding are deeply engrained in discursive practices during parenthood (e.g. Callaghan & Lazard, 2012; Kent et al, 2025) and have implications for decisions regarding when to transition to solid food. Interactional approaches could be used to investigate how and when talk about stopping milk-feeding becomes topicalised in different settings and the immediate consequences of this. Understanding how situational encounters unfold in real time could be used to develop concrete resources for empowering parents to be able to navigate social settings as and when they arise.

Physical difficulties

The ability to eat independently requires physical skills such as fine-motor control of hands and fingers but may also be affected by difficulties with swallowing such as dysphagia (e.g. Manno et al, 2005; Rudolph & Link, 2002). Infants with cognitive or motor difficulties or other disabilities require different forms of assistance at various stages of eating. Interactional approaches could be used to identify potential issues before these arise and explore how specific challenges during mealtimes might be addressed through practical support for caregivers and healthcare professionals working in these fields.

Multiple participants

The management of milk-feeding or complementary feeding often takes place in settings in which there are several participants (sometimes referred to as 'multiparty interaction'). This might be, for instance, when siblings or peers are present or when there are distractions, such as in busy play areas. Examining the nuances of how infant eating is accomplished in such settings would be of use not only for interactional research on children's peer interactions (e.g. Gunnarsdóttir & Bateman, 2022), but also for psychological research on peer and other social influences on children's eating behaviour (e.g. Houldcraft et al, 2014).

Summary

Social interaction is at the heart of children's eating practices, and this is particularly evident in the first mealtimes of milk and solid food. This chapter has introduced readers to a research area that encapsulates some core issues relating to eating, such as establishing hunger and a readiness to eat and responding to infant cues in an appropriate manner. The data examples and analyses in this chapter have demonstrated how these issues can be analytically interrogated using interactional approaches. The focus on identifying moments of joint attention (i.e. participation frameworks) is key to establishing responsiveness as it unfolds in real time. The chapter has further demonstrated that assisted eating can be broken down into a series of overlapping stages that highlight not only the importance of subtle details (e.g. establishing joint attention on the food and the pacing of moving a spoon to mouth) but also the ways in which eating becomes a collaborative activity. It is from this starting point of early mealtimes that all other eating practices follow, such as developing tastes, which is addressed in the next chapter.

5

DEVELOPING TASTES

Eating opens up a world of sensoriality – an explosion of flavour and texture, sights and smells. Research into taste and the senses is a particularly dynamic area spanning an extraordinary range of disciplines, from philosophy to anthropology, sensory science to nutrition. This chapter demonstrates how interactional research on children's tasting practices (and other sensory practices) can contribute to this vast landscape and how to address the core concepts of flavour learning and sensory development that to date have defined empirical research on children's tastes.

The chapter opens with a guide to navigating the multidisciplinary landscape of research on the senses, providing starting points for literature searches and highlighting some of the core concepts that have shaped this field. The principles of how to research tasting practices in children's mealtimes using interactional approaches are demonstrated using data clips from family meals, with a focus on how tasting emerges as an embodied and social activity and the role of food offers in sensory development. An illustrated research example is taken from a published paper on tasting in preschool lunches, which shows the importance of the sequential and temporal elements of sensory practices. The chapter also provides a detailed guide to interactional research that has already been conducted in this area before offering practical suggestions for future work that might be developed. In sum, the chapter aims to open up the world of the senses in children's eating and demonstrate how this can be investigated using interactional approaches within everyday mealtimes.

DOI: 10.4324/9781003529620-5

Navigating the multidisciplinary landscape on tastes and the senses

Scholarly writing on taste has a deep history that stretches back as far as Aristotle's work on the five core senses (see Korsmeyer, 1999, for an overview). Despite this historical engagement, empirical research on tasting is relatively new. There has been something of an intellectual hierarchy of the senses, tracing back to Aristotle and prevailing until at least the mid 20th century, in which taste (alongside smell) has been regarded as a 'lower' sense and too primitive or animalistic to study scientifically (see Barwich, 2017; Eccleston, 2016; Korsmeyer, 1999; Mol, 2024). Recent decades, however, have seen an explosion of research on biological tastes (see Meiselman et al, 2022; McQuaid, 2016; Shepherd, 2012), incorporating topics such as supertasters (e.g. Bartoshuk et al, 1994), multisensory tasting (e.g. Spence, 2017), and associations between taste and gut microbiota (e.g. Mameli et al, 2019). Taste is also a unique sense in that a distinction can be made between gustatory taste and aesthetic taste, relating to biological/sensory versus cultural/quality issues, each with varying moral values (Bourdieu, 1984; Korsmeyer, 2017; Mennell, 1996). Taste is not only about a sensing body but also about the cultural and social practices within which it is situated (Counihan & Højlund, 2018; Korsmeyer & Sutton, 2011; Hennion, 2007; Højlund, 2015; Mann et al, 2011; Sutton, 2010; Vannini et al, 2014). Nestled within this diverse landscape on the senses is a small section of work that focuses specifically on children's tastes.

BOX 5.1 THE TERMINOLOGY OF TASTE

Within the gustatory system, the taste receptors (or 'tastebuds') on the tongue detect the five basic tastes: sweet, bitter, salt, sour, and umami (this last one was discovered in 1908 but was only listed as a basic taste in the 1990s; see Kurihara, 2015). What is often referred to as 'taste' (i.e. what is experienced when food is placed in the mouth) is more accurately defined as 'flavour' – a combination of smell and taste (Bartoshuk, 1991) blended with other sensory inputs such as sight and sound (e.g. Auvray & Spence, 2008). 'Taste' might also be used interchangeably with 'food preference' (see Chapter 6); and there are remnants of judgement in its etymology, from the Latin '*taxer*' – to feel, touch sharply, or judge (Classen et al., 2002; Mol, 2024). In this way, it is not always possible to disentangle taste from how it is assessed by the taster (see also Mann & Mol, 2019, on the limitations of the English language in relation to taste words).

Navigating this rich landscape to find work on children's senses around eating leads to a large extent to biopsychological and sensory sciences research on infants. Work conducted in this area has been consistent in terms of a core message: the first years of tasting are foundational for flavour learning. Evidence has established the importance of early flavour exposure in newborns (and even *in utero* via the ingestion of amniotic fluid; see Forestell, 2024, Ustun et al, 2022) for subsequent acceptance of flavours later in childhood (e.g. Beauchamp & Mennella, 2009; Cooke & Fildes 2011; Forestell & Mennella, 2007; Mennella et al, 2009). The flavour variety found in breastmilk compared to the uniform content of formula has also been shown to affect the acceptance of different flavours during complementary feeding (Hausner et al, 2009; Mennella & Castor, 2012). This does not mean, however, that mere exposure to breastmilk is enough. Some of the most established findings in this area are that infants are born with an innate preference for sweetened flavours and an aversion to bitter or sour flavours (e.g. Mennella & Bobowski, 2015; Steiner, 1979), which changes gradually throughout childhood and into adolescence (Desor & Beauchamp, 1987).

In the years following infancy, there is thought to be a developmental window between the ages of around two to six years old, during which children are considered to be more receptive to new flavours and textures (e.g. Mura Paroche et al, 2017, Nicklaus, 2017; Nicklaus & Schwartz, 2019). It is also around this age that children may show signs of neophobia: a rejection of, or unwillingness to try, new or unfamiliar foods (e.g. Birch & Fisher, 1998; see also Chapter 7). A considerable amount of research has therefore focused on methods to develop children's sensory experiences to take advantage of this developmental window and overcome neophobia. The most common methods are the use of repeated exposure (i.e. multiple offers of food; e.g. Ahern et al, 2019; Caton et al, 2014), flavour learning (pairing new flavours with already-liked or familiar flavours, e.g. Hausner et al, 2012), and modelling behaviours (peers or adults eating the same foods, e.g. Blissett, 2018, Edwards et al, 2022). Concepts such as 'willingness to try' (Pelchat & Pliner, 1995) have also been used to ascertain how children might be encouraged to try different foods, using parental rating scales (e.g. the Child Food Neophobia Scale, Pliner, 1994), children's reports on various measures (e.g. the Food Situation Questionnaire, Loewen & Pliner, 2000; WillTry instrument, Thomson et al, 2010), or coded observations of children's behaviour (e.g. Momin et al, 2018; Wetherill et al, 2021). Sensory education programmes, or 'food-related sensory activities' (Weiser et al, 2026) such as the Sapere method (e.g. Helland et al, 2016; Sepp & Höijer, 2016) and the '*Classes du Goût*' (e.g. Reverdy, 2011), provide more structured means of teaching children about tastes and the senses, and their potential implications for future food likes (Reverdy et al, 2010).

Conducting research on young children's tastes presents similar challenges to those discussed in Chapter 4 concerning infant eating practices. Investigating taste experiences in infants is heavily reliant on observational methods of facial expressions and sucking rate (Forestell & Mennella, 2017), or even, in some cases, animal studies (e.g. Forestell, 2024). Interpreting individual gestures and bodily movements has become the core means through which taste might be 'observed' by caregivers or researchers. Taste has, however, often been 'relegated to the unanalyzable interiority of the individual' (Wiggins & Keevallik, 2021a: 2).

As noted throughout this book, the importance of the social context is paramount: the environment in which taste is experienced matters (Falconer, 2021) and the specific context of eating can affect willingness to try new foods (e.g. Wilkinson et al, 2025). Capturing the nuances of the social environment has so far proved elusive in tasting studies (Köster, 2003, 2009; Lahne et al, 2014). It has also been argued that the dominant research paradigm treats children's sensory practices as being problematic and as at risk of being led astray if not given appropriate education (Højlund, 2015; Leer & Wistoft, 2018). That is, for children, tasting is often treated not just as something to be experienced but as something that needs to be actively developed.

In summary, what is known about children's senses – and taste in particular– is that it develops before birth and is affected by maternal diet, and that active measures are put into place to try to educate children's taste and encourage an acceptance and increased intake of fruit and vegetables. Social context and parental interaction are known to be important for how infants sense and taste food, but the details are missing. What remains to be understood is how 'taste is learned, shared, adapted, and communicated in everyday interactions' (Højlund, 2015: 100). Interactional approaches thus offer a research tool for investigating how children's tasting as a practice happens in everyday settings.

How to research children's sensory practices using interactional approaches

The centrality of the senses for children's eating practices makes this an engaging issue to investigate using interactional approaches. Sensory practices are not only experiential, however – they are also embedded within the organisation of situated social actions (Mondada, 2021). This section demonstrates how to analyse children's sensory practices using interactional approaches, using examples from mealtimes in family homes. The analysis explains how caregivers interpret children's sensory practices and make food offers, providing an alternative perspective on how concepts such as flavour learning and sensory development can be empirically investigated.

On tasting as a social action

One of the distinctions noted across the literature on the senses is that between examining taste as a phenomenon and tasting as a practice – that is, between individual experience and social action – something that we have or something we do (e.g. Hennion, 2007; Højlund, 2015; Sutton, 2010). An interactional approach takes the latter as its starting point, examining how tasting practices are embedded within social interaction during children's everyday mealtimes. In doing so, it becomes apparent that trying to understand infant sensory experiences is an issue for caregivers just as much as it is for researchers. Extract 5.1 provides an example of this, taken from an infant mealtime, with a mum and her five-month-old son, Christopher. The clip is taken from the start of the meal, before any food has been consumed. A multimodal transcript is provided to illustrate more closely the interplay between talk and gesture, parent and child. Mum is gazing towards Christopher throughout this sequence from line 02 onwards.

Extract 5.1

```
01 Mum   €mmm- oops!
   mum   €stirs food, some spills out

02       €(2.0)        €& (2.0)    & (0.6)    &€(1.4)
   mum   €stirs food €spoon near mouth       €retracts spoon
   chr                 &gaze up  &hands up  &hands down, gaze away

03 Mum   €°hm:° (0.4) not so sure?
   mum   €spoon held resting on table

04       (1.8)
05 Mum   s'nice< cauliflower and carr:ots and ↑peas,
06       €&      (2.0)           €(1.2)
   mum   €spoon towards infant €spoon into mouth
   chr    &gaze and hands to spoon

07       €&(1.0)
   mum   €withdraws spoon
   chr    &pursed lips, forehead wrinkle

08       &(1.4)
   chr   &open mouth, eyes closed, turns head

09 Chr   >cah cah cuh,< ((coughing))
10 Mum   o::(hh)h (0.2) wha(hh)t's tha(hh)t face,
11       (1.2)
12 Mum   not so sure of this combination? (0.2) are we not?
```

The details regarding hand movements (stirring food, moving spoons to mouth or hands to spoon) and other non-verbal features in this transcript enable a closer investigation of how language, bodies, and food are intertwined during eating practices. The turn-by-turn layout of the transcript allows for an examination of the event as a series of unfolding social actions, each of which is collaboratively achieved. The clip begins with Mum stirring the puréed food while producing a gustatory '*mmm*' (line 01); this orients to the food being tasty before it has reached Christopher's mouth (Wiggins, 2019; see Chapter 6 for more on gustatory *mmms*). The spoonful of food is held close to his mouth for a few seconds, in which his hands seem poised to take the food, but he then drops them and he gazes away (line 02). These hand and eye movements are situated within a specific moment in time, and it is their combination and sequence that are particularly important: they suggest potential interest in the food which subsequently disappears.

These first few seconds are enough for Mum to recognise that something is up. She retracts the spoon at the same point at which Christopher turns away. This is synchronised timing, visible only through close attention to the video recording and the temporal details presented in the transcript. The verbalised 'not so sure' (line 03) formulates Mum's interpretation of Christopher's movements as pertaining to a problem with the food rather than relating to, for instance, a lack of appetite or hunger. Having pre-empted the food as being pleasurable, the conversation now turns to whether the food might not actually be that tasty. Christopher does not need to say anything; his movements within the interactional sequence provide a means through which Mum can formulate an interpretation of his sensory response. All this in less than ten seconds of interaction.

The rest of the sequence – from line 04 onwards – builds on this initial 'abandoned' food offer. After a brief silence, in which Christopher makes no move towards the food, Mum does some additional work to emphasise the tastiness of the food (line 05) with an object-side assessment (Edwards & Potter, 2017; Wiggins & Potter, 2003) and lists the constituent parts of the food without further elaboration. As with the gustatory '*mmm*' (Wiggins, 2002, 2019) on line 01, the taste of the food is already being constructed as being pleasurable or 'nice' (line 05). Note the timing of this utterance, produced immediately before the spoon is placed into the mouth.

It is within this specific interactional sequence, immediately following the small mouthful of food, that Christopher's facial expressions and body movements (lines 07 and 08) and coughing (line 09) are visible. Mum gazes intently at his face and furrows her own forehead before uttering, 'oh, what's that face' with interpolated laughter particles (line 10) and a repeat of the suggestion that he might be unsure about the food (line 12). Christopher's sensory practices are embedded within the unfolding social actions and surrounding interactional context – that is, his sensory experience is constructed through various multimodal resources. Regardless of how the senses (taste, smell, sight, touch) are experienced by Christopher, therefore, what becomes important are the various multimodal resources (e.g. eyes, hands, mouths) embedded within the interactional sequence that enable the participants to collaboratively accomplish tasting as a social action.

Another data extract can be used to illustrate how tasting can be foregrounded during the introduction of a new flavour–what is sometimes referred to as 'flavour learning' – and thus another example of how tasting can become part of social actions. Extract 5.2 is taken from another mealtime from the same family as in Extract 5.1. The transcript again includes multimodal details to indicate eye gaze and body movements.

Extract 5.2

```
01       €(2.0)             €(1.0) &  (1.6)
   mum   €spoon in mouth  €spoon out
   chr                          &glance Mum then away

02 Mum   is this mango nice?
03       €&(6.0)
   mum   €holds spoon steady, watches infant
   chr    &gaze ahead, hand to mouth

04 Chr   €°hh°
   mum   €moves infant's hand away from mouth

05 Mum   't's €mango and banana (0.2) €>you like banana<
   mum        €raises spoon to mouth  €spoon into mouth

06 Mum   €(.) and apple.
   mum   €spoon out of mouth

07       &(0.4)    &(0.6)     &(3.0)
   inf   &gaze Mum &gaze down &eyes closed, eyebrow raise,
                              pursed lips
08 Mum   nice and smoo::th isn't it
```

This sequence of spoon-feeding begins and unfolds in quite a different way from that seen in Extract 5.1. Here, the spoonfuls of food are taken without hesitation (lines 01, 05–06) and this time Mum asks whether, rather than stating that, the food is nice (line 02). There is a similar naming of the food (lines 05–06), though this time it is produced at exactly the same time as the spoon is placed into Christopher's mouth. Note the exquisite timing here as the spoon is placed into and then moved out of the mouth in synchrony with Mum's utterances; in particular, Mum states that Christopher likes banana precisely as the spoon enters the mouth (line 05; see Chapter 6 for more on food likes). It is only when the spoon is retracted from the mouth that Mum mentions the third flavour: apple, with an emphasised tone (line 06). In doing so, it is vocally marked as being different from the other flavours. The social action that unfolds here is not just a food offer but also one which embeds the introduction of a new flavour alongside an orientation to pre-established food likes.

Christopher's facial expressions (pursed lips and eyebrow raise, line 07) once the food is in his mouth might also be treated as indicating a particular taste experience; but in this case – possibly as Mum's gaze is on the spoon rather than Christopher's face – they are not commented upon. In contrast to Extract 5.1, the facial expressions are not oriented to as being indicative of an uncertain tasting experience. Instead, Mum notes the consistency of the food and the rest of the mealtime progresses in a similar manner. This extract provides an example of how tasting can be topicalised during mealtimes in different ways: through language use (Mum's description of the food and Christopher's food likes), as well as through the coordination of body movements and facial expressions alongside the interaction. Tasting and sensing food, even in infancy, can be examined in terms of how and when it is situated within social interaction.

Developing the senses

Introducing new tastes is not confined to infancy and developing the senses can continue throughout childhood. As noted in the literature overview section, one common technique for encouraging children to try new foods is through repeated exposure and by offering food on multiple occasions. How this works in practice, however, is largely unknown. The next extract demonstrates how interactional approaches can be used to study such issues as they occur in everyday settings. Extract 5.3 is taken from a family mealtime in which a mum is eating dinner with her daughters Poppy (ten years old) and Isla (five years old). The extract is taken from near the start of the meal as Mum is about to put some mint sauce onto her plate. She is being watched by Isla. It is worth considering a slightly longer transcript here to unpack some of the complexity of how food offers and 'encouraging to taste' are not a single behaviour but rather a progressive sequence of social actions that unfolds incrementally. The multimodal details have been added in written form to allow for a clearer focus on the progression rather than specific timings of the interaction.

Extract 5.3

```
01 Isl   what's that (.) is it gravy, ((gaze at Mum's plate))
02 Mum   this is mint sauce:= ((puts sauce onto plate))
03 Isl   yu:ck.
04        (1.2)
```

```
05 Mum   it's very nice:=it's minty- well you like minty
06       things
07 Pop   it sme:lls- (0.4) min-
08       (0.8)
09 Mum   it smells ↑minty
10       (0.2)
11 Mum   d'y'want to smell it Isla?
12       (1.2) ((Mum holds sauce towards Isla, who
13       leans back with downturned mouth))
14 Mum   well tictacs are minty=have a sniff
15       (2.0) ((Mum holds sauce close, Isla leans in,
16       then sharply back again, sauce is withdrawn))
17 Pop   just smell it
18       (1.8)
19 Mum   you can even taste it if you like
20       (.)
21 Mum   it's on[ly minty
22 Pop          [no [way
23 Isl              [NO
24       (0.4)
25 Mum   it's minty!
26       (0.2)
27 Pop   no::,
28 Mum   but you ↑like minty
29 Pop   I like mint (.) but I don't like minty things
30       like that (0.4) or minty ↓chocolate or anything
31       minty apart from ↑mints
32 Mum   °apart from mints yeah° but it is quite vinegary
33       too cos its like in a sharp sauce
34 Pop   yucky
35 Isl   yuck (.) I hate vinegar
36 Mum   right, >°fine fine fine°<
```

There are many aspects to this clip that could be examined, including those that relate to food likes (Chapter 6) and disgust (Chapter 7); but the focus here is on the interplay between offering food and sensory practices. To begin with, there are elements of some of the same practices seen in Extracts 5.1 and 5.2, in which Mum uses both an object-side assessment ('very nice', line 05) and a subject-side assessment ('you like minty things', lines 05–06, line 28) early on in the interaction and possibly as a counter to the disgust expression by Isla on line 03. The food, therefore, is already presented vocally as a specific type of taste object and one that is grounded in Isla's existing food preferences (see more on these practices in Chapter 6).

What happens next is that Mum does more work to encourage Isla to smell (line 11) or even taste the sauce (line 19). Note the use of various expressions here by both Mum and Poppy to minimise the level of effort required on

Isla's behalf: 'have a sniff' (line 14), 'just smell it' (line 17). This is an example of how the sense of smell can be analysed in terms of how it is organised within sequences of social action (cf Mondada, 2020a, 2023), and of the use of different categories of words to construct different versions of events (Edwards, 1991). A 'sniff', for instance, suggests that minimal effort is required on Isla's part to engage with the food. While olfactory aspects might be present throughout mealtimes, therefore, there may be specific moments in which *active smelling* is constructed as relevant for the ongoing social interaction. Here, for instance, it is used as a way to bring Isla closer to the food object and, potentially, one step closer to tasting.

Offering the food to Isla, or 'exposing' her to it, is achieved in several ways. There are only two points at which Mum says something that might otherwise be treated as a direct offer, in which she asks Isla whether she wants to smell it (line 11) or presents the option of tasting it (line 19). Woven throughout the interaction are various other practices that involve physically moving the food closer to Isla, invoking a food like, associating the taste with other liked foods ('tictacs are minty', line 14) and minimising its status ('it's only minty', line 21). All of these moves might be treated as building towards, or in themselves, a food offer. That they are so is evidenced in Isla's (and to some extent, Poppy's) counter-moves in leaning away from the food and verbalising disgust, as well as in the more direct 'no's (lines 22, 23, 27). Food offers can involve holding out a spoon (e.g. Extracts 5.1 and 5.2) or asking someone whether they want to try a food; but they can also be accomplished in multiple multimodal ways.

In summary, the examples in this section have demonstrated how interactional approaches can provide a route to examining sensory practices as these are embedded within sequences of social action during everyday mealtimes. The analyses demonstrate how and when tasting is topicalised: that sequentiality and the details of interaction are consequential for how tasting is understood. The examples illustrate how this works with young infants and older children, and in situations where there may be more than one child present (as in Extract 5.3). Sensing food is not only an individual experience but also a collaborative one, in which sensory practices are intricately part of the interaction between adult(s) and child(ren) and made accessible for others.

Illustrated Research Example #2: Daring to taste during preschool lunches

This section illustrates in more detail an interactional analysis of children's tasting practices, with a specific focus on how tasting is organised in interactions involving several children. The analysis is taken from a published paper by Wiggins, Cromdal, and Willemsen (2024), entitled 'Daring to taste: The organisation of children's tasting practices during preschool lunches', published in the journal *Appetite*. Using conversation analysis and discursive psychology as the analytical approaches, the paper aimed to explicate the form and occurrence of tasting practices as they spontaneously occurred – that is, without prompting or intervention by researchers – during everyday eating practices. The data was taken from the Swedish preschool lunch corpus and comprised 35 instances in which tasting food was topicalised, with children between the ages of three and six. These instances were identified by manually searching the corpus for cases in which 'tasting' or 'trying' food was explicitly mentioned or demonstrated, such as through offering a small spoonful of a new sauce or requesting to try a different food. As will be seen from the analysis, it was not necessary for participants to verbally name 'tasting' for this to be included as a tasting example.

The main findings of the paper were that: a) young children's tasting of unfamiliar food was sequentially and multimodally organised in a particular order and similar to adult tasting practices; b) tasting was oriented to as a means of expanding the child's personal development – as being brave, for instance; and c) tasting was formulated in terms of individual food preferences and thus 'knowledge' about the child. Examples of each of these points are presented below. The analysis demonstrates the collaborative and organisational features of tasting practices and how these might also, in some situations, be associated with institutional goals of developing the child.

The multimodal organisation of children's tasting practices

The organisation of children's tasting sequences demonstrates that, as with adult tasting practices (e.g. Mondada, 2018, 2021, 2025), tasting is a very different kind of activity from eating (Mondada, 2023). That is, while taste as an *experience* might occur at any point while eating, tasting as a *practice* is structured in a way that is markedly different from regular food consumption. The child is first offered or takes a small piece of food that is presented and handled as a 'tasting sample'; the morsel is placed in the mouth and the interaction between the child and other persons is suspended as visible manipulation of the food is underway (i.e. chewing or lip-smacking); then the child resumes engagement with another person (usually an adult) to make an assessment of the taste. In this way, tasting has observable steps that make relevant tasting as the main interactional activity for the participants and thus also observable for researchers.

The first indication that a tasting sequence is imminent is visible in the recordings through the way in which a child or adult handles the food in a particular way: taking a small piece or amount of food and treating this as something separate from the rest of the meal. In Extract 5.4, Pippi (4;5) is about to serve herself cottage cheese from a bowl on the table and the manner in which she does so – alongside her talk – denotes this as a separate kind of activity.

Extract 5.4

```
01 Pip   så ta ja lite här
         then I'll take a little here

02        (0.9) % (0.3)
   pip          %micro-pause holding spoon in bowl

03 Pip   ja ska bara ta %lite för ja %gi- (0.2) ja tror
         I'll only take a little because I don-  I think
   pip                  %lifts spoon %scoops out small amount

03 Pip   ja inte gillar det hära
         I don't like this
```

Pippi serves herself food while vocalising her actions. She states what she is doing (taking a little), repeats 'little', and accounts for this in terms of not being sure whether she likes it. As she does so, she removes the spoon from the bowl and reinserts it to select a smaller amount of food on the spoon (lines 02–03). It takes more effort to take less food; taking a small amount is a deliberate and visibly accountable process. Note that there is no verbal mention of 'trying' or 'tasting' here; rather, Pippi talks about 'taking' a small amount. Word choice is important here, in terms of how people's actions are formulated in relation to the ongoing interaction. There is no mention of 'tasting' the food but of 'taking' it; it becomes something that Pippi is then responsible for eating (or not) later in the mealtime. In this way, it is an example of a tasting sequence that is not explicitly named as 'tasting'; instead, this particular item of food is marked out as different in some way and handled accordingly.

The remaining parts of the tasting sequences unfold in a manner which treats the food as something *to be tasted* rather than simply *to be eaten*. Food is sampled in small mouthfuls or bites, with the child disengaging from interacting with other persons present during the tasting itself. Similarly, teachers monitor the tasting visually but wait until the child themselves has responded with an assessment of the food. Extract 5.5 provides an example of this, in which Jennifer (5;9) is tasting a sauce that she has just put on her plate and uses a fork (not a spoon) to taste a tiny amount. There is only one other child present at this mealtime (Fiona, 3;5), who is telling the teacher about a story that she has read about a well-known book character called Pippi Longstocking (i.e. not Pippi from Extract 5.4).

Extract 5.5

```
01 Fio   och- och- (0.4) %vet du vad piraterna gjort-
         and- and-    do you know what the pirates done-
  jen                  %picks up fork, into sauce

02       %(1.0)
   jen   %fork into mouth, gz to side-->

03 Fio   gjorde
         did
04       &(0.8)
  tea    &glance to Jen

05 Fio   &låst in %pap&pa
          locked in Dad
  tea    &gz Jen      &eyebrow raise, smile
  jen          -->%gaze teacher

06       (.)
07 Fio   .hh %ehm Pippi's &pappa i fängelse
         .hh ehm Pippi's Dad in prison
  jen        %smile, thumbs up
  tea                     &thumbs up
```

The eye gaze during this sequence is particularly important for tasting sequences, since it is somewhat asymmetrical (Mondada, 2021). Jennifer is gazing away from the table as she places the sauce into her mouth and there are visible jaw movements that indicate she is moving the sauce around on her tongue. Her averted eye gaze demonstrates to others that she is engaged in the tasting and not available to talk, and the teacher's own eye gaze is mainly towards Fiona (who is telling a story) – although she briefly glances towards Jennifer, monitoring her progress. As such, the tasting is individual but not private (Mondada, 2018): it is, despite it taking place within one person's body, an observable activity. Once Jennifer has finished tasting the sauce, she resumes engagement with the teacher, turning back towards her (line 05), smiling and giving a 'thumbs-up' gesture (line 07) to indicate a positive response; the smile and thumbs-up are reciprocated by the teacher. In this way, the tasting concludes with an assessment that is produced by the child and directed towards the teacher as the recipient of this information.

This organisational pattern of tasting sequences – of taking a small piece, averting eye gaze while tasting, then resuming mutual eye contact to deliver an assessment – was consistent across the data corpus. Tasting as an activity in this particular setting can be understood as something that is not only about individual experiences but also an observable process that temporarily halts the child's participation in other mealtime activities (e.g. eating the food or joining in a conversation) and prioritising tasting as the main focus of activity at that time.

Tasting to develop the child

An important aspect of the analysis in the paper is an illustration not only of how tasting was multimodally organised, but also of how tasting becomes a means through which the teachers can demonstrate the development of the child. That is, tasting is often presented to the children not necessarily to develop their sensory experiences but as a way to develop *themselves*: to dare to try something new and to be brave. It is here that the constructive nature of talk is particularly important, in line with DP analyses. Extract 5.6 is a clear example of the use of categories of behaviour that construct the tasting sequence in a specific manner. There are five children at this meal and the teacher is asking whether they would like to try the spinach sauce; at this point, only Kaspar (3;11) responds.

Extract 5.6

01	Tea	om, (.) man vill,
		if (.) one wants,
02		**(1.0)**
03	Tea	så kan man faktiskt få smaka på såsen me' en sked
		so one can actually get to taste the sauce wi' a spoon
04		**(0.6)**
05	Kas	men jag [(vi- (jag våga)-
		but I wa- (I dare)
06	Tea	[ba:ra, (0.2) bara för att va' modig å våga
		ju:st (0.2) just to b' brave and dare
07	Tea	testa nånting nytt
		to test something new
08		(2.0)
09	Tea	det finns den möjligheten
		there's that possibility

In contrast to the previous two extracts, this example illustrates how a teacher introduces food to the children as something to taste. It is already markedly different from the earlier examples, in that tasting is introduced here as an activity for one or more children at the table and so becomes the central focus for this part of the mealtime. Extracts 5.4 and 5.5, by comparison, involve the tasting being announced by the children as a side activity that does not halt the progression of other activities (e.g. Fiona's story in Extract 5.5). There are other notable features to the extract. Tasting is talked about as something that is optional (line 01, 09) and which can be done 'just to be brave and dare' (line 06). These discursive practices construct tasting, in this setting at least, as being about bravery rather than the senses. The sequence formulates tasting as an opportunity that the children can do, not as a requirement, but as something to be a certain kind of person: brave and daring – that is, to develop themselves as a person. It might be considered a way in which children are given the chance to express a willingness to try the food; though here there is no explication of different sensory experiences (e.g. touching, smelling, looking) but rather a suggestion that tasting something new (line 07) is in itself a courageous thing to do. In this way, it also aligns with institutional goals of preschools to develop the *child* rather than necessarily to develop their sensory practices.

Tasting as individual knowledge

The final core analytical point from this paper may seem rather obvious and trivial: that tasting is oriented to as primarily an individual property – something that a child can claim for their own. What is meant, however, is that the tasting sequences almost always end with an assessment of some kind, such as Jennifer's thumbs-up gesture in Extract 5.5. Moreover, this assessment is typically done while the child resumes mutual eye gaze with, or is looking towards, the teacher. The assessment is produced at a specific point in time and is directed towards a particular recipient: it is a social action being done for the purposes of the interaction. Extract 5.7 provides an example of this, towards the end of a sequence in which Lucas (4;1) has been encouraged to try a small amount of veggie burger near the start of his meal. Seated beside him is Josephine (4;8), who is watching this activity (see Figures 5.1 and 5.2); the teacher is directly opposite, facing Lucas.

Extract 5.7

```
01 Tea   du vet inte om du ↑prova &#inte
         you won't know if you don't ↑try
   luc                              &food in mouth
   fig                               #fig 5.1
```

FIGURE 5.1 Lucas takes a forkful

```
02         %&(2.8)
   luc     %chews food
   tea      &watches Lucas
03 Tea     var den god?
           was it good?
04         %#(0.7)
   luc     %shakes head
   fig      #fig 5.2
```

FIGURE 5.2 Lucas shakes his head

```
05 Tea     du tycker inte om den
           you don't like it
06         (0.2)
07 Tea     du behöver inte om du vill inte
           you don't need to if you don't want to
08         (0.2)
09 Tea     men duktig att du ↑provade
           but good that you ↑tried
```

The teacher in this sequence initiates the tasting of the veggie burger and pursues its reception, asking Lucas whether it was good (line 03). Both she and Josephine (see Figure 5.1) are watching Lucas intently; the process is observable and accountable, as with Extract 5.5). His non-verbal response – a head shake, indicating no (line 04, Figure 5.2) – is reformulated by the teacher as a subject-side assessment ('you don't like it', line 05), which construes it as an individual reaction rather than something about the food. As with the earlier examples, the conclusion of a tasting session is an assessment rather than necessarily a discussion about sensory properties. In this way, it works to say more about the child and their tastes (or likes) than about the food itself. The switch to a personal assessment not only validates Lucas' right to be able to make judgements about the food, but also avoids stating something that might have consequences for the shared meal: that 'it wasn't good' (cf Edwards & Potter, 2017). Josephine's smile (Figure 5.2), while not attended to by either Lucas or his teacher, hints at the possibility of further interactional work that might explore how sensory practices are negotiated by several children within a social setting (see also Extract 7.6 in Chapter 7, where a child asks to taste a food directly after another child has expressed disgust about it). Tasting is not just about Lucas's individual experience but also something that has consequences for the rest of the mealtime.

Lucas is praised for trying the food (line 09) – a further example of tasting being associated with bravery. This tasting sequence focuses on establishing Lucas's individual assessment of the food and of what he might (or might not) be prepared to eat. In line with research that is discussed in Chapter 6, it also establishes 'knowledge' about the child (that Lucas didn't like the veggie burger), rather than necessarily anything about sensory practices or the nuances of tastes and textures. Encouraging children to taste food and noting their assessments of this food is therefore also a way in which early years institutions such as preschools might promote the development of the child as a competent member of society – as knowing their tastes and sharing these with teachers so that staff members can learn and support the child by attending to their needs and preferred foods.

Concluding comments

In conclusion, this research example illustrates how examining sensorial states as interactional practices can reveal the ways in which tasting is formulated in terms of individual development rather than necessarily sensory practices. It also demonstrates a regular pattern in how tasting was organised within children's preschool mealtimes, involving the careful manipulation of the food, averted eye gaze, momentary disengagement from participation, and finally an assessment. The conclusion of this tasting sequence was that taste was frequently given a binary status: liked or disliked, good or bad. The discussion of flavours or textures was much less common in the preschool data corpus. Taste was formulated instead as being about developing oneself and daring to try new foods and then ascertaining whether those foods were accepted or not.

What interactional research has already been conducted in this area?

Children's tasting practices, in their broadest possible sense (as cultural as well as physiological taste), have been examined through a wide range of interactional approaches. A broad platform of work has already been conducted that can be used as a starting point for future work in this field. This section provides an overview of work that has been conducted on sensory (and specifically tasting) practices – including that specifically on children's food consumption – to orient readers within existing work from ethnomethodology and conversation analysis (EMCA), DP, and language socialisation (LS).

The field of EMCA has been particularly important in the development of analyses of sensory practices in various settings, for the most part involving adults (e.g. Fele & Liberman, 2021; Liberman, 2024; Mondada, 2020ab, Vannini et al, 2010, 2014; see also Goico et al, 2021) but also children (Wiggins & Laurier, 2020; Wiggins et al, 2024). One concept used within this field is that of multisensoriality: how sensory practices are embedded within a range of social practices (e.g. Mondada, 2018). This work has provided detailed empirical evidence of how sensing is a collective enterprise, coordinated and sequentially and temporally organised across participants within social interaction – that is, how tasting is a situated practice. This includes work on sensory practices around specific food types such as cheese (Mondada, 2018, 2020b), coffee (Fele, 2016, 2019; Fele & Liberman, 2021; Liberman, 2022) and wine (Vannini et al, 2010); and tasting in the absence of visual cues (Hänggi & Mondada, 2025). Mondada's research on adult tasting is particularly important for demonstrating the importance of multimodal analyses for research on tasting, and that tasting is an entirely different activity from eating (e.g. Mondada 2018, 2020b, 2021, 2023; see also Wiggins & Keevallik, 2021a). EMCA research on touch in social interaction has also been shown to be an important resource within adult-child interaction (e.g. Cekaite & Kvist Holm, 2017; Cekaite & Mondada, 2020) and could be used to expand the sensory repertoire around children's eating practices beyond taste.

DP research on tasting to date has focused primarily on the evaluative work done by tasting practices to construct the subject (the eater) or the object (the food) through various assessment practices (Seymour-Smith et al, 2020; Sneijder & te Molder, 2006; Wiggins, 2004; Wiggins & Potter, 2003; Wiggins, Potter, & Wildsmith, 2001). It is here that the overlap between tasting as sensory practice and tasting as evaluative practice is most clearly seen. As discussed earlier in the chapter, tasting often ends with an assessment and DP research has illuminated how tasting becomes intricately bound up with individual likes and dislikes (Wiggins, 2014a, 2023; Wiggins & Potter, 2003); this is discussed further in Chapter 6 on establishing food likes. Further, the overlap between DP and EMCA research is evident in research on gustatory pleasures in which the multimodal organisation of sound objects such as the gustatory *mmm* is also part of the construction of psychological and individual states of food enjoyment (Wiggins, 2002, 2019; Wiggins & Keevallik, 2021a); again, these are discussed further in Chapter 6.

A substantial part of the research into children's tasting is located within LS, which demonstrates the various interactional processes through which children are socialised into socio-cultural moral orders of food. The classic work in this field examines the mealtime practices of Italian and American families, arguing that children are socialised into four different notions of taste – food as nutrition, material good, reward, and pleasure – and that the Italian families were more likely to prioritise food as pleasure (Ochs, Pontecorvo, & Fasulo, 1996). Other LS research has examined the socialisation of children's tasting practices in family homes (Blum-Kulka, 2012; Kremer-Sadlik & Morgenstern, 2022; Kremer-Sadlik et al, 2015; Ochs & Shohet, 2006) and in preschools and schools (Burdelski, 2014, 2025; Karrabæk, 2012, 2013). Burdelski's analysis (2025), for instance, demonstrates how two to three-year-olds in preschool in Japan not only produced their own food taste assessments but also verbally transformed those of their peers. Being socialised into taste is as much about learning language as it is about learning about the moral order of food (and about what constitutes good taste within a particular culture; see also Karrabæk, 2012, 2013 on how this was made relevant within a Danish school context). Kremer-Sadlik and Morgenstern's (2022) analysis of French family dinners demonstrates how children are not just encouraged to taste food but taught *how* to eat a food, such as using particular garnishes to enhance flavours or using touch to determine the ripeness of fruit. LS research illustrates how tasting is not only about the quality of foods but also inextricably bound up with the language practices that situate eating within specific cultural and social contexts.

How can interactional approaches be used to research developing tastes?

The potential for interactional approaches to be used to examine children's tasting and sensory practices in everyday settings is substantial. Given the breadth of research on sensory practices within the social and natural sciences, there is much that could be done to develop a richer understanding of how children develop tastes and other senses in relation to eating practices. The following are just a few suggested areas for future analyses.

Milk sensory experiences

The earliest months of milk-feeding provide a 'unique interactive space of taste socialisation for exploration' (Van Esterik, 2002: 11) and have implications for later food acceptance (e.g. Mennella et al, 2017). The sensoriality of milk-feeding in everyday settings is, however, less well understood. Interactional research could offer a multimodal analysis of how these sensory experiences – including not only taste but also touch, sight, and smell – are collaboratively accomplished during milk-feeding sessions. These findings could contribute not only to sensory and eating research but also to work on early infant development (e.g. Chen & Monroy, 2026).

Tactile eating

Eating solid food in the early years is a very tactile activity, in which infants use hands and faces to familiarise themselves with food. While exploring food with all the senses is considered important (Sepp & Höijer, 2016), there are various cultural and social (as well as individual) norms that relate to touching food with the fingers (Mann et al, 2011), particularly in cultures where utensils are used. Interactional research, such as that relating to multisensoriality or haptics, provides a tool for examining how tactile behaviours become part of eating in different contexts and how children are socialised into appropriate eating practices.

Early sensory sensitivities

Food sensory sensitivities can have a substantial impact on eating practices, especially for children with autism or other neurological diversities (e.g. Chistol et al, 2018). Early identification of sensory issues is a vital step, but it relies on caregivers being able to distinguish sensitivities from other food-related responses. The detailed analyses of interactional approaches make them ideally placed to examine how sensory sensitivities become recognised and acted upon in complex and variable eating situations. Such knowledge is invaluable for caregivers and health professionals in terms of the everyday management of sensory processing issues in young children.

Repeated exposure in practice

The importance of repeated exposure and multiple offers of food is firmly established in the literature (e.g. Ahern et al, 2019), though little is known about how this plays out in practice and through different stages of childhood. Interactional research provides a unique opportunity to research the ways in which offers and 'exposures' can be presented in everyday settings, particularly when food has previously been rejected. Work in this area might also be combined with investigations into how food likes (see Chapter 6) and food refusals (see Chapter 7) are negotiated during children's mealtimes.

Accepting bitter flavours

As children progress through childhood, the early preference for sweet foods evolves into a greater acceptance of bitter flavours (Mennella & Bobowski, 2015), which in turn has implications for health outcomes. Interactional research could be used to investigate how and when this transition begins to emerge – including, for instance, the impact of peers, different eating environments, as well as cultural variations in foods that are introduced to children at different ages. Understanding more about these everyday practices of developing tastes could be invaluable for health and nutritional professionals and sensory scientists.

Summary

Eating is a richly sensorial activity and there is significant potential to develop interactional research into children's eating practices in this particular area. This chapter has introduced readers to a diverse landscape of work on the senses, from philosophy to sensory science, but within which only a small fraction to date has examined children's sensory practices in everyday settings. Researching sensory practices using interactional approaches reveals the ways in which apparently 'individual' states are invoked, interrogated, and become consequential for the immediate social environment. Sensory practices are deeply social events and interactional research provides the analytical tools through which they can be empirically investigated. The assessable or evaluative aspects of tasting were also emphasised, in that children's tasting practices are often formulated in terms of likes or dislikes. The assessment of food and the establishment of food likes and pleasures are examined in the next chapter.

6

ESTABLISHING LIKES

The enjoyment of food can be one of life's greatest pleasures. In recent decades, children's food preferences have become one of the predominant domains of research within eating studies, particularly in psychological research. Work on gustatory pleasure, by contrast, has received much less attention. This chapter focuses on the enjoyable aspects of eating and how these can be examined using interactional approaches. Central to this area is the use of specific lexical formulations (e.g. 'like') and non-lexical vocalisations (e.g. the gustatory *mmm*) to construct eating as about preferences or pleasures. Interactional research that examines all aspects of language therefore provides an important analytical tool to empirically interrogate moments of food pleasure.

This chapter introduces readers to the landscape of research that stretches from hedonic responses to food preferences. In the first section, the expansive work on food enjoyment is sketched out, with a particular focus on how food preferences came to be such a dominant feature of psychological research into children's eating practices. The chapter proceeds with a step-by-step account of how food likes can be examined in terms of their lexical formulation and gustatory pleasure through non-lexical vocalisations in data clips from family mealtimes: both words and sounds can thus be used to examine food enjoyment. The illustrated research example features a published paper on how food likes become established as knowledge during infant mealtimes. The chapter also provides an overview of interactional research that has already been conducted within this area, creating a platform from which new work can be developed. Ideas and specific suggestions for future projects are then presented at the close of the chapter. In summary, the chapter contains all that is needed to get started in exploring the enjoyable aspects of eating in children's mealtimes.

DOI: 10.4324/9781003529620-6

Navigating the multidisciplinary landscape on children's food likes and gustatory pleasures

Scholarly writing on the enjoyment of eating offers a rich array of contributions from across the social and cognate sciences, from neuroscience (e.g. Kringelbach, 2015) to psychology (e.g., Avena, 2015; Bolles, 2014), sensory and consumer science (e.g. Meiselman et al, 2022), and sociology (e.g. Coveney, 2006). This is also a research area that is variably defined and divergent, peppered as it is with synonyms such as 'enjoyment', 'gustatory pleasure', 'hedonic response', 'liking', and 'preferences'. Research into the pleasures of eating has been criticised for being, at best, 'fleeting' (Coveney & Bunton, 2003: 163) or 'excluded from serious research as too private, too corporeal, too female, or too frivolous' (Mol, 2024: 17). Food pleasure or enjoyment barely gets a mention in psychological textbooks on eating (e.g. Chaffee & Da Silva, 2022; Splane et al, 2024). Instead, psychological research into food enjoyment has focused primarily on food preferences (or likes; see Box 6.1) and their development in children (Birch, 1999). A substantial proportion of this research has examined how preferences might be changed – for instance, to increase children's consumption of fruit and vegetables (e.g., Ahern et al, 2019; Cooke et al, 2003, 2011), such as through modelling other's behaviour (e.g. Edwards et al, 2022) or through repeated exposure (e.g. Ahern et al, 2014; Caton et al, 2014). Research into food likes also closely overlaps with research into developing children's tastes, as discussed in Chapter 5.

BOX 6.1 HOW FOOD PREFERENCES BECAME MEASURABLE

The history of research into food preferences is unique and can be traced back to Duncker's (1938) and Lamb and Ling's (1946) studies of the influences on two to five-year-olds' food choices. It was not until research funded by the US army that a standardised rating scale was developed (Peryam & Haynes, 1957; Peryam & Pilgrim, 1957) to examine food acceptance and consumption among army personnel (see Meiselman & Schutz, 2003, for an extensive review of the history of food research in the US army). The numerical rating scale, often referred to as the 'nine-point hedonic scale', has rating points ranging from 'like extremely' to 'dislike extremely'. The scale became popular for its simplicity and its general accessibility; pictorial versions for children have also been developed (e.g. Chen & Resurreccion, 1996). Since then, there has been much debate around the hedonic scale, such as on the use of numbers versus words (Nicolas et al, 2010; Wichchukit & O'Mahony, 2015) and on the distinction between hedonic states and food preference (e.g. Booth, 2016); but the scale remains firmly established within sensory and consumer science (Meiselman et al, 2022; see Lim, 2011, for alternative scales). While the term 'food preference' predominates, it is defined as a 'measure of how much a person likes a given stimulus relative to another' (Mennella et al, 2018: 9), compared with a 'food like' as a 'a measure of hedonic response to a single stimulus' (Mennella et al, 2018: 9). Liking food is thus considered a part of, but not the whole of, a food preference (Birch, 1999: 42; see also Mela, 2006, for confusions between 'liking' and 'preference').

Some of the earliest research on children's eating practices focused on what are referred to as 'innate' and 'learned' food preferences (e.g. Birch, 1999; Birch et al, 1982; Steiner, 1979). Innate preferences are the genetic predispositions to prefer sweet foods and reject bitter foods, while learned preferences comprise the environmental impact of experiences to which the infant is exposed at an early age. Both of these preferences are typically measured via rating scales or observations of facial gestures. Similar to the research on flavour learning, as discussed in Chapter 5, this body of work has demonstrated the establishment of food preferences at a very early age and the importance of the social context for the development of these preferences. Research with very young infants relies on the coding of facial expressions and gestures to indicate a liking or acceptance of a food (e.g. Forestell & Mennella, 2017; Hetherington, 2017; Madrelle et al, 2017). The importance of parental influence is considered to be particularly meaningful and some research designs require parents to wear face masks during observed feeding sessions to reduce the likelihood that infants will imitate parental facial expressions (e.g. Forestell & Mennella, 2012: 1139).

Underlying research into food preferences is the assumption that liking a food is strongly correlated with consumption – that children will eat those foods which they like or prefer – even though it has been argued that there is limited empirical evidence for this association (Keller et al, 2022). There is, moreover, a conceptual distinction between liking (hedonic drive) and wanting (motivation to eat; Berridge, 2009) – though again, concerns have been raised as to whether it is possible to analytically disentangle these components of food reward in practice (Havermans, 2011). Regardless of whether this conceptual puzzle might be solved, the association between liking and wanting food remains.

Research into gustatory pleasure in relation to children's food consumption, by contrast, is more complex and less often studied (Nicklaus, 2016a). 'Pleasure' not only is treated as conceptually distinct from 'liking' but may also be defined variably in terms of sensory pleasure (hedonic experience), the social pleasure of eating with others, or a form of cognitive assessment (Marty et al, 2018). Conceptually as well as empirically, pleasure is an elusive issue (see Bolles, 2014, for hedonic research that exemplifies this) and laden with moral concerns. The perils of taking *too much* pleasure in eating have been noted by psychologists in relation to healthy eating (e.g. Birch, 1999; Marty et al, 2018; see also Chapter 8). If children have an innate preference for sweet foods, for instance, too much enjoyment of this could counteract measures to broaden their tastes (see Chapter 5).

Anthropological and sociological work on food pleasure is similarly rather limited (though see Coveney, 2006; Mann & Mol, 2019; Warde & Martens, 2000), and has discussed the apparent dichotomy between health and pleasure and its associations with morality – though often in relation to adult rather than children's eating practices (Coveney, 2006; Vogel & Mol, 2014). In what has been referred to as the 'asceticism versus consumption dialectic' (Lupton, 1996), resisting the pleasures of eating is in many situations treated as more virtuous than embracing enjoyment. The pursuit of pleasure in itself has been portrayed as morally inferior, at times associated with religious beliefs about abstinence (Coveney, 2006). The pleasures of eating have thus, to their detriment, often been pitted against healthy eating (Warde, 1997). Much of this work is based on adult eating practices and very little has focused specifically on children's gustatory pleasures.

In summary, research into children's enjoyment of food is primarily focused on food preferences (or food likes) and follows a similar pattern to that seen in relation to developing tastes (Chapter 5): early experiences and the social context are incredibly important for the establishment and potential evolution of food likes. What is not known, however, are the specific processes through which food enjoyment is established in infancy and how this is associated with eating practices throughout childhood. Food pleasure is a particularly complex topic, fraught with moral and health implications, and one that demands closer attention. Interactional research has much to offer in relation to these issues: through a close examination of what happens when children eat with other people, one can investigate how food *becomes* pleasurable and how food likes emerge in specific social settings.

How to research children's food likes and pleasures using interactional approaches

Examining the pleasurable aspects of eating using interactional approaches affords a chance to examine how and when enjoyment becomes topicalised during mealtimes. As seen in Chapter 5, food likes might be used to encourage children to taste food; and this chapter shows how they become established during the earliest mealtimes. This section demonstrates how food likes and gustatory pleasures can be analysed using interactional approaches, with a specific focus on the use of subject and object-side assessments, and the way in which the multimodal organisation of non-lexical vocalisations is essential for invoking the body. In this way, the chapter builds on the analyses presented in Chapter 5 and demonstrates the importance of language for understanding how food likes have become such an established concept.

Food assessments as constructing likes

One of the foundational arguments of interactional approaches is that talk is action (see Chapter 2) – that is, language *does* things – and this performative aspect of talk is essential for understanding how children's eating practices are organised in everyday settings. This is particularly pertinent regarding food likes, which rely to a large extent on being expressed through certain linguistic formulations. The next data extract (6.1) provides an illustration of this. This clip is taken from a different mealtime with the family seen in Extract 5.3, this time with just Mum and Poppy (ten years old) eating lunch together. Poppy is eating chicken nuggets and Mum is eating chicken soup.

Extract 6.1

```
01 Mum   want to try a wee taste o' chicken soup,
02       (2.0) ((Poppy gaze to Mum then to her food))
03 Pop   no thank you
04 Mum   it's rea:lly ni:ce,
05       (0.6)
06 Pop   no thank [you
07 Mum             [you like chicken=you're eating chicken
08       anyway:,
09 Pop   no thank you
10 Mum   okay that's a shame it's REALLY lovely it's,
11       very mild it's very plain >cos its not spicy
12       or anything< it's just really creamy and,
13       (1.0)
14 Mum   mmmm just makes you feel all warm and good inside.
```

The extract begins with a very clear offer to taste the soup (line 01) and adds to the repertoire of ways in which food might be offered (as discussed in Chapter 5). Poppy politely declines. What happens next is that Mum produces several food assessments (lines 04, 06, 09), which are treated by Poppy as *also* being offers. That is, the assessments work, in their sequential placement following the original offer, not as being simply about evaluating the food but as doing something extra. The assessments become part of a social action that could be defined as offering food or trying to persuade Poppy to taste the soup. The extract provides an example of how parents might use different resources to broaden children's tastes (as seen in Chapter 5) – though the focus here is on how food likes, in particular, become interactional resources.

A focus on the different lexical forms of the food assessments reveals something that is not only a linguistic matter but also has interactional implications. Two core distinctions can be made about the assessments produced by Mum in Extract 6.1: 'it's really nice' (line 04) and 'you like chicken' (line 06). The first refers to a specific item of food ('it's') and uses an assessment form that describes the food itself ('really nice'). The second mentions a category of food ('chicken') and a personalised assessment ('you like'). These two distinctions can be characterised as item-category and subject-object, in which the latter refers to subject-side assessments which foreground the person doing the assessment and object-side assessments which foreground the assessable item itself (Wiggins & Potter, 2003). These distinctions between subject-object and item-category food assessments are summarised in Table 6.1.

The different format of these assessments not only is about syntax but also has implications for the people involved. Take the subject-side assessments: they make an assessment on behalf of a specific person. Stating an assessment in this way also stakes a claim about the speaker's entitlement to be able to access that experience: that Mum in Extract 6.1 can claim knowledge about Poppy liking chicken, for instance. This is referred to as a 'Type 1 knowable' (Pomerantz, 1980) – personal information that one can be held accountable for knowing or claiming on behalf of another person. Object-side assessments, by contrast, make a claim about the food (i.e. the object) itself and could potentially be produced by anyone who has access to the object (Heritage & Raymond, 2005; Pomerantz, 1984a). Mum's assessment of the soup as 'really nice' also claims that she is in a position to make that judgement – that she has eaten the soup herself.

The variability of food assessments renders them amenable to numerous social actions, such as persuading someone to have something to eat or

TABLE 6.1 Two core distinctions of food assessments

	Category	*Item*
Subject-side	Pronoun + assessment term + food category E.g. *you like chicken*	Pronoun + assessment term + food item E.g. *you like this chicken*
Object-side	Food category + assessment term E.g. *chicken is nice*	Food item + assessment term E.g. *this chicken is nice*

Source: Adapted from Wiggins & Potter, 2003.

refusing a particular kind of food (Wiggins & Potter, 2003; see also Edwards & Potter, 2017 on subject and object-side assessments). As is seen in the next section, it is subject-side category assessments that can be most consequential for children's mealtimes. The sequential or temporal position of assessments within social interaction is also important. Consider Extract 6.2, taken from a preschool lunch in Sweden in which Pippi (4;5) and her peers are passing serving dishes to each other so that they can put their own food onto their plates.

Extract 6.2

```
01 Tea   Pippi vill du börja me:d (.) blomkål?
         Pippi do you want to start with cauliflower?
02 Pip   ja gillar inte det ((gaze to teacher))
         I don't like it
03 Tea   nähe, vill du börja me' lite morötter då kanske=
         nope do you want to start wi' some carrots then maybe
04       =skicka vidare till (.) Oscar
         pass onto Oscar
```

In this example, the food assessment is in the form of a subject-side item assessment (line 02), thus referencing the assessment as being a personal dislike (i.e. concerning Pippi) of a particular item of food. Produced immediately after the teacher's invitation for Pippi to serve herself some cauliflower, it functions to decline the food. The teacher receipts the assessment with a 'nope' (line 03) and continues to offer an alternative food instead. The social action here begins as an offer to Pippi to serve herself food, which is declined through an expression of a food dislike that embeds within it the assumption that eating food is dependent on liking it. That is, Pippi did not need to say anything about not wanting to take any cauliflower; a simple food assessment – while gazing towards the teacher – worked perfectly adequately in its place. The announcement of a food (dis)preference in this particular temporal location did more than express an internal state; it also had consequences for the progressivity of the serving dishes and the mealtime itself.

What these examples show, therefore, is that the format and placement of food assessments matter: they have implications for how children's eating practices are understood and managed and they can be used for different social actions. Assessments were used to try to encourage Poppy to try the soup in Extract 6.1 and to decline the offer of food in Extract 6.2. Taken from two different contexts (family dinner in Scotland; preschool lunch in Sweden), they nevertheless indicate how food like constructions can be used as part of the negotiations of what children might eat (see Chapter 7 for further negotiations of eating).

The embodiment of gustatory pleasure

In contrast to food likes, which may often be expressed or produced through lexical formulations, gustatory pleasure is a more elusive concept. While the conceptual distinction between concepts such as liking, preference, pleasure, and enjoyment might be difficult to unravel in practice (as noted earlier), an interactional approach focuses on how these concepts are produced within everyday mealtimes to examine the implications of these for children's eating practices. This sub-section focuses on how food pleasure or enjoyment might be expressed through not a word but a sound: the gustatory *mmm*. Described as '(a) accompanying eating or talk about food and drink (or both) and (b) hearably evaluative in a positive direction' (Wiggins, 2002: 315), the *mmm* is typically more emphasised and elongated than the conversational *mm* (Gardner, 1997) and can have a rising or falling intonation. Extract 6.3 provides two examples produced by a mum who is watching her seven-month-old daughter, Sarah, chewing on a rice cracker, while eating lunch at home in Scotland. The clip begins as Sarah puts the cracker into her mouth.

Extract 6.3

```
01 Mum    °mmmm: °  (0.2) >nice<
02        (4.0) ((infant gaze to Mum, food out of mouth))
03 Mum    mm↑mm:  (.)  ↑yummy
```

What is unique about the gustatory *mmm* is that it expresses something that is, like other sensory practices, putatively individual and visceral (i.e. a hedonic expression; see previous section and Chapter 5), but which nonetheless is embedded within social interaction in specific ways. By examining how and when it is produced during eating practices, certain features can be observed that suggest that it also has a social function – that it is produced as immediate, spontaneous, and semantically vague (Wiggins, 2002). The immediacy of the expression means that *mmms* are typically produced at time-sensitive locations in social interaction, such as when food is placed in the mouth. In line 02, for instance, Mum produces the sound while Sarah is chewing and while Sarah is gazing towards Mum. The immediacy of the *mmm* sound secures its position as seemingly responding to the visceral experience of the food, and as something that can be produced while food is still in the mouth (with lips closed and mouth full). The flipside is that an *mmm* that is delayed can appear disingenuous or faked.

By virtue of being a sound that putatively relates to the pleasures of eating, it can be produced spontaneously during the consumption of food without any need to preface or account for its production. The enjoyment of eating might be said to be omnirelevant during a meal when food is being consumed.

Note again, however, Mum's production of the sound following Sarah's eye gaze. It is not simply that these sounds can be produced at any point, but rather that there are specific sequential positions in which they may become relevant. Extract 6.4 provides another example from an infant mealtime, this time with Christopher (five months, as seen in Chapter 5). The transcript here includes both anonymised still images and multimodal details to depict the exact timing of the food being placed in the mouth, the eye gaze of parent and infant, and the production of the gustatory *mmm*. The extract begins at the precise moment when Christopher opens his mouth to receive the spoon (this extract is analysed in more detail in Wiggins, 2019).

Extract 6.4

```
01 Chr   &^mts(.)#(0.7)
   chr   &opens mouth
   mum    ^smile broadens
   fig             #6.1
```

FIGURE 6.1 Christopher takes a spoonful of food

```
02 Mum   ^     m#mm&mmm.#     ^
   mum   ^spoon into mouth^
   chr      -->&gaze to Mum
   fig        #6.2     #6.3
```

FIGURE 6.2 Mum produces a gustatory *mmm*

FIGURE 6.3 Mutual eye gaze and Mum smiles

This is a very short sequence of interaction, though the multimodal transcript captures some of the complex embodied details. The '*mts*' sound on line 01 is a lip-smack sound (Wiggins & Keevallik, 2021b), made as Christopher's mouth opens to receive the spoon that is moving towards his mouth (Figure 6.1). Mum is smiling and gazing at Christopher throughout this sequence and the coordination of their bodies (mouth opening to receive the spoon, gaze and smile) establishes the participation framework and mutual attention on the eating process. Christopher's opening mouth movements anticipate the trajectory of the spoon, demonstrating how even young infants can coordinate their movements during feeding episodes (see Toyama, 2013, and other references noted in Chapter 4). The short pause (0.7 seconds) is similar to the micro-pauses seen during the assisted eating episodes in Chapter 4, as the spoon is held still while Christopher moves his head to align with the spoon. These are highly synchronised movements and analytically available due to the video recording and the focus on the details of the interaction.

It is within this carefully coordinated interactional space that the gustatory *mmm* is produced, following the trajectory of the spoon (Figure 6.2): the up-down contour of the long '*mmm*' mirrors the movement of the spoon up and down and out of the mouth. Christopher gazes towards Mum during its production and mutual gaze is achieved as the spoon is retracted (Figure 6.3), with Mum gently smiling. This is an exquisite coordination of bodies, sounds, and food to produce a moment embodying pleasure. The movements of Mum and Christopher cannot be coded separately, since it is only through the mutual coordination of their actions that the sequence is produced. In particular, it is the precise timing of the '*mmm*' sound when the infant's mouth closes around the spoon that enables a strong connection between the sound itself and the experience of food in the mouth. In short, Mum is expressing pleasure on behalf of her infant (Wiggins & Keevallik, 2021a); one might argue that these are socialisation practices through which pleasure is tied to eating.

In summary, the analyses in this section have demonstrated some of the ways in which language (and sounds at the edge of language; Ogden & Keevallik, 2020) can be used to construct and make relevant food likes and gustatory pleasure at specific moments during children's mealtimes. As with the analysis in previous chapters, the sequentiality and temporal position of the talk and sounds within the interaction are crucial features: it matters not just how but also when actions are produced. Together, they demonstrate how interactional approaches can be used to investigate how food *becomes* pleasurable in everyday settings.

Illustrated Research Example #3: How infant food likes become established as knowledge

This section of the chapter focuses specifically on the issue of food likes and illustrates in more detail how these can become established from some of the earliest mealtimes with infants in family homes. The extracts and analyses are taken from the paper by Wiggins (2023), entitled 'How infant food likes become established as knowledge: Parental food assessments during infant mealtimes in the home', published in the journal *Appetite*. The research used discursive psychology (DP) to address the research question, 'How and when are infant dis/likes constructed by parents using food assessments during infant mealtimes in the home?' The data was taken from a corpus of infant mealtimes recorded in six family homes in Scotland and Sweden (with English-speaking families) and comprising 77 mealtimes in total. The instances analysed were identified by manually searching the corpus for instances in which the parents made use of food assessment terms in relation to the infant's food consumption.

The main findings were that infants' food likes were verbally constructed by parents from the very first mouthfuls of food, with a specific use of subject-side category assessments (e.g. 'You like X'). These assessments were collaboratively established between parents and anchored in previous tastes, and any potential dislikes were calibrated to endeavour to steer the infant towards accepting the food. All of these things occurred on the basis of parental interpretation of infants' responses to the food. The following sub-sections illustrate how this process was established. The paper demonstrates the importance not only of how food likes can become established in the early years of eating but also of the intertwining of assisted eating (Chapter 4) and sensing food (Chapter 5) alongside establishing food likes. It also demonstrates how the concept of parental influence can be examined in a way that attends to the details of social interaction.

Establishing infants' rights to assess food

The analysis of the data corpus first demonstrated that parents oriented to taste not only as a purely oral sensation (i.e. not related to sight or smell), but also as something that infants would be able to distinguish at first mouthful. Extract 6.4 is taken from an infant mealtime with five-month-old Daisy (seen in Chapter 4), who is now beginning to eat solid food and is trying sweet potato for the first time. Both Mum and Dad are present in this clip, and the extract is taken from the second at which a spoonful of food has been placed in Daisy's mouth.

Extract 6.4

```
01          (3.0) ((food into mouth, some falls out))
02 Dad      [°like that°
02 Mum      [what d'you think of tha: Daisy
03          (1.6) ((Daisy gazes at Mum))
04          £what do you think of tha(h)::t=is that yummy£
```

There are many ways in which this sequence of interaction could be analysed, such as by examining how Daisy begins to move the food in her mouth or how the parents collaboratively achieve spoon-feeding (see Chapter 4). What happens next begins to focus more on the child's reception of the food (as with Lucas, in Chapter 5). As Mum and Dad lean towards and gaze intently at Daisy while she eats, they begin to talk to her about the food. The language socialisation (LS) literature has long established that parents in Euro-American cultures scaffold children's language development through treating them as already competent and independent conversational partners (Ochs & Schieffelin, 1979; Schieffelin & Ochs, 1986). That is, children 'learn to *do* food through language' (Cavanaugh et al, 2014: 92). In this example, the talk constructs the food as not only something to be consumed but also something to be assessed, or suggests that the infant might have their own, independent opinion about it.

Daisy's parents were not alone in how they talked about food during these first mealtimes. The next three extracts illustrate very similar phrasing in other examples from the data corpus.

Extract 6.5

```
01 Mum   what you thinkin' (0.8) what you thinkin'
```

Extract 6.6

```
01 Mum   >what d'you think<=she's like what is this bullshit
```

Extract 6.7

```
01 Dad   's that nice (0.2) >heh heh< (1.0) that good.
```

While all three of these extracts were recorded by different families, each of them uses similar words or phrases, such as about what the infant 'thinks' or whether the food is 'nice' or 'good'. The assessments are formulated in terms of psychological states (thinking) and so not only about the food but also about the child (c.f. the earlier discussion on subject-side versus object-side assessments). While Extract 6.7 uses an object-side assessment, it is produced in a way as if it is merely confirming what the infant has already expressed. Through these formulations, the assessment is produced as if on behalf of the infant themselves – that is, the talk oriented to the infant as having primary access to their taste experience.

It is through these discursive practices during early mealtimes that the distinction between sensing and assessing becomes blurred: at what point is the food experienced and subsequently translated into a verbal output? The social action being accomplished here orients to the infant's tasting practices as being something that can be assessed and something to which the infant themselves has primary access. Food is not just to be experienced but also to be evaluated. When it is produced at these time-sensitive moments – immediately after food is placed in the mouth – it further constructs this evaluation as being based on mouth experience rather than anything prior to this (e.g., the sight or smell of the food).

Establishing food likes as knowledge

What happens following these initial 'verbal checks' is that parental talk shifts to formulations that not only positively assess the food but also do so in a way that personalises it. That is, they are constructed as something that is individual 'knowledge' about the child that might also be anchored in previous food experiences or familial food preferences. What begins as a judgement about the food progresses into establishing a more permanent understanding of the child's food likes. The next example provides an illustration of this, taken from the sequence immediately following Extract 6.4 with Daisy.

Extract 6.8

```
01 Dad   &%try another ↑wee bit
   dad   &spoon touching infant's mouth
   dai    %gaze to Mum, chewing-->

02       (1.2)
03 Mum   I think you li:ke that, (0.8) you do: %don't you
   dai                                    -->%gaze down

04 Dad   °mmh°
05 Mum   that's one- that's Mum's favourite as we:ll,
06       &%(2.2)
   dad   &scoops up food from chin and into mouth
   dai    %opens mouth, tongue out, to receive food

07 Dad   .h heh=
08 Mum   =&%>hh heh heh< she lo(hh)ves it doesn't ↑she .hh heh
   dad    &holding spoon in or near mouth
   dai     %chewing on food and spoon
```

This section of interaction follows Mum and Dad's close attention to both Daisy and each other and demonstrates the delicacy of attributing food likes to a child. In Mum's claims about what Daisy 'loves', for instance, she not only attends to Daisy as an active participant (asking 'you do, don't you', line 03) but also to Dad as having equal observer rights to be able to make judgements ('doesn't she', line 08). There are various other things also going on here, such as addressing the potential for infants to choke (or 'gag', line 11) and responding to this as required; and Daisy herself is an active participant in gazing towards Mum (line 02) and moving her head to receive food (lines 06, 12–13). In terms of establishing food likes, this is a clear example of not only how food is treated as assessable (to be liked) but also how multimodal discursive practices are important for establishing these assessments *as if* originating from the infant themselves. It is worth considering, for instance, how this section of interaction might have looked almost identical but focused on how hungry the infant was and how much she needed to eat.

The analysis in the published paper illustrated how infant food likes were not just produced by parents individually but unfolded in such a way as to produce the 'knowledge' about the food like as something that is shared between family members and, on occasion, anchored in family food preferences. Analysis of these kinds of discursive practices can also be a way to examine how cultural food practices are realised in language, such as how people might talk about family favourites or foods that tie people to specific cultural groups (e.g. as being a 'Scottish' delicacy).

Calibrating potential dislikes

The final section of the paper demonstrated how the establishment of infants' food likes has implications for situations in which food is not eaten. While there are many reasons why food might not be consumed, orienting to this specifically as a dislike was a reasonably common occurrence within the data corpus. Moreover, just as a 'like' was formulated entirely by the parents, so too were dislikes. Sometimes these were treated as unproblematic (see Extract 6.6); but in other examples, the parents treated the infant's facial expressions as being symptomatic of a particular response to the food (see also Extract 5.1 in Chapter 5). In Extract 6.9, Mum has prepared some cooked eggs for seven-month-old Sarah, who appears to be more interested in playing with the spoon than in eating.

Extract 6.9

```
01 Mum   put it in your [mouth then
02 Sar                  [%<mm::::h::>
   sar                   %gaze down, manipulates spoon

03       (1.0)
04 Sar   %mm:::MH:::
   sar   %gaze down, manipulates spoon

05 Mum   ↑seem to have developed an aversion to eggs.
06       &(0.2) why don't you like eggs anymore
   mum   &moves bowl to side
```

```
07          %(0.8)
   sar      %gaze down, picks up and drops spoon

08 Mum      you ↑used to like them
09          %(2.2)
   sar      %picks up and gazes at spoon
```

In this family, the parents have been using baby-led weaning, so Sarah is quite familiar with picking up food (or a spoon) to guide it towards her mouth, unaided by her parents. While Mum's turn on line 01 might appear abrupt, it serves as a prompt to bring Sarah's attention back to the food. When Sarah does not comply with this request (see lines 02–05), Mum treats this as 'an aversion to eggs' (line 06) rather than some other cause, such as being tired or not hungry. The point is that Mum treats Sarah's behaviour, both immediately prior to this turn and following, as actively ***not eating*** when eating is the expected behaviour. These kinds of interactions between caregiver and child can become particularly important for understanding how food refusals might be negotiated, as is discussed in Chapter 7.

Extract 6.9 is an example of how interactional research focuses on how the participants themselves make sense of the behaviour of others. In this case, Mum treats the lack of interest in the food not as an unwillingness to eat (c.f. Chapter 4) but as something specific to this food. She then states that Sarah 'used to like eggs' (lines 09, 11) and subsequently tries to account not just for a dislike but for a change from liking to disliking. Given that Sarah is unable to verbalise any responses to the food, what transpires during these mealtime interactions is based entirely on parental formulations of her facial expressions and bodily responses.

Concluding comments

In summary, this paper demonstrates how interactional research can examine the interplay between language and eating in relation to how something as fundamental as food 'likes' can be established in the earliest months of eating. Of importance were the particular lexical formulations – the use of words such as 'like' was central – and the use of different kinds of assessments. Shifting from an item to a category assessment was crucial to the reformulation not just of enjoyment of a specific food but of that category of food that might be eaten on future occasions. It is here that language and eating become intertwined: that the words used to help understand early eating experiences can, in some situations, become a trap that constrains both children and parents when endeavouring to change food likes and dislikes (Wiggins, 2025). Given that food preferences are a central feature of research into children's eating practices and are known to be heavily influenced by parental practices, this research sheds a more nuanced light on how food likes become collaboratively established within and through language and social interaction.

What interactional research has already been conducted in this area?

The previous sections have demonstrated how the broad area of food enjoyment spans a considerable number of disciplines and how it might be examined with a focus on language and social interaction during children's mealtimes. This section provides an overview of work that has already been conducted in this area, using ethnomethodology and conversation analysis (EMCA), DP, and LS. In so doing, the aim is to provide a solid foundation on which future research can be built.

Within EMCA research, conversation analysis (CA) work in particular has been central in establishing the basis of interactional work into food likes, through explicating the interactional organisation of assessments. Some of the earlier CA work into assessments, for instance, illustrated that there is a regular organisation to how assessments are produced in conversation (Pomerantz, 1984a), and that producing an assessment in social interaction stakes a claim to having experience of or access to the assessable object: a 'Type 1 knowable' (Pomerantz, 1980; see also Heritage & Raymond, 2005).) Food assessments used within adult mealtimes have been shown to be situated at particular moments during mealtimes, when: a) food is brought to the table; b) there is a close or shift in a conversational topic; and c) there is some potentially delicate interactional business (Mondada, 2009). Other CA and DP work has examined the organisation and production of the gustatory *mmm* (Wiggins, 2002, 2019; Wiggins & Keevallik, 2021a) as discussed earlier in this chapter and found parental use of *mmms* during UK infant meals to occur at four temporal positions: a) during announcements of food immediately prior to eating; b) as a receipt, when food was placed in the infant's mouth (as in Extract 6.4); c) as modelling behaviour, when parents were also eating and enacting their enjoyment of food; and d) as encouragement to continue eating, when the infant's food consumption slowed or stopped (Wiggins, 2019). Again, the temporality and sequentiality of language within social interaction are paramount.

Work that uses both CA and DP has been especially important for advancing understandings of children's food likes in everyday mealtimes in the UK. The earliest work outlined the subject-side and object-side format of food assessments and their role in constructing eating practices (Wiggins, 2004; Wiggins & Potter, 2003; Wiggins et al, 2001), while later work focused more specifically on how distinctions could be made in terms of adult and child use of various food assessment terms ('love', 'like', 'don't like', 'hate'; Wiggins, 2014a) and the subsequent implications of this for how food preferences are established in infant mealtimes (Wiggins, 2023) and become resistant to change (Wiggins, 2025). The negotiation of children's formulated food likes contra dislikes has also been examined in family mealtimes in Chinese-American

(Waring, 2025) and Dutch homes (Van der Heijden et al, 2022). Collectively, this body of work begins to pick apart the ways in which parental 'influence' on children's food likes can be understood as the construction and negotiation of food assessments and highlights the importance of language and social interaction throughout this process.

Much of the LS research on family mealtimes is also highly relevant for research into food enjoyment, in terms of how children are socialised into various food likes through the ways in which they are encouraged to taste and assess food in everyday meals. In the Ochs et al (1996) paper on socialising taste, for example, the authors note how 'part of what it means to be a member of these families is knowledge of individual tastes' (p. 40) – that is, that one learns to *do family* through learning likes and dislikes (see also Wiggins & Laurier, 2020). Liking food demands that one has first tasted it, for instance. There is also a body of LS research that has demonstrated how children are socialised into assessing food in various ways in homes in France (Kremer-Sadlik & Morgenstern, 2022; Kremer-Sadlik et al, 2015), Italy and the US (Ochs, Pontecorvo, & Fasulo, 1996); in Japanese preschools (Burdelski, 2025); and in Danish primary schools (Karrabæk, 2012, 2013). Ochs et al (1996) demonstrated how individual food preferences were encouraged within Italian families: if the child expressed a dislike, this was not challenged by the parents. Other examples of work in this research area have further demonstrated how food likes and assessments can be caught up in discourses around health and the compromise between individual responsibility and parental control in American households (Paugh & Izquierdo, 2009).

How can interactional approaches be used to research food likes and pleasures?

The topic of food preferences is undeniably one of the predominant fields of research within children's eating practices, at least within certain disciplines. Gustatory pleasure, by contrast, has received far less attention. Given the assumed associations between the enjoyment of food and its consumption – as well as the overlap between tasting and assessments – it is essential that more research is developed in this area. The following are concrete suggestions for research avenues that might be explored using interactional approaches.

Encouraging food likes

While children's expressed food dislikes are often challenged by parents (Waring, 2025; Wiggins, 2014a, 2025), expressions of food likes are often ignored (Van der Heijden et al, 2022), leading to a focus on trying to change something that is considered problematic. Further research in this field could examine the conversational norms through which this pattern might be subverted, enabling a greater focus on the encouragement of talk about food likes. This work could then help parents to navigate dislikes talk in more productive ways.

Exploring gustatory pleasures

The limited research into children's gustatory pleasures is a concerning omission from the literature and very little is known about how infants are socialised specifically into this experience aside from work on gustatory *mmms* (Wiggins, 2019; Wiggins & Keevallik, 2021a). There is ample space to explore how gustatory pleasure is enacted and topicalised in a range of settings, in infancy and throughout childhood, and across cultural variations. Building a stronger research base in this area would be invaluable, not least for a range of scholarly research in psychology and the sensory sciences.

Enjoyable mealtimes

Institutional contexts such as early childcare and education centres often aim to provide a 'positive mealtime environment' (e.g. Mita et al, 2015) while respecting the needs of all children present. Interactional research is perfectly placed to examine the details of how enjoyment might be established in subtle ways through language and embodied interaction (e.g. through food play, as seen in Chapter 2). Analyses of this kind could enable educational practitioners to navigate the delicate balance of providing an enjoyable but calm mealtime environment.

Enjoying too much?

The distinction between pleasure and health has been noted across the literature, with concerns that enjoying food too much may be problematic if the food is not considered good for one's health (e.g. Marty et al, 2018). The dichotomy established between health and pleasure has implications for how food enjoyment is handled during children's mealtimes. Discursive and interactional research could examine how constructions of food enjoyment (in all its variations) are embedded in different settings and the consequences of these for children's eating practices.

Enjoying too little?

It has been assumed, for the most part, that food enjoyment is universal – that all children might be encouraged to take pleasure in eating. Children who have temporary or permanent impairments in taste (dysgeusia) or conditions that impact on oral sensations such as Sjögren's syndrome (e.g. Cartner, 2023) may have limited resources to enjoy food by mouth alone. Interactional research could be used to explore other ways in which food enjoyment (and gustatory pleasure) can be enhanced for those with gustatory impairments. This work might also consider how varieties of eating experiences might be normalised in social interaction.

Summary

The pleasures of eating can be a driving force for many adults, but the realm of research into children's eating practices looks very different. This chapter has discussed how much of the field is focused on children's food likes rather than gustatory pleasures and thus the research currently represents a narrow range of what might be considered as food enjoyment. The importance of language, in both lexical and non-lexical form, has been explicated through data examples from early infancy. The discursive practices that are used to orient to children's tasting practices, as discussed in Chapter 5, involve assessments that then become consequential for future eating practices. Food likes can become a label or 'sticky category' (Wiggins, 2025) that has implications for negotiating food dislikes. The negotiation of situations in which food is disliked (or not eaten) is the focus of the next chapter.

7

NEGOTIATING REFUSALS

Children's mealtimes are not only about ingesting food; they can also involve numerous situations in which food is avoided, resisted, or refused. Researching how children eat almost inevitably involves, at some point, researching what happens when they do not eat. The research captured in this chapter covers a vast multidisciplinary area, including research on neophobia, 'fussy' or 'picky' eating, food aversions or sensitivities, disgust, food refusals, and eating disorders. Central to this area is the negotiation of eating between caregiver and child, and the concept of parental strategies has become a useful concept in psychological research in this field. Interactional research is ideally placed to examine how these negotiations play out in real time.

This chapter illustrates how interactional research can be used to examine situations in which food is not eaten. It begins with an overview of research across the topic areas of neophobia, fussy eating, and sensory sensitivities, presenting some of the core concepts across the field and orienting readers to literature areas. The chapter continues by using data clips to demonstrate how interactional approaches can be used to examine refusals, focusing specifically on children's expressions of disgust and how refusals can be examined as interactional resistance to different trajectories of social action. An illustrated example from a published paper then shows how disgust expressions can be positioned at transitional moments within children's mealtimes, with implications for the progression of the meal. The chapter closes with an overview of interactional research that has already been conducted within this area and future research areas that might be developed.

DOI: 10.4324/9781003529620-7

Navigating the multidisciplinary landscape on food refusals

Of all the eating practices discussed in this book, considering situations in which *not eating* occurs is perhaps the most elusive, since it concerns the absence rather than the presence of ingestion. There are various ways into and through this landscape. A starting point can be the term 'food refusal', which has been used as an umbrella term that encompasses aversions to or repulsions by a limited or more extensive range of foods, such as those referred to as 'neophobia', 'picky eating', 'food aversions', 'avoidance', 'restrictions', 'feeding difficulties', 'sensory issues', and 'eating disorders' (e.g. Campbell & Peebles, 2014; Dovey et al, 2008; Farrow & Coulthard, 2012; Taquet et al, 2024). A substantial volume of empirical research across this area is situated within developmental medicine, paediatric nutrition, and psychology; but there are other routes into the landscape from an anthropological or sociological perspective (e.g. Eli, 2018; Lupton, 1996; Shohet, 2018) or speech and language pathology (e.g. Thompson et al, 2025). The ramifications of not eating – regardless of the form it takes or how it is conceptualised – can lead to serious nutritional problems and lack of development, and research in this area is thus of vital importance.

Research into refusals begins as early as the first mealtimes, with babies refusing or rejecting the bottle (Maxwell et al, 2023) or the breast (Karaburun & Yalçin, 2024) during milk-feeding. Once complementary feeding begins, the possibilities of not eating increase exponentially and infancy can be a particularly challenging period for caregivers. It is within the first few years of life that food neophobia – the avoidance of, or reluctance to eat, new or unfamiliar food – has been most notably reported (Addessi, Galloway, Visalberghi, & Birch, 2005; Cashdan 1994). While some degree of neophobia is argued to be adaptive in protecting children from consuming harmful substances (Pliner & Hobden, 1992), this can become difficult to negotiate for caregivers who are also endeavouring to develop children's tastes (see Chapter 5).

Neophobia is sometimes included as a subset of 'picky' or 'fussy' eating (e.g. Dovey et al, 2008; Mitchell et al, 2013; van der Horst, 2012; Wolstenholme et al, 2022), though an operational definition or measure of this concept does not exist (Taylor & Emmett, 2019; Wolstenholme et al, 2022). Given that many studies rely on parental reports of their children's behaviour (e.g. Carruth et al, 1998), the lack of a clear definition may lead to over-reporting of the phenomenon. A further challenge – for caregivers as well as researchers – is establishing whether neophobia or picky eating behaviour is part of a 'normal' transitional phase (Bialek-Dratwa et al, 2022; Cardano Cono et al, 2015) or indicative of a longer-term issue and potentially an eating disorder such as avoidant/restrictive food intake disorder (Bryant-Waugh, 2019; Kramer et al, 2025). Mealtimes can become emotionally charged arenas, which in turn can lead to non-responsive feeding practices from parents (Harris et al, 2017).

A particular subset of research investigates the range of sensory sensitivities that may underlie food refusals, such as those related to tactility (Nederkoorn et al, 2018) or texture (Chow et al, 2024). This area overlaps with work on developing tastes and the senses (see Chapter 5) and includes research that examines genetic and environmental influences (e.g. Cooke, Haworth, & Wardle, 2007), as well as associations between sensory sensitivities and neurological diverse conditions such as autism and attention deficit hyperactivity disorder (e.g. Smith et al, 2020). An increased sensory sensitivity can further be associated with food disgust (van den Brand et al 2023; see Douglas, 1966; Miller, 1997, for conceptual discussions of disgust) – as much a visceral, emotional response as it is associated with conceptual understanding (Rozin et al, 2000). It has been argued that children may experience but not fully understand disgust before the age of three years old (Widen & Russell, 2011) and studying or measuring disgust in very young children is therefore a challenge. Research has typically focused on children's understanding of facial expressions (Barthomeuf et al, 2012; Widen & Russell, 2010) or sounds (Widen & Russell, 2011) of disgust as expressed by other people, or on how it may be 'transmitted' between parent and child (Barthomeuf et al, 2012; Stevenson et al, 2010).

As with many other aspects of children's eating practices, the involvement of parents in situations of food refusal is crucial. One concern, however, is that much of the research – at least that into picky eating – relies on parental reports (Wolstenholme et al, 2022). Research which uses observational studies often focuses on categorising children's behaviours as being problematic in some way – for example, covering the mouth, negative vocalisations, or spitting out food may be coded as 'disruptive behaviour' (Borrero et al, 2010). There is a risk here not only that children's behaviours are being labelled as problematic, but also that parents are being treated as morally responsible. The importance of parental feeding styles or strategies has been highlighted as vital to understanding refusal behaviour (Kerzner et al, 2015). For instance, parental pressure on getting children to eat has been shown to be related to an increase in food rejections (e.g. Galloway, et al 2006); though, as Lafraire et al (2016: 352) note, 'we do not know whether children's food rejections elicit more parental pressure, or whether parental pressure and restriction foster food rejections in children.' Others have argued instead that 'feeding difficulties must be conceptualised as a relational disorder between the feeder and the child' (Kerzner et al, 2015: 345). There have also been calls to take a more relational or bi-directional approach to understand how children's and parents' behaviour might impact on each other (Walton et al, 2017).

In summary, the diverse landscape of research into food refusals (or not eating) is complex and sensitive terrain. It is hampered by issues such as the diversity of terms and definitions used, the methods of measuring refusal, the range of causes or contextual factors that can impact on eating practices, and the ethical considerations surrounding what can be a traumatic experience for children and caregivers. Very little is known about the social or cultural aspects of food rejection (Rioux et al, 2019) and specifically how refusals emerge in everyday mealtimes. Yet the interaction between children and caregivers is known to be crucial and interactional approaches are ideally placed to contribute to this expansive area of research, since they allow for an examination of the details of what happens when (and how) food is not eaten. That is, they enable researchers to investigate how these behaviours become manifest in social interaction and how they might be resolved.

How to research children's food refusals using interactional approaches

The various ways in which food refusals become manifest within daily mealtimes might appear to present a challenge: how can one analyse picky eating in the same way as sensory sensitivity? There are, however, some common interactional features that can be examined – namely how and when not eating becomes an accountable issue. Regardless of the severity or longevity of the issue, moments of food refusal can be studied as and when they become interactionally relevant. This section demonstrates how food refusals (or not eating) can be analysed using interactional approaches, with a specific focus on disgust sounds and interactional resistance. In so doing, the section illustrates how concepts such as disgust and parental strategies can be approached from an entirely different perspective.

Sounding disgusted

Interacting with other people around food involves not only talk and gestures, but also the sounds that lie at the edges of language – known as 'non-lexical vocalisations', 'sound objects', or 'liminal sounds' within interactional research (Dingemanse, 2020; Ogden & Keevallik, 2020; Reber, 2012). These are quite different from what are sometimes referred to as 'babbling' and 'cooing' in infant speech development; by contrast, non-lexical vocalisations are used by adults as well as children and can occur across languages. One example is the gustatory *mmm* (Wiggins, 2002; 2019), seen in Chapter 6, which can be used to express pleasure on behalf of oneself or someone else (Keevallik et al, 2023; Wiggins & Keevallik, 2021a). This chapter considers food-related non-lexical vocalisations used to enact disgust, such as the '*bleughh*' seen in Extract 2.1/2.2 in Chapter 2 and reproduced in

Extract 7.1. As a sound that can be used to express revulsion towards food, it is a particularly useful route into analysing situations in which food refusal might arise.

Extract 7.1

```
01 Mum   ^&d'y'want pepper?
   mum   ^holds veg dish in front of Emma
   emm    &gaze to veg dish

02           (0.4)
03 Mum    &want a bit of pepper?
   emm    &gaze to own plate

04 Emm    &ble&^ughh            no^pe& hh
   emm    &head shake
   emm        &gaze to veg          &gaze to mum
   mum         ^withdraws veg    ^starts to lift in chair

05       ^&(2.3)
   mum   ^places veg dish in centre of table
   emm    &gaze to own plate

06 Emm   never tasting it.
```

One of the first things that can be noted about transcribing non-lexical vocalisations is that there is no standardised orthographic representation, as compared with lexical items (i.e. words). Disgust expressions or revulsion sounds (Goffman, 1981) are often transcribed as '*bleugh*', '*ew*', '*urgh*', or the more word-like 'yuck' and 'yucky' (seen in Extract 5.3): but these do not always capture the nuances of these sounds and their production (see Wiggins & Keevallik, 2023, for some variations in adults). They are sounds and not words for a reason: they accomplish different things in interaction. Transcribing non-lexical vocalisations requires a more phonetic representation of the sound to convey its unique qualities and to avoid layering on interpretations that can undermine the analysis. For instance, using a descriptive word such as 'disgust' does not quite capture the nuances of how a sound can be produced, stretched, and otherwise adapted to the specific sequential context. In Extract 7.1, therefore, the '*bleughh*' on line 04 provides a closer representation of how the sound was produced and enables a more detailed analysis, though it still has its limitations.

To analyse this '*bleughh*' sound, it is important to consider how it is situated within the social interaction: what happens before and what happens immediately after. On lines 01 and 03, Mum asks Emma whether she wants some pepper (pieces of bell pepper amid a plate of salad items): the social action here is thus putatively an offer of food. Emma has already glanced up at the food and then back to her own plate while Mum is talking and starts to produce the '*bleughh*' sound while still looking down. Her gaze lifts back up to the salad plate while making the sound, before stating 'nope' and gazing up to Mum. She is also shaking her head at the same time. Meanwhile, Mum begins to withdraw the salad dish midway through Emma's production of the sound, and it is this that might have caught Emma's gaze. This is a subtle but important point: Mum displays her recognition of the very start of the '*bleughh*' sound as indicating that Emma will not take the pepper, before Emma has even completed the sound or uttered the definitive 'nope'. The vocalisation works as a remarkably efficient way of responding to the food offer while also providing a stance on the matter (c.f. how Pippi's 'I don't like it' declined the cauliflower in Extract 6.2 in Chapter 6).

There is another feature of the disgust sound that is important to note here: the '*bleughh*' sound is produced at the start of Emma's turn; it precedes the 'nope'. This turn-initial placement of the sound has been evidenced in adults' as well as children's disgust expressions (Wiggins, 2013, 2014b), and it works to construct the sound as if it were purely a visceral reaction to the food – that is, as if the sound were an involuntary response from the body, before the explicit (and lexical) declining of the offer. Emma has already gazed at the food, however, while Mum was making the offer, and if it had been a purely bodily reaction, it might have been produced then. Instead, it is placed perfectly in the sequential slot when Emma's turn is expected.

Non-lexical vocalisations such as those associated with disgust provide a novel route into analysing what happens when children appear to avoid or are sceptical of food (see also Extract 5.3 in Chapter 5). This is further evidence of how words, sounds, and bodies are analysed as coordinated within social action. Rather than coding individual behaviour as indicative of a putative internal state, interactional research examines the progression of eating practices and how these unfold as an interplay between adults and children. It starts with examining how 'not eating' becomes the current relevant thing that is happening.

Food refusal as interactional resistance

Another route into examining food refusal using interactional approaches is to consider more closely the interplay between adults and children while food intake is being negotiated. This requires a focus on the immediate social interaction within which the 'not eating' becomes topicalised or noted as problematic in some way. Extract 7.2 provides an example of how one child's lack of consumption of a specific item of food is attended to vocally by a parent. This clip is taken from a family dinner, with two parents

(Mum, Dad) and three children (Joseph, nine; Samuel, seven; and Emma, five). The focus here is on Samuel and Emma. The family are eating pasta and green beans, and there is a plate of garlic bread in the centre of the table. The data clip is taken from a point towards the end of the meal, though consumption is still ongoing.

Extract 7.2

```
01        (9.6)
           family members chewing silently

02 Dad    Samuel and Emma, €(0.4) you've not done %very well
   sam                     €gaze to Dad
   emm                                                %gaze to Dad

03 Dad    in the gree:n bea:ns: stakes tonight >hav' you<
04 Jos    >ah have<
05        @(0.4)
   jos    @gaze to Dad

06 Mum    °mmhm°=
07 Dad    =I know you've >gone an scoffed all (yours) up<
          (2.4)

08 Dad    while they were still wa:rm
09 Mum    °mmhm°
10        €(2.5)
   sam    €gaze to bread in hand, chewing

11 Dad    you like your greens Samuel,
12 Jos    they're very nice::@
   jos                       @gaze to Mum

13 Dad    mmhm
14        €(1.6)
   sam    €chewing bread, gaze middle distance
```

Unlike data examples seen in earlier chapters, what happens in this section of interaction is not a food offer or a request to eat, but rather a noticing of a particular food that remains lying on the children's plates. Dad makes relevant the green beans on Samuel's and Emma's plates not simply as food but as food *not yet eaten*; there is some hint here that it might be consumed (c.f. Sarah's lack of consumption of the eggs in Extract 6.9 in Chapter 6). There is also some sense of a competition with the reference to 'stakes' and the hint that this might be an ongoing issue, marking it out as specifically 'tonight' (line 03). Since the children are visibly chewing (line 01), it is not eating *per se* that is the problem, but rather a specific type of food that has not been consumed. While Joseph responds immediately (line 04) regarding his consumption of the beans – which is acknowledged (lines 07–08) – Samuel and Emma gaze briefly towards Dad (line 02) but otherwise remain silent. Up to around line 10, therefore, what appears to be going on is a check as to who has or has not eaten the green beans on their plates.

What happens next is that Dad invokes a subject-side category assessment ('you like your greens Samuel'; see Wiggins, 2014a) of the kind seen in Chapter 6. In this sequential position, it suggests that food likes are a sufficient reason to eat the food (Waring, 2025) and that Samuel might be deviating from usual routines by not doing so (Wiggins, 2025). This is a further example of how food likes can be implicated within various aspects of children's mealtimes and bound up with different social actions. This might be similar to the way in which Poppy was encouraged to try the chicken soup in Extract 6.1 in Chapter 6; but the specific sequential unfolding of this sequence is very different. Here, for instance, Joseph also joins in, using an object-side assessment to add further weight to Dad's turn.

So far, the extract demonstrates how negotiations around food (and not eating) might be broken down into shorter sequences of social actions, such as pointing out that something has not been eaten when eating is expected. The progression of the meal is important here, with eating the beans necessary for completion of the meal (see also Chapter 8). Regardless of what else might be going on, food refusals are time-sensitive issues. It matters *when* as well as *how* children are not eating. Interactional approaches, with a focus on social actions, can enable an identification of those moments when there is a lack of progression of eating. Extract 7.3 picks up directly after Extract 7.2, illustrating this further.

Extract 7.3

```
15 Dad     >m'eat yer beans up< (.) @mhh
   dad                              @lifts food into mouth

16         @€(1.8)
   jos     @moves hand towards bread
   sam      €moves hand towards bread

17 Dad  no, (0.2) no, (0.2) +>no no ↓no< (0.4) +€beans.
   dad                      +lifts Sam's hand off bread
   dad                                         +points to plate
   sam                                          €gaze to Dad

18      €(1.6)
   sam  €turns away, shifts in chair
```

```
19 Dad   come on (0.8) €°not° gonna stuff yerself w'↓bread.
   sam                €puts fork down on plate

20       €(1.0)
   sam   €leaves table
```

The situation has escalated somewhat. What began with an observation about food not eaten has morphed into a sequence that might be more readily classified as 'food refusal'. Samuel – still chewing on his bread (line 14, Extract 7.2) – is now explicitly told to eat up his beans (line 15, Extract 7.3) using a form of directive observed in other family mealtime interaction (Craven & Potter, 2010). Samuel does not verbally refuse this request. His reaching towards the bread (rather than the beans) on line 16 is, however, treated by Dad as defying the directive (lines 17 and 19), and Dad actively prevents Samuel from taking more bread by lifting his hand away from the food. Soon after, Samuel leaves the table.

By breaking down the sequence into separate chunks of action and examining how different trajectories of action are invoked by features such as directives (Goodwin & Cekaite, 2018), what might be glossed as 'refusal' can start to be seen as something more akin to resistance – or at least, not following the same trajectory as the parent within the turn-taking sequence and temporal slot that was made available (see Wiggins & Humă, 2026a, for further analysis of this extract). The two extracts shown here demonstrate how what might be glossed as 'food refusal' can be broken down into much smaller sequences of social action, each of which might progress along different trajectories. What might turn into a sequence of refusing food can begin as a seemingly innocuous comment about food on plates. Examining social actions within unfolding sequences of interaction enables a closer analysis of how and when not eating occurs in terms of timing and progression of the meal. Participants' behaviours (whether vocal, verbal, or embodied) are analysed in terms of how they are oriented to and become consequential. Samuel's reaching for bread, for instance, is not in itself a 'problem' or refusing behaviour – he is still eating something, after all – but it is treated as problematic by Dad because it is not aligned with the immediately prior request. The meaning of the behaviour is embedded within its placement within the unfolding social action and is therefore analysed as part of an interactional sequence.

In summary, the analyses in this section have demonstrated how interactional approaches can provide a means of examining various forms of food refusal by focusing on the details of how and when the lack of consumption or a disgust response towards food is produced within situated social actions. Children's behaviour might be defined as refusal because it is working against the trajectory of a social action that is being projected by an adult: to eat a particular food, to eat more of it, or to engage in some other food-related activity. While there are many more issues at stake in instances of not eating, an interactional approach nevertheless provides important insights into how food refusal might emerge within everyday settings and how caregiver-child interaction in such settings can be analysed.

Illustrated Research Example #4: Sequences of disgust during children's mealtimes

Having demonstrated how interactional approaches can be used to analyse non-lexical vocalisations of disgust and unpack sequences of food refusal in terms of opposing trajectories of social action, this section illustrates an example that brings together these two components. The analysis is taken from a published study by Wiggins and Keevallik (2026), entitled 'Disgust at the table: The sequential location and production of young children's food disgust expressions in the home and preschool' and published in the journal *Research on Children and Social Interaction*. The data was taken from two separate corpora – a large corpus of family mealtimes recorded in Scotland and preschool lunches recorded in Sweden – and comprised over 200 mealtimes in total. The recordings were searched manually to identify those sequences in which children used a disgust expression (whether lexical, non-lexical, or facial); previous analyses of disgust responses within the family mealtime corpus (Wiggins, 2013, 2014a) meant that some of these cases had already been identified (see Chapter 3 for a discussion of multiple analyses). The search collated both English (*bleurgh, ugh, yucky*) and Swedish (*blä, ick*) expressions of disgust.

The findings demonstrated that children's disgust expressions were produced at sequential locations that were intricately tied to transitional moments within the eating trajectory – that is, when the food object was moved ever closer to the requirement for the child to eat it. The analysis used discursive psychology (DP) to examine how psychological aspects of disgust were embedded within social actions, and how disgust became not only an individual concern but also interactionally relevant. The paper explicated how the temporal and sequential positions of the disgust expressions were important in terms of their relevance for the progression of the meal.

Disgust at transitional phases

The focus of the analysis on the format and the placement of disgust expressions demonstrated how the timing of the expressions was crucial in terms of their production within the turn-taking sequence as well as the location within a meal. The disgust expressions were produced during transition phases within the progressivity of eating: when food was brought to the table, moved from serving dish to plate, or moved from plate to mouth.

There were some examples of disgust produced after food was expelled from the mouth, though for the most part these occurred before food was ingested. In Extract 7.1 seen earlier in this chapter, Emma's '*bleughh*' is uttered at the exact point at which the food might be transferred to her plate. The stakes can be higher when the food is already on a child's plate and they may be expected to eat it, as seen in Extracts 7.2 and 7.3. Extract 7.4 is taken from shortly after these earlier sequences, when the pressure is mounting on Samuel to eat the green beans on his plate. Further negotiations have taken place in the meantime (see Wiggins & Humă, 2026a, for further analysis of the extended sequence); and at this point, Samuel returns to the table having established with his parents that he just needs to 'eat two' green beans and then can have more bread.

Extract 7.4

```
01 Dad   you can [do tha-
02 Sam           [€and that's (.) all I- °need° €to do.
   sam            €returns to sit down at the table
   sam                                           €looks to Mum

03 Dad   you can do tha:t,
04        (0.6)
05 Dad   >come on<
06        €(0.6)
   sam    €looks down at plate

07 Sam   €cha- (.) nn- (.) [m- (.) ugh, (.) uh- .hh ghh
   sam   €turns head away, eyes closed, downturned mouth

08 Dad                     [eat two only look
09       (0.8)
10 Sam   they're yucky
11       (0.6)
12 Mum   §they're not yucky:,
   mum   §turns to Samuel
```

In the sequences prior to this clip, there has been much discussion of the green beans, in which Samuel claims not to like them and states that he will 'never eat those things'. There is no question, therefore, as to whether he might be ambivalent about the food. Up until now, however, there have been no disgust expressions. It is only when Dad reiterates the task that has been set and cajoles further with the 'come on' in line 05 that Samuel looks down at his plate and produces a sound that begins as a cut-off '*cha*' and then becomes a series of sounds that are suggestive of vomiting. At the same time, his head is pulled sharply back, his eyes are closed, and his mouth is downturned in a manner reminiscent of the 'disgust face' (Rozin et al, 1994). The non-lexical vocalisation is produced at exactly the point in the interactional sequence when his turn is anticipated. In terms of its location within trajectories of eating, it occurs at a pivotal moment when other options to avoid the food have already been tested and failed.

A further point to note about this extract is the distinction between the disgust-relevant sound produced on line 07 and the lexical form 'yucky' on line 10. It is here that a clear difference can be observed in the way in which the non-lexical versus the lexical vocalisation is handled within the interaction. The parents continue with the negotiations (line 08) following the '*ugh*' sound and there is no direct response to this by either Mum or Dad. By contrast, when Samuel claims that 'they're yucky' (line 10), this is immediately countered by Mum with a negation: 'they're not yucky' (line 12). One of the interactional nuances of non-lexical vocalisations is that they are not response relevant in the same way as lexical items (Keevallik et al, 2025). Due to the way in which they are produced as if an involuntary visceral response – despite being intricately situated within the unfolding social interaction – they are often not challenged in the same way as one might challenge a lexical turn.

A second example illustrates the performative nature of disgust expressions and of how they can emerge in situations when children may not be required to eat an item of food, but nonetheless provides a means through which a stance on eating can be produced. Extract 7.5 is taken from a preschool lunch in Sweden, in which several children are eating lunch with their teacher. Johan (5;5) is serving himself potatoes when he notices a mark on one of the potatoes and comments on this to the teacher. Sitting beside Johan is Peter (4;4), also seen in this transcript.

Extract 7.5

```
01 Joh   .hh det är nån MA^sk& s^om har
         .hh there's some worm that has
   joh    body forward -->^      ^head towards Tea -->
   tea                          &gaze to bowl-->

02 Joh   har k^rypit i^n här^ tror jag
         has crawled in here I think
   joh     -->^gaze Tea^head to bowl
                               ^point at potato-->

03 Tea   TRo&r ^du
         do you think?
   tea   -->& gaze away
   joh          ^gaze to Tea
```

```
04 Joh   el[ler] JOrd el&ler nåt [(XX)]
         or mud or something
05 Tea     [men-]                 [ aa ]
           but-                    yeah
   tea                    &gaze to joh

06 Tea   det var ett &lit- ett litet märke på &potatisen dårå
         it's a lit-        a little spot on the potato then
    tea              &gaze away                 &gaze to joh

07       ^(0.6)^
   joh   ^nods ^

08 Pet   ska du ha ^det (.)^
         will you have it
   joh             ^head shake^

09 Joh   nää-ä^
         no way
   joh   body lean, head turn away^

10 Tea   nej du be^höver inte ^ta den(.)&
         no you don't need to take it
   joh   gaze back^           ^spoon towards potato
   tea                                  &gaze away

11 Joh   ^bläää
   joh   ^spoon touches another potato

12       (0.6)
   joh   takes potato -->
```

Of particular interest in this section of interaction is the length of the discussion about the potentially disgust-relevant object – mud on or a worm in the potato – before the disgust expression itself is produced (on line 11). As previously mentioned, the timing and placement of non-lexical vocalisations are crucial for understanding how they are embedded within social actions and also how they construct specific understandings of eating practices – that visceral reactions should be spontaneous, not planned, for instance (see gustatory *mmms* in Chapter 6). Johan's expression here is produced immediately after Peter asks whether he will have the potato (line 08) and the teacher confirms that he doesn't need to take it (line 10). It is only when the subject of possible ingestion is raised that the sound is used to bolster the 'no way' declining of the suggestion that he might take the potato, while also constructing a particular stance and justification for doing so.

That disgust expressions are not simply sounds but also embodied movements is evident in this transcript and in Extract 7.4. In both examples, the child's head turns away from the food in question; and in the second, the body also leans backward. The bodily stance enables a physical distancing away from the disgust-relevant object. These movements are also dynamic, shifting alongside the conversational turns in talk, and present a more fully bodied representation of how disgust can be expressed: not just as a static face or a sound, but as a combination of faces, voices, and bodies (see also Wiggins & Keevallik, 2023).

A final extract (Extract 7.6) provides an example from *after* the food has been placed in the mouth. This data clip is also taken from the preschool lunch corpus, this time with Emma (5;8), Maria (5;2), and Alex (4;2), who have been involved in a discussion about the 'stringy' bit in the green beans that they are eating. Prior to this clip, Maria has asked the teacher what they are and, when told they are edible, performed a disgust response. This time, Maria has put the 'string' into her mouth and the clip is taken from the point at which she visibly removes it from her mouth with her fingers.

Extract 7.6

```
01 Emm   det är som  [om man-
            it's like [if you-
02 Tea               [^st^rängar
                     [strings
   mar                ^food out
                        ^gaze to food

03 Emm   hhhe[he
04 Mar      ^[BLÄÄ[Ä, +det HÄ-
              BLAH it THI-
   mar      ^hand down
   tea                +gaze to mar

05 Tea       [fibrer
             fibres
06 Mar   .h det SMAkar som STREck-
         it TAStes like a line
07       .h som ÄR ett [BAND.
         .h like IS a band
08 Tea                 [khrm khrm
09        (0.4)
10 Ale   får ↑JA::G smaka.
         can I taste (it)
```

In this example, the disgust sound '*BLÄÄÄ*' (line 04) is produced in the immediate aftermath of the tasting, as soon as the food is removed from the mouth. Indeed, it might be noted that it is difficult to produce a disgust sound while food is still in the mouth. Its placement in this immediately sequential position produces it as if it is a visceral response that cannot be avoided. Maria's gaze on the food (line 02) and her hand movement to place the food back on the plate (line 04) also construct the food as being the locus of the problem. The disgust sound attracts the teacher's gaze (line 04) and the attention of others at the table, and subsequently the curiosity of Alex (line 10). Maria proceeds to specify the taste experience by using the formulation 'tastes like X', which has previously been seen in research on sensoriality (Majid, 2021; Mondada, 2020b) – though notably it is not seen in the tasting examples in Chapter 5. While the disgust expression may convey a sensorial experience, its production and subsequent description are incorporated into the turn-taking sequence of the interaction. It is not only an individual experience but also part of a situated social action.

Concluding comments

In summary, this illustrated example has demonstrated the potential for analysing sounds that are often dismissed as inconsequential or beyond the realms of particular disciplines: non-lexical vocalisations. The form analysed here – non-lexical vocalisations associated with disgust – has important implications for understanding how children might resist or refuse certain foods and how these practices are embedded within sequences of social interaction. The sequential position of these sounds was shown to be particularly important for producing a stance on the food at time-sensitive moments in the progression of the mealtime. The analysis further illustrates the importance of examining not only the details of talk but also the sequentiality and temporality of eating practices: things happen in a particular order and this order is consequential for the mealtime.

What interactional research has already been conducted in this area?

Having navigated some of the wider literature on food refusals and examined how interactional approaches can be used to address some of the core concepts, this section presents an overview of existing work from ethnomethodology and conversation analysis (EMCA), DP, and language socialisation (LS) within this field. The aim here is to familiarise readers with relevant literature and provide a basis on which future research can be built. The good news is that there is an extensive base on which to stand and some that interconnects with work discussed in other chapters, such as research on sensoriality (see Chapter 5) and dislikes (see Chapter 6).

EMCA research, and specifically conversation analysis (CA), hosts a particularly rich seam of work on examining the interactional practices through which eating is negotiated. Directives – 'utterances designed to get someone to do something' (MH Goodwin, 1990: 65) – are a prime example that has already been studied in UK family mealtimes (Antaki & Kent, 2012; Craven & Potter, 2010; Kent, 2012; see also Pauletto et al, 2017, on requests in Italian and Swedish families). Directives can vary in terms of entitlement and contingency (Curl & Drew, 2008) and can be calibrated using verbal and embodied resources (Goodwin & Cekaite, 2018; Waring, 2025), demonstrating how social responsibilities for eating are managed through language practices. Children's responses to directives include the enactment of incipient compliance or 'a performance of compliance' (Kent 2012: 718) or 'reluctant compliance' (Wiggins & Humă, 2026a), building on an emerging body of CA and DP research into interactional forms of resistance (Flint & Rhys, 2023; Humă & Stokoe, 2023; Humă et al, 2023).

Related work within CA and DP has examined the various discursive practices that can be used to negotiate children's consumption in UK family mealtimes, including threats (Hepburn & Potter, 2011), admonishments (Hepburn, 2020a; Hepburn & Mandelbaum, 2018), or the use of 'shaming interrogatives' to encourage children themselves to adapt their behaviour by making them publicly accountable (Potter & Hepburn, 2020). The use of rules to achieve compliance during mealtimes in English, Finnish, German, and Polish languages (Küttner et al, 2022), or to negotiate with children in playful situations during Swedish family meals (Zotevska & Martín-Bylund, 2022), has also been examined. The CA and DP research discussed in Chapter 6 on negotiating likes and dislikes (Van der Heijden et al, 2022; Waring, 2025; Wiggins, 2023) is also useful here.

Research into disgust has been examined in work from across EMCA, DP, and LS, such as that discussed earlier in the chapter. This includes research into children's expressions of disgust in US school playgrounds (Goodwin, Cekaite, & Goodwin, 2012) and UK family dinners (Wiggins, 2013, 2014b; Wiggins & Osvaldsson Cromdal, 2020), with further work examining the variation and transformation of adult disgust expressions during a UK family meal (Wiggins & Keevallik, 2023). The morality of expressing disgust has also been examined as a topic of negotiation during Swedish family mealtimes (Aronsson & Gottzén, 2011). Work on multisensoriality within EMCA research, such as that discussed in relation to tasting in Chapter 5 (e.g. Mondada, 2018, 2021, 2023), provides a further entry point into examining disgust responses in everyday interaction.

Family dinner interaction has long been a cornerstone of LS research, so there is a wealth of literature on how children are socialised into culturally normative eating practices in the US and Italy (e.g. Ochs et al, 1996), including in relation to negotiations around table manners and rules of eating in family meals in Italy (Caronia & Colla, 2024; Galatolo & Caronia, 2018; Pontecorvo, Fasulo, & Sterponi, 2001; Sterponi, 2009), the US and Israel (Blum-Kulka, 1990, 2012), and Sweden (De Geer, 2004). This body of work has demonstrated the centrality of language for children's socialisation into eating practices within specific cultural and social settings, including negotiations around what should be eaten and argumentation between parents and children. This work has examined American (Paugh & Izquierdo, 2009), American and French (Kremer-Sadlik et al, 2015), French (Kremer-Sadlik & Morgenstern, 2022), Italian (Arcidiacono & Bova, 2015; Arcidiacono, Pontecorvo, & Bova, 2022; Bova, 2021; Bova & Arcidiacono, 2014) and Swedish (Brumark, 2006, 2008) family dinners.

How can interactional approaches be used to research food refusals?

Interactional research to date has already begun to unravel some of the discursive practices through which caregivers and children negotiate eating practices during family mealtimes in the home in certain cultural contexts. Given the importance of dealing with not eating in a broader variety of settings and languages, there is much more that could be done to develop this empirical base. The following research areas are concrete suggestions for some of the ways in which interactional research could be developed to address issues around food refusal.

Milk refusals

The earliest instances of not eating can occur within the first moments of milk-feeding, when infants refuse the breast or the bottle. Feeding difficulties can occur for a range of reasons and distinguishing between physiological problems such as ankyloglossia (when the infant is 'tongue tied'; Tomara et al, 2023) and other issues is important for both caregivers and healthcare professionals. Interactional research could be used to examine in detail how latching or other feeding difficulties become manifest in everyday situations and how these might be resolved.

Early disgust sensitivities

While the association between disgust and picky eating in adults is becoming clearer (e.g. Coulthard et al, 2022), much less is known about disgust responses in early childhood (Widen & Russell, 2011). A closer examination of infant interactions around food in relation to disgust would be extremely useful for understanding the aetiology of food aversions and disgust sensitivities. Interactional approaches could further be used to unpick the nuanced ways in which dislikes, disgust, and similar responses to food are distinguished in everyday eating practices and the implications of these for children's food consumption.

The 'fussy/picky eating' label

The stigmatising label of 'fussy/picky eating' and the heavy reliance on parental reports have already been recognised (e.g. Wolstenholme et al, 2022), and the term is pervasive throughout the literature on children's eating. The focus of interactional approaches on talk as constructive of the social world makes them ideally placed to examine how this label has come to define and shape caregivers' as well as children's own understandings of their eating practices. This could be considered in mealtimes as well as other situations featuring talk about children's eating, such as in classroom or kindergarten settings.

Refusals of food refusal

Negotiating what is or is not to be eaten is a common practice throughout children's mealtimes and spans a range of practices, from turning down a single food offer to complete refusal to eat. Much of the research to date, however, has been conducted in contexts where children have the ability and right to negotiate, to a limited extent (Kent, 2012; Wiggins & Humă, 2026a). There are, of course, many situations in which children have no freedom in this regard. Interactional research is needed in eating situations in which food refusals are refused – when the possibilities of negotiation are restricted or non-existent.

Early detection of 'disordered' eating

Eating practices that are defined as clinically disordered have a serious impact on children and their families. Early detection of potentially problematic eating practices is thus extremely important for preventative intervention (e.g. Kalindjian et al, 2022). Interactional research on eating in everyday settings could be used to help caregivers and health professionals to investigate the varieties of 'normal' and transitional phases of eating (Bialek-Dratwa et al, 2022), and to provide practical support through which mealtime interactions can be navigated during sensitive periods in children's lives.

Summary

Situations in which children do not (or will not) eat are perhaps more common than those in which they are actively eating. This chapter has navigated an expansive landscape that deals with eating challenges ranging from the inconsequential to the life-threatening. Grouped under the heading of 'food refusals', this literature has noted the need to focus more attention on the emergence of refusals in everyday mealtimes. Examining this research area using interactional approaches requires a shift from categorising individual behaviour as 'refusal' to more closely examining the conversational and interactional practices through which 'not eating' becomes relevant at particular moments during children's mealtimes. The analysis of non-lexical vocalisations, such as disgust expressions, provides an illustration of how different forms of language can be investigated as a route into analysis. Approaching refusal as interactional resistance and of diverging or conflicting trajectories of action provides a further analytical tool to unpack processes of not eating. In sum, the chapter has demonstrated the importance of examining not only *how* not eating arises but also *when*, in relation to the progression of social actions and the temporality of mealtimes. As is seen in the final analytical chapter, progressivity is central to everyday mealtimes.

8

ACHIEVING SATIETY

Like all good things, eating must inevitably come to an end. Ingestion stops; meals finish. This chapter focuses on the things that take place towards the end of children's mealtimes, including stopping eating, achieving satiety, and closing a meal. Research in this area ranges from biopsychological research on gastric fullness to sociological work on appetites and finishing meals. The concept of satiety is central, alongside responsive feeding and attending to the interoceptive states of children. Taking an interactional approach to this area enables the possibility of examining how satiety and finishing the meal are closely intertwined.

The chapter begins by sketching out the multidisciplinary landscape within which research on satiety has been conducted, particularly in relation to children's appetites and interoceptive states of fullness. This first section aims to help readers to navigate the literature in this area and gain a sense of what trajectories of work have been developed to date. The chapter continues by demonstrating, using data examples from family meals and preschool lunches, how satiety and the end of mealtimes can be analysed using interactional approaches. An illustrated example from a published paper on finishing the meal complements this section, going into more detail on how offers, satiety, and endings are intertwined. Towards the end of the chapter are two sections that describe some of the interactional work that has already been conducted across this area and offer concrete suggestions for what might come next. In sum, the chapter aims to immerse the reader in this research area and to provide the means through which to find their way forward.

DOI: 10.4324/9781003529620-8

Navigating the multidisciplinary landscape on satiety

There are several routes into and through the multidisciplinary landscape of research on satiety and closing meals (see Box 8.1 for a guide to terminology). On the one hand, satiety is typically treated as an individual and/or biological concern and research is often situated within fields that traverse biology, nutrition, physiology, and psychology (e.g. Blundell et al, 2010; Forde, 2018; Yeomans, 2020). On the other hand, research into meals as events (and how they might be brought to a close) is typically situated within anthropological and sociological work (e.g. Cappellini & Parsons, 2012; Germov & Williams, 2017; Wilhite, 1983). Research on children's satiety spans these two domains and the tension between individual and the social influences on satiety – what are sometimes termed 'internal' and 'external' cues to satiety – is evident throughout. Early research into children's abilities to self-regulate food intake, for instance, suggests that it is learned or developed in the right (social and interactional) circumstances (Birch & Fisher, 1998; Davis, 1939; see also Splane at al, 2024). Even in those fields that examine purely biological or cognitive factors of satiety, it is conceded that eating usually takes place in a social context, and that social influences affect how much food is consumed (Yeomans, 2020). Satiety is both an individual and a social concern.

BOX 8.1 TERMINOLOGY USED WITHIN SATIETY RESEARCH

Familiarity with the various terminologies used across disciplines will help when navigating the literature. The following are common terms used in empirical research across this area.

- ***'Ab libitum* meal paradigm':** An experimental set-up in which participants are encouraged to eat as much as they want without restrictions.
- **'Gastric fullness':** Perceptions of stomach distension corresponding to feeling 'full'.
- **'Meal termination':** The physiological and psychological processes through which a person stops eating during a meal.
- **'Satiety':** The suppression of appetite or the absence of hunger.
- **'Satiation':** The processes that lead to the termination of eating (i.e. to satiety).
- **'Sensory-specific satiety':** The suppression of appetite for a specific food as it is consumed, but not necessarily full satiety.

In terms of satiety in early infancy, the concept of responsive feeding has become particularly important (as with hunger; see Chapter 4). This concept refers to the process through which the caregiver is attentive to, and responds appropriately to, the child's satiety cues (Ventura, 2022). Parental responsiveness to satiety cues has been investigated in relation to milk-feeding (e.g. Hetherington & McNally, 2019; Ventura et al, 2021) and different styles of complementary feeding (e.g. Di Prete et al 2023; McNally et al 2020; Shloim et al, 2018). Infant cues of satiety may be ambiguous and even more of a challenge than deciphering those for hunger (DiSantis et al, 2011; McNally et al, 2016; Yu et al, 2025a). There is widespread consensus, across the psychological literature at least, that a mismatch between responsiveness and satiety cues is associated with infant weight gain or health issues (DiSantis et al, 2011; Lumeng et al, 2012; Redsell et al, 2021). It is in part because of these concerns that various coding scales (e.g. the Responsiveness to Child Feeding Cues scale; Hodges et al, 2013) have been developed to provide valid observational measures. The situation can be complicated if parents themselves find it difficult to recognise and express their own bodily sensations, as in the case of alexithymia (Yu et al, 2025b); or if infants are considered 'avid eaters' with an increased responsiveness to food cues and lower sensitivity to satiety (e.g. Pickard et al, 2025).

Related to the literature on responsive feeding is a parallel research area that focuses on parental strategies that require children to eat up or finish all the food on their plate (sometimes referred to as 'cleaning the plate' – though note that this is different from, but perhaps has implications for, the 'clean plate movement', which aims to reduce food waste in adults – see Wang et al, 2022). Often coded in self-report (e.g. Fildes et al, 2015) or observational studies (e.g. Bergmeier et al, 2016) as 'pressure to eat' behaviour or 'controlling feeding practices' (e.g. Dev et al, 2016), this can include both verbal commands and behavioural practices that are used to determine how much children eat. It is also included in questionnaires such as the Child Feeding Questionnaire (Birch et al, 2001) and the Parental Feeding Style Questionnaire (Wardle et al, 2002). Parental strategies of this kind have typically been focused on requiring children to eat a specific amount of food (eg, Orrell-Valente et al, 2007).

While parental reports are commonly used to measure satiety in young children (e.g. Qu et al, 2025), other methods are also being developed. These can include observational studies in which behaviours that might suggest 'mealtime disengagement' (moving away from the table) or 'mealtime negativity' (saying 'yuck' or eating slowly) are treated as indicative of satiety (Tan et al, 2021). With older children who can express their interoceptive states, studies have used various methods such as picture scales with teddy bears (Bennett & Blissett, 2014; Edwards et al, 2025) or dolls (Keller et al, 2006) to measure satiety states. While such scales have been found more suitable for over four-year-olds, it is not clear whether younger children do not understand the scales or whether they are unable to recognise satiety cues (Edwards et al, 2025).

Researching children's satiety states involves a range of issues, from abilities to express and report on interoceptive states to other behavioural cues that might indicate a lack of appetite. For instance, research into children's language development has shown that children can typically produce internal state words (e.g. 'I'm full') at around two to three years of age (Bretherton & Beeghly, 1982; Razuri et al, 2017); but very little is known about how this language is produced in everyday settings. Studies within early childhood education and care settings suggest that teachers might ask children about external rather than internal satiety cues (Ramsay et al, 2010; Swindle et al, 2017). The speed of consumption has also been addressed as an eating behaviour that may be associated with obesity; in other words, that faster eaters are likely to be heavier than slower eaters (Keller et al, 2024) and that obesity can be a heritable trait (Llewellyn et al, 2008). Moreover, nuances in terms of the ability to express sensory-specific satiety – that is, reduced levels of appetite for a specific food while still having an appetite for other foods – have been shown in children (Birch & Deysher, 1986; Cunningham et al, 2026).

Other issues involved in the closing of a meal do not necessarily relate to individual satiety, but rather to what are referred to as 'external' or 'environmental cues' to meal termination. These can include things such as portion size (e.g. Fisher et al, 2007); the amount of time available for eating (e.g. Burton et al, 2022); and nudging or choice architecture, in which features of the material environment might be used for behaviour change (e.g. Lycett et al, 2017) – though the latter has mainly been used to alter choices of food rather than amount. Work within anthropological and sociological literature, which is typically focused on issues related to appetite rather than satiety *per se*, offers perspectives on the social processes through which appetites might be tempered within specific social contexts (e.g. Germov & Williams, 2017). Other work within this field explicates the details of how children acquire the rituals of stopping eating and ending a meal, or how food is defined as 'leftovers' (Cappellini & Parsons, 2012). Wilhite's (1983) work on end-of-meal routines in Guatemalan Indian households, for example, details the verbal and non-verbal practices from over 1,200 meals to illustrate language acquisition in children, as well as how routines around meal endings are acquired.

In summary, research into satiety in children has predominantly focused on individual (or 'internal') factors of satiety, while still acknowledging the importance of the social context. What is still not known is how children express satiety in everyday settings or how they might be socialised into the skills necessary to maintain healthy eating practices through their life. While much is understood about how to start eating (see Chapter 4), very little is known about how to finish.

How to research children's satiety using interactional approaches

Interactional approaches are perfectly placed to examine the intricate ways in which satiety is both an individual and a social concern. This section demonstrates how satiety and meal endings are inseparable. The achievement of children's satiety, at least in those situations where there is sufficient food to be eaten, is as much an interactional concern as it is an individual one. Finishing a meal may be dependent on establishing that people have had enough to eat and satiety itself might foreground the closing of a meal. Progressivity and temporality are also fundamental issues, since the amount of time available for a meal and how it progresses can put constraints on satiety or on what can or should be eaten. This section demonstrates how to get started with researching endings, with a particular focus on how satiety checks and expressions are used by caregivers and children to negotiate the closing of a meal.

Establishing satiety in infants

One of the first things to note about children's mealtimes, particularly those involving infants, is that it is not always possible to know in advance when the meal will end. Infants may stop eating at any time (or never start, in some cases); and the closing of the meal is only observable after the event. This may seem a rather obvious point, but for those living through infant mealtimes – that is, caregivers and infants – this means that checks might need to be conducted several times during the meal to determine whether the infant might eat more or whether they have finished. Much of this needs to be done non-verbally, so determining 'satiety' is very much an embodied and collaborative activity within social interaction. Extract 8.1 provides an example of this, taken from an infant mealtime at home in Scotland, with eight-month-old Jessie and her mum; they are seated beside each other. At this point in the recording, Jessie has been eating pieces of bread and jam after finishing her main meal. Around 30 seconds prior to this clip, Jessie took a bite of the bread and then passed it back to Mum; she then begins to look around and vocalise. Mum is gazing at Jessie throughout this sequence. The transcript features both multimodal details to pick out eye gaze, facial expressions, and hand movements, and figures to provide further clarity at key points.

Extract 8.1

```
01 Jes   %hhff::
   jes   %gaze ahead, facing forward

02       (1.0)   %    (1.8)   %
   jes           %head turns %body turns
```

```
03 Jes   %Ck- heh &>HHh hh<
   jes   %brow furrows
   mum        --->&hand to J's shoulder

04 Mum   are we done,
05       (0.6) % (0.2) & (0.6)
   jes         %gaze to floor
   mum                 &hand drops

06 Mum   &shall we call& it a [day,
   mum   &-moves food--&

07 Jes                         [m:: m:: AA &#AAH >hhh hhhh hhh<
   mum                                     &holds food up
   fig                                      #Fig 8.1

08 Mum   las[t chance
09 Jes      [Hheeh >HH HH hHH (.) %mmmhh
   jes                            %hand to food-->

10       (0.6) %#    (0.4) %#    (0.2)     %(0.8)
   jes   ---->%grabs food %moves hand back %drops food
   fig         #Fig 8.2    #Fig 8.3
```

FIGURE 8.1 Mum holds up food

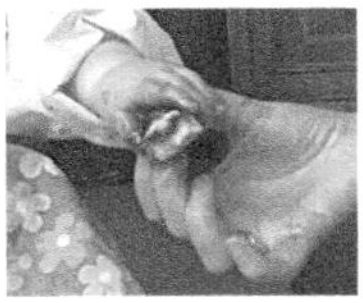

FIGURE 8.2 Jessie takes the food

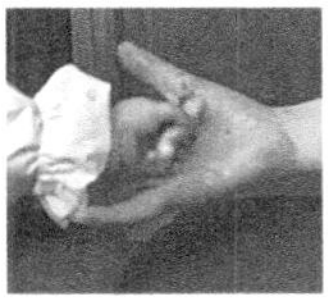

FIGURE 8.3 Jessie drops the food

```
12 Mum   °righ.° (0.4) call it a day:
```

One of the advantages of having a video recording of a mealtime is the benefit of hindsight: closings can easily be identified by starting from the end of the recording and working backwards. Parents and other caregivers, on the other hand, are living through the meal in real time and therefore have to do a lot of work to establish, second by second, the point at which the infant might be finished eating. In Extract 8.1, this begins to emerge around line 01 – though the 'start' of the end might have been allocated sooner, of course – when Jessie, who no longer has food in her hands or mouth, begins to sigh and gaze ahead. As she starts to turn her body to face Mum, her vocalisations become louder and more cry-like, accompanied by a furrowed brow; in response, Mum puts a supporting hand on her shoulder with a comforting touch (Cekaite & Holm Kvist, 2017). These first three lines indicate a shift in the interaction from one sequence of action to another.

It is at this point that Mum produces the first completion check (Laurier & Wiggins, 2011): 'are we done' (line 04), which sets up the next action as establishing whether the meal might be at its end. There follow two more checks (lines 06 and 12, using the English idiom 'call it a day' to indicate stopping an activity) and a final food offer (lines 07–09; Figure 8.1), which is taken by Jessie but then dropped immediately after (lines 09–12; Figures 8.2 and 8.3). Jessie's eye gaze and hand movements clearly demonstrate acknowledgement but then dismissal of the food offer. What transpires is that several interactional slots are opened in which the 'closing' could begin, in which Jessie's vocalisations and movements could be treated as related to hunger or satiety, boredom, or tiredness. As seen in Chapter 4, caregivers can calibrate their interaction with infants to collaboratively establish the status of infant vocalisations and movements and their meaning within the progression of the mealtime. Mum's use of the collective pronoun 'we' neatly reflects the idea that closing a meal is a collaborative endeavour, presenting the action as not only about Mum's decision, but also about establishing a consensus with Jessie.

On finishing the food to finish the meal

Once children can talk and interact more fully during mealtimes, achieving satiety and closing a meal become a site of complex verbal negotiations. This might involve, in some settings, a requirement to finish the food on one's plate before the meal is brought to a close. Satiety may or may not be involved in such situations and progression of the mealtime may become the greater concern. The next two examples demonstrate how interactional analyses can unpack the discursive and embodied practices through which this is accomplished. In Extract 8.2, the family (Mum, Dad, Magnus, five years and Rob, two years) have been eating dinner together at home (this example was also used to illustrate transcription in Chapter 3). Mum, Dad, and Rob have finished eating; but Magnus, who is now sitting on Dad's lap, still has some food on his plate. Mum has already left the table to fetch something and Rob is busy throwing things onto the floor; the meal is not entirely over but there are moves that indicate it is coming to an end.

Extract 8.2

```
01 Dad   do- >&y'going to- d'y' [want
02 Rob                          [ay::
   dad          &gaze to Magnus' plate

03       (0.4)
04 Dad   have you had enough (0.2) %fishfinger or
```

05 d'y'want more fish.
mag %gaze to plate

06 Mag I want %<some:: more (.) of thish>
mag %picks up fork and into beans

Achieving satiety for a five-year-old takes on a very different format from that for an eight-month-old: questions can be asked that allow the child to respond verbally and to make choices about what they might like to eat. In this example, Dad specifically asks about the fish (or rather, fishfinger) on Magnus's plate; to which Magnus replies that he wants more of the beans instead. Of importance here are the various verbal and embodied resources that are used to check for satiety. Dad's initial turn (line 01) involves two formulations that work on slightly different trajectories: the first leans more towards Magnus' intentions to eat ('going to'), while the second relates more explicitly to his desires ('want'). Both of these are abandoned before he restarts (Goodwin, 1980) and produces a more direct satiety check: 'have you had enough' (line 04). These kinds of formulations – such as those used to ascertain children's internal states – are an incredible resource for researchers in examining the end of mealtimes. It is in this way that psychological and interoceptive states such as hunger, satiety, and appetite are invoked and become embedded within social actions (see more on this in the next section). Dad's convoluted question (lines 04–05) offers an alternative – to eat more or not – even though it effectively offers the same food (Antaki & Kent, 2012). It relates not only to individual satiety, but also to what might be eaten in relation to the remaining food (and thus serves as an intriguing comparison with the green beans in Extract 7.2 in Chapter 7).

What might be examined further is the way in which issues related to satiety and remaining food are handled. As noted earlier, these may be referred to as internal versus external cues to satiety (e.g. parental pressure to eat versus interpretation of one's interoceptive state of 'gastric fullness'). In everyday situations, however, it is not so easy to distinguish between what is internal and what is external. This problem becomes apparent when embodied resources are considered. In Extract 8.2, it is eye gaze that is of particular interest. Despite asking Magnus a question about what he wants or whether he has had enough, Dad does not gaze at Magnus but rather gazes at his plate (line 02). Magnus, who had previously been looking up at Dad, gazes down at his plate (line 05). The visual focus of attention is established in this way as being on the remaining food rather than on Magnus himself. Dad asks Magnus whether he has had enough (thus suggesting interoceptive states), while joint attention on the food (orienting to external cues) is also achieved. Satiety may be considered to be not only about what can be eaten but also about what *might* or *should* be eaten.

The next data clip offers a very different example of how the progression of the meal might involve aspects of eating more, without necessarily any reference to satiety. This clip is taken from a different family dinner in Scotland with two parents (Mum, Dad) and two children (Bethan, five years, and Ali, two years). The clip is also taken from towards the end of the meal, when the children have started playing a game ('Duck, duck, goose') that Bethan is demonstrating by walking around the table. Ali is sitting on the floor. The parents are focused on getting them back to the table so that they can finish their soup and close the meal.

Extract 8.3

```
01 Mum   Ali you need to come and eat some [more -soup please
02 Dad                                     [yeah::
03 Ali   no:::,
04 Mum   [no cake [then.
05 Dad   [°used to do that°
06 Bet            [duck, ((walking around table))
07       (0.6)
08 Ali   °mmh° (.) [°((unclear))°
09 Bet             [duck (0.6) duck.
10 Dad   used t'=
11 Mum   =you only get [cake if you eat your soup honey.
12 Bet                 [duck
```

A first thing to notice about this extract is that it includes a clear example of what, in some fields of research, is referred to as a 'pressure to eat' parental strategy (e.g. Bergmeier et al, 2016; Fildes et al, 2015) or a 'controlling' feeding practice (e.g. Dev et al, 2016) – specifically, using food as a reward. If the sequence is instead considered in terms of social actions, a different picture emerges. The challenge here is that both children are away from the table and a first step is to get them back to the table before eating can re-commence. Each family member is engaged in a different action trajectory: Bethan is demonstrating the game; Ali is sitting out; Dad is reminiscing about playing the game ('used to do that', line 05); while Mum is trying to get Ali (but not Bethan) back to the table to eat more soup so that the meal can finish.

Mum begins with a directive that Ali 'need[s] to come and eat some more soup' (line 01; Craven & Potter, 2010), not dissimilar to that seen in Extract 7.3 in Chapter 7 with Samuel and the green beans. Ali's negative response – a stretched out 'no:::' in a slightly whiny voice (line 03) – shuts down that line of negotiation and Mum progresses to using cake as a reward. The discursive practice here is what is known as an 'if-then' formulation (if you eat soup, then you get cake), which functions as a conditional threat (Hepburn & Potter, 2011). What is particularly interesting about this formulation is that Ali's agency – his ability to influence the course of events – is embedded within it. That is, his actions in eating the soup (or not) will determine whether he gets the cake, rather than this being something that Mum controls (which, of course, she does). Ali responds with a whimper and muffled speech (line 08) and Mum repeats the conditions of the threat (line 11). The progression of the meal is subsequently dependent on what Ali does next.

Announcing satiety

The final example presents a situation in which a child themselves announces that they are 'full' and cannot eat any more, towards the end of the meal. It is taken from a preschool lunch, in which five children are eating with their teacher, and closing the meal is not only dependent on one appetite but is a collective endeavour. In this clip, the teacher is turned towards Amine (5;1), who is seated beside her and who is asking for more food. At the same time, Simon (3;0), seated diagonally opposite the teacher, announces that he cannot manage to eat any more.

Extract 8.4

```
01 Ami   °mera°&
         °more°
   Tea         &gaze to Amine--->

02 Sim   ja [or%kar inte
         I can't manage
   sim         %gaze to teacher--->

03 Tea      [va sa du
             what did you say
04 Sim   [halå jag orkar [inte mer,
          hey I can't manage any more
05 Ami   [mera
          more
06 Tea                    [vad
                           what
07 Ami   [mera (.) mat
          more (.) food
08 Sim   [jag or:kar inte mer mat
         I can't man:age any more food
09 Tea   vad &är det du vill ha då [&utav maten&
         what do you want then from the food
   tea   --->&gaze to food         -->&gz Amine->&gz Simon
```

```
10 Sim                                    [jag är mätt
                                           I'm full
11 Tea      °a° då kan du sätta ihop be%sticken så så ser man
            yeah then you can put the cutlery together like
            this so so one can see
   sim                                ---->%gaze to plate
```

The teacher is visually focused on Amine throughout this sequence and verbally draws out more information about the food that he would like. It is only when the teacher's gaze shifts towards the food on the table (line 09) and Simon repeats his turn (line 10) that her gaze moves to Simon and she gives him an instruction – without hesitation – about what to do with his cutlery (line 11). Simon's satiety expressions, meanwhile, not only are repeated to pursue a response (Pomerantz, 1984b) but also change in form, progressively building from 'can't manage' (line 02) to 'can't manage any more' (line 04) to 'can't manage any more food' (line 08), and then changing to 'I'm full' (line 10). The increasing specificity of Simon's turns and the finality of the satiety expression on line 10 are neat examples of how a child can express their interoceptive states even at a young age. They also demonstrate an orientation to the importance of other people (specifically, the teacher) knowing about satiety states: that this is something which the teacher should know about. In other words, satiety is not just about an experience but has social relevance. The teacher confirms this understanding by commenting not on Simon's internal state, but on what he should do with his cutlery, thereby associating an expression of satiety with the finishing of his meal.

In summary, the analyses throughout this section have demonstrated how issues related to satiety – being 'done', having 'enough', eating 'more soup', and being 'full' – are as much about progressing a meal and bringing it to a close as they are about an individual child's physical capacity to consume more food. Closing a meal and achieving satiety can also be considered as a set of interactional projects, rather than a single event: several actions must be taken between actively ingesting food and engaging in the next activity. In a mirror image to the start of mealtimes, there is rarely a clear line between meal-not meal but rather a transition into a different set of activities. By focusing on situated social actions, how these are collaboratively produced through verbal and embodied resources, and how these unfold over a sequence of interaction, interactional research can provide a tool to investigate *how* satiety ***and*** closing a meal are achieved.

Illustrated Research Example #5: Finishing the family meal

Examining the ways in which satiety and finishing a meal are intertwined is illustrated in more detail using a data clip and analyses from a published paper by Laurier and Wiggins (2011), entitled 'Finishing the family meal: The interactional organisation of satiety', published in the journal *Appetite*. Using conversation analysis (CA), the paper aims to open up the field of interaction research on satiety within everyday settings and is more exploratory than some of the other papers discussed as research examples. The paper is based on data examples from family mealtimes recorded in Scotland, which are used as illustrative examples of the kinds of issues that can be examined within everyday meals. At the core of the paper is a concern with how family members manage the transition from eating to not eating: those threshold moments in which the children may continue to eat the same food, start to eat a different food, or stop eating altogether. That is, it focuses on the transition from finishing one food item to perhaps moving to another 'course' in the meal or to finishing the meal completely.

The main arguments of the paper are that a more integrative approach is needed to understand the work involved in finishing meals, and that issues of satiety are closely interwoven with transitioning to different stages of a meal or to closing a meal, as seen in the earlier examples in this chapter. The paper argues that much more needs to be done to examine the intricate details of family mealtimes (and other examples of children's eating practices) to understand the social and interactional relevance of satiety. The analysis in this section focuses on one of the extracts used in the paper to discuss further how these various ways of 'finishing' can be interwoven. The extract itself is quite long, but its length demonstrates the ways in which these issues unfold; it is also used to illustrate how a single case analysis (see Chapter 3) can offer benefits over a collection of instances. The extracts have been retranscribed from the original recording to add more details and divided into three sections for a closer and more detailed analysis than in the original paper.

Progressing the meal

One of the issues raised in the paper is how the finishing of a meal can be organised in different ways and how individual satiety may not necessarily become topicalised. Eating *more* might be necessary primarily to progress the meal. Requesting that children eat up the food on their plates is one way in which this might be done. Extract 8.5 is taken from the first part of the sequence in which Mum makes relevant the remaining food on Robin's (age four) plate. The family have been eating a barbecue outside and Robin is standing near the table, looking around at the garden and at the cameras that are recording the dinner.

Extract 8.5

```
01 Mum   come on,
02       (0.4)
```

```
03 Mum  you've only got two bits of sausage left Robin,
04      (5.6) ((Robin looks around, parents watch))
05      (1.2) ((Dad taps Robin's chair))
06 Dad  hh::
07      (8.0) ((Robin walks to different chair))
08 Dad  oh:: Robi::n ((sing-song voice))i
09      (2.0) ((Robin walks closer to Dad))
10      (1.0) ((holds out fork with sausage))
11 Dad  we're almost there (0.4) and then you [know what's next
12 Rob                                        [where's Bean?
13 Mum  if you finish this=
14 Dad  =well he's waiting patient[ly for us to (.) finish
15 Mum                            [yeh (0.4) you have to finish,
16 Dad  our [dinner >so you can play with him again<
17 Mum      [so we- ((Robin starts to move away))
18 Dad  no LEAVE HIM [Robin::
19 Mum               [>Robin<
```

Several things in this extract are reminiscent of sequences of interaction noted in the previous chapter and highlight some of the complexity of distinguishing between what might be classed as 'not eating' (or food refusal) and attempts to close a meal and finish eating. Mum's 'come on' (line 01) may be heard as an attempt to cajole Robin and harks back to Extract 7.4 in Chapter 7, in which consuming two green beans was made relevant as the next action (and the noticing of the beans in line 03). In the current extract, there are also two pieces of food left, formulated specifically as 'bits' (c.f. Orrell-Valente et al, 2007). This is not merely highlighting remaining food but formulating it as an observable and minimal amount. Ostensibly, this formulation might lower the threshold for what is required to be eaten; though it also becomes a means through which 'not eating' can be measured. Both parents in this case work together to pursue compliance (c.f. Kent, 2012) and make moves towards orienting Robin to this shared focus of attention. Mum's turn, the mutual gaze on Robin (line 04), the tapping of the chair (line 05), and Dad calling his name (line 08) and holding out the sausage on the fork (line 10) collaboratively accomplish this action. This sequence is further stretched over a relatively long period. While tapping the chair makes relevant a move back to the table, the spatial organisation of this sequence means that Dad is close enough to reach forward with the fork. Eating does not, therefore, rely on Robin sitting down again (as with Ali in Extract 8.3).

The sequence is quite different from other negotiation sequences involving the pursuit of consumption, since what is raised here is the relevance of progressing to a closing point. This is foregrounded in the reference to what is 'only . . . left' (line 02), but also in Dad's reference to being 'almost there' and projecting forward to what is next (line 11). While there are several social actions that might be unpacked further in this sequence, the interactional project might be something along the lines of 'progressing to the next stage' of the meal, discussed below.

Robin's question about Bean (the dog) pursues a different action trajectory from that focused on the food, and Mum and Dad use the question to redirect Robin back to the task of finishing the meal (lines 14–16). Playing with the dog might become an option if the food is eaten. Note how the verb 'to finish' is used, rather than 'to eat', which is never mentioned in this particular sequence. That is, the parents do not request that Robin eat the food but rather ask him to finish his dinner. While ostensibly the same physical behaviour is required (consuming the food), this is a clear example of how language practices shape particular sequences of interaction. What happens next is that Robin walks away from the food and towards the dog – at which point the parents' requests become more urgent as they attempt, without success, to halt the trajectory.

An alternative food offer

The sequence continues in Extract 8.6 and involves a change of tactic to bring Robin back to the table. At this point, it is clear that the dog has become a distraction, or rather an alternative participation framework for Robin, and there is a shift in tactics to attempt to progress the meal: the introduction of another, desirable, food item.

Extract 8.6

20		(4.0) *((Robin looks towards the dog))*
21	Mum	Robin,
22		(1.2)
23	Mum	do you want ice cream
24		(4.0) *((Robin turns around))*
25	Rob	°(what did you)° say
26	Dad	°°do you want some ic[e-cream°°
27	Mum	[°°do you want some ice-cream°°
28		(2.2) *((Robin hesitates))*
29	Mum	can you sit down at [the table please
30	Rob	[what about ham?
31		(2.0) *((Robin moves towards his chair))*

Introducing another item of food (or the next course in the meal) is a delicate business – not only because it could mean that the child abandons the first food but also because it sets up one food item as preferable to another. In a similar manner to that seen in Extract 8.3 earlier in the chapter, the offer of ice cream (rather than cake) is also positioned at a pivotal moment in the interaction. There have already been attempts to encourage Robin back to his chair (in Extract 8.5) and he has now moved further away from the table, apparently with his attention on the dog. An upgraded move pursues the action trajectory of getting Robin back to the table, following a lengthy gap in the talk (line 20), in which Robin remains focused on the dog. Note that the offer is formulated as a 'want' (Childs, 2012) and is thus constructed as if originating from Robin's personal desires rather than from parental decision-making. It makes no reference to needing to eat the sausage first (c.f. Extract 8.3) but rather introduces an alternative course of action.

After another substantial gap in the talk (line 24), in which Robin turns back to his parents, the mishearing on line 25 is a classic example of what is known in CA as an 'other-initiated repair' (Sacks, Schegloff, & Jefferson, 1974), where someone other than the speaker initiates a sequence that requires them to repeat (or repair) their previous turn. In this case, the long gap, Robin's turning around, and his 'what did you say' prompt Mum to initiate a repair of her question on line 23. What happens next is that both parents repeat the question but do so in ***quieter*** voices – almost as a performed whisper. This alone suggests that this is not being handled as a hearing issue, but rather as a request to repeat the offer. Following another period of silence (line 28), Mum relaunches the focus on convincing Robin to return to the table (line 29), which he then does. The alternative food offer accomplishes the original action trajectory (of returning to the table) through the introduction of a possible new sequence of actions involving ice cream.

Completion check

The possibilities for progressing forward with the meal continue now that Robin is moving back to his chair. In this final section of the data clip, the sausage is tentatively eaten and the parents conduct a completion check ('are you finished . . .?') as a means to move the meal towards the next step.

Extract 8.7

32	Dad	well (.) finish your sausage *((holds out fork))*
33	Mum	without ham?
34		(1.2) *((fork near mouth))*
35	Dad	°what about (ham)°
36		(0.8) *((Robin starts to bite))*
37	Mum	°big mouth >come on<° *((Robin closes in on fork))*
38	Dad	>go go< *((Robin retracts mouth, starts to pull away))*
39		(3.0) *((Robin walks away, Dad retracts fork))*
40	Dad	are you finished then Rob?
41		(1.8)
42	Dad	are you finished? *((Robin walks further away))*

43 Rob °°yes°°
44 (2.0)
45 Dad I can't hea::r you (.) can you turn round
46 Rob °I'm finished°
47 (0.8)
48 Dad all right. (.) do you want ice cream (.) strawberries
49 Rob yes
50 Dad 'kay *((sausages put back on plate, Robin returns to chair))*

The original request to finish (note the verb 'finish' rather than 'eat') the sausage is reiterated once Robin is back at the table. The mishearing of Robin's comment about ham is clarified by Dad (lines 30–35) – ham in this case being an alternative food that has previously been attributed as one of Robin's favourites. At around line 34, the sausage is once again poised on the fork ready to be eaten in a manner that is reminiscent of line 10 in Extract 8.5. All Robin needs to do is take a bite. In this case, however, he makes a slow move to open his mouth – the progress of this action being cajoled again by Mum through indicating the necessary mouth movements (line 37) and further coached by Dad (line 38) – but then abandons the bite and walks away (lines 38–39). The embodied and collaborative coordination of this possible mouthful is a further example of the various ways in which caregivers can be actively involved in the eating practices of children. The walking away on the second occasion prompts the repeated completion check ('are you finished?', lines 40 and 42), which is pursued until Robin himself explicitly states it (line 46).

The interactional work to establish the final moments at which food might be offered have been seen previously (see Extract 8.1) and illustrate the endeavours that can be undertaken to establish what is not necessarily a clear-cut case. While there is food remaining (or 'drinks to be drunk', Laurier, 2008: 175), the mealtime can potentially continue. Work needs to be done to bring it to a close and this work is undertaken through a series of social actions, such as offers of more food or alternative food, as seen in this sequence. Having confirmed that Robin is finished, the interaction moves onto the next stage: clearing away the sausages and returning to the topic of ice cream. The closing of this phase of the meal is merely the beginning of the next phase; it is not necessarily a finish but rather a transition to the next activity.

Concluding comments

In summary, this illustrated example has demonstrated how interactional analyses can begin to unpack the complex interactional work that goes into finishing meals (or parts of meals), involving a sequence of social actions (e.g. offering food, returning to the table, checking completion) that in themselves can unfold in variable ways. Many of these social actions are reminiscent of things that can occur at various moments throughout mealtimes, as seen in data examples in the previous chapters. What this paper demonstrates, therefore, is the complexity of closing meals and achieving satiety, which requires a much closer examination of the details of children's eating practices in everyday settings.

What interactional research has already been conducted in this area?

The chapter so far has provided an overview of research into children's satiety and the closing of meals, a demonstration of how interactional research can be used to analyse this aspect of eating practices, and an illustrated research example from a published paper. Satiety is an essential aspect of eating, intertwined with concepts of appetite and hunger, as well as elements of sensory practices and food likes; as a result, this is a complex research area. Much work remains to be done to understand the interactional processes and practices through which children's satiety, in particular, is managed. In terms of interactional research that has already been conducted, there is surprisingly little on satiety. Identifying a foundation on which to build future research requires consideration of a broader area of work. As before, work from ethnomethodology and conversation analysis (EMCA), discursive psychology (DP), and language socialisation (LS) is showcased here to guide readers through this landscape.

EMCA research into the closing of events or the transition to the next activity in an interaction is a suitable place to start, and much can be gleaned from this in terms of how children's eating practices are not simply brought to a 'close' but are a moment of transition to a new activity. Some early conversation analysis (CA) research on 'closings' (Schegloff & Sacks, 1973) detailed how these can be sequentially organised, turn by turn; while later work has demonstrated the interdependence of talking alongside bodily movements as a means to accomplish the close of one sequence of action and the transition to another (Broth & Mondada, 2013). Laurier's (2008) paper on the closing of a coffee-drinking encounter in a café deserves particular attention, since it details the multimodal ways in which the drinking (c.f. a meal) was collaboratively achieved. As with the analysis detailed above (Laurier & Wiggins, 2011; also CA), the paper illustrates that it is neither the drink nor the conversation in itself that brings the meal to a close, but rather how language and food (or drink) are inextricably interlinked. Other EMCA work on the management of children's everyday activities, such as moving them towards cleaning their teeth or going to bed (Goodwin & Cekaite, 2018), also provides valuable inspiration.

DP is a particularly useful approach to address the issue of satiety from the perspective of examining how what is putatively an individual and physiological (though also, arguably, cognitive and experiential state) becomes consequential for social actions. Initial work on the management of children's appetites in preschool lunches (Wiggins et al, 2026) has demonstrated how establishing satiety is a collaborative achievement – and one that might also be positioned near the start of the meal. Using the Swedish verb '*orka*' – to be able to manage or have the effort to complete a task (see Simon's use of this in Extract 8.4) – teachers and children negotiated amounts that might be eaten while food was being served, as well as towards the close of meals. Other DP work on family mealtimes has briefly addressed the issue of satiety (Wiggins et al, 2001); though it is work on children's interoceptive states (e.g. expressions of pain; Jenkins, 2015) that could help to develop further work on how bodily states (in relation to eating) are discursively constructed and embedded within social actions. This might also include, for instance, examining how epistemic authority over children's rights to 'know' and claim satiety is negotiated (c.f. food likes; see Wiggins, 2023 and Chapter 6).

LS has provided a considerable range of research into how mealtimes as an event are navigated by parents and children. While not necessarily addressing satiety explicitly, this body of work nevertheless demonstrates how children are socialised into cultural appetites (e.g. Kremer-Sadlik & Morgenstern, 2022; Kremer-Sadlik et al, 2015; Ochs et al, 1996). Research in this area has also demonstrated the language practices through which children learn politeness routines, such as being excused from the table (Gleason et al, 1984) and other table manners (Blum-Kulka, 1990, 2012; Caronia & Colla, 2024; Ochs & Shohet, 2006). LS provides a means through which to specifically focus on the language practices through which children are socialised into culturally normative routines concerning appetite, satiety, and the closing of mealtimes.

How can interactional approaches be used to research satiety and closing meals?

This final section aims to provide inspiration for research that might be developed next; to build on the work discussed in the previous sections and to consider various research trajectories forward. As noted, there is much still to be done to examine how satiety is handled within children's everyday mealtimes and further research is essential for dealing with issues such as health and food waste. It is an area which has great potential for developing new lines of research to understand how it is that children come to stop eating.

Closing a feed

Beginning milk-feeding and establishing a latch can be crucial interactional moments, but closing a feed can also be a delicate negotiation between caregiver and infant. Interactional research is perfectly placed to examine how caregivers distinguish between infants 'playing' or 'snacking' during a feed and indications that they may be sated. The duration of individual feeds (or milk meals) is particularly important in situations where there are concerns about undernutrition or 'failure to thrive' (e.g. Krugman & Dubowitz, 2003), when caregivers might attempt to prolong feeding sessions to ensure adequate nutrition.

Collective satiety

When children eat with their peers in settings such as preschool or kindergarten, achieving satiety is not just an individual issue; it is also a collective concern. Interactional approaches could be used to unpack the various stages that comprise the close of a meal – such as finishing food, clearing dishes, and leaving the table – to examine how these are negotiated collaboratively. Such knowledge would be useful for practitioners within early childhood education and care (ECEC) settings, where encouraging children to finish their food can be a delicate matter (e.g. Swindle et al, 2017; Podanovitch et al, 2025).

Preventing 'overeating'

The examples presented in this chapter typically involved checking whether the child would like to eat more food before the meal finished. In some situations, however, there are concerns about children eating too much – who are sometimes referred to as 'avid eaters' (e.g. Pickard et al, 2025). Interactional research could examine the language used to define 'overeating' in various situations; investigate the social actions through which eating is terminated prematurely (before satiation is reached); and explicate the ways in which epistemic authority over satiety states (and rights to eat) is negotiated. The potential for this to contribute to health and nutrition research and policy is substantial.

Developing interoceptive language

The role of language in the development of emotion regulation skills in children (e.g. Cole et al, 2010) is becoming increasingly important, particularly in ECEC settings (e.g. Silkenbeumer et al, 2024). The ability to articulate interoceptive states such as appetite and satiety is a valuable step in fostering children's understanding of their own eating practices and caregivers' scaffolding of these skills. Interactional research could be used to explore how language around interoceptive states could be developed within everyday contexts while being sensitive to the complex interactional structures that support children's eating practices.

Reducing food waste

There is a delicate balance to be struck around the end of mealtimes between children's satiety and their willingness to eat and the potential food waste which might remain on plates, as seen in research on controlling feeding practices (e.g. Dev et al, 2016) or what is defined as 'waste' (e.g. Cappellini & Parsons, 2012). Interactional research into satiety is beginning to show how such issues might be managed even in the earlier parts of mealtimes (Wiggins et al, 2026); and more work could be done to explore how the details of mealtime interaction become consequential for navigating this balance between individual appetite and reduced food waste.

Summary

Meals do not simply end; work is done to bring them to a close. This chapter has examined research into what happens at the end of mealtimes. A central concept within this research area is that of satiety – which is typically treated as primarily an individual state but is also shown in this chapter to have interactional relevance as families and preschools collectively bring meals to a close. The temporal aspects of eating are especially important at the ends of mealtimes, since it is progressivity towards the close of a meal that raises issues of satiety and vice versa. Interactional approaches provide the analytical tools needed to unpack the various social actions involved in bringing meals to a close, from food offers to satiety checks, and the language and bodily resources used by parents and children to achieve this. The finishing of a meal might also be considered not necessarily as a closing, but rather as a transition to the next activity. Ending a meal is also the beginning of the next social action.

9

BEYOND MEALTIMES

Eating, in its most basic definition as the ingestion of food, does not just happen. Food does not simply fall into children's mouths. Things need to be done in order to arrive at the point at which food can be ingested: collaborative social actions that facilitate not only children's eating but also a myriad of other activities involving language, food, and bodies. The preceding chapters have explicated some of the ways in which children's eating takes place. Not everything that is important for children's food consumption happens at the dinner table, however. There are other vast landscapes of research relevant for children's eating beyond mealtimes and beyond that described in Chapter 1. This final chapter draws together some of the core contributions of the book before considering how interactional research might do more, go further, and develop in new directions. Quite simply, it reflects on what has been shown, what could be done next, and what might be done better.

Unpacking mealtimes

There is nothing particularly glamorous about children's mealtimes. As Bugge and Almås (2006: 206) have noted, 'the everyday dinner at home and all it entails carries little prestige; it is practical, commonplace and repetitive.' It is precisely these characteristics that make mealtimes an ideal setting for research into how children eat. Few other research areas can be researched several times a day, in spectacular variety, ***ad infinitum***. Mealtimes are ubiquitous events, but it is perhaps because of this that their status as a research object has often been overlooked, dismissed as trivial or mundane, or considered too unpredictable for the demands of certain methods. And it is not just mealtimes that have received limited attention. Research into the consumption of food in

DOI: 10.4324/9781003529620-9

general has, at times, been regarded as a lower form of science. Typically associated with the body rather than the brain, it has fallen foul of the Cartesian mind-body dualism that has pervaded much of the natural and social sciences (Korsmeyer, 1999). The cognate aspects of eating – of how people perceive or think about food – have been privileged over the visceral realities of how people eat, as evident in discussions of the senses in Chapter 5 and gustatory pleasure in Chapter 6. This is particularly true of research into children's eating as distinct from adults' food consumption. Eating is often modified or mediated through other methods to render it acceptable for the scholarly gaze. It is rarely studied in situations where it occurs naturally.

Children's mealtimes nevertheless enjoy an exalted status. The *idea* of eating together and its moral value for individuals and society commonly go unquestioned. Writing on the importance of commensality, and the family meal in particular, can be unapologetically sentimental. This is not to suggest the opposite, but rather to direct closer attention to the details of a research object that too often has been put on a moral pedestal. Mealtimes can thus be said to have a liminal status: simultaneously considered too ordinary or complicated for many research methodologies while also revered as a panacea for societal and individual ills. Mundane and trivial, but also fundamental and essential.

The interactional analyses presented throughout this book demonstrate that it is possible to conduct rigorous and detailed analyses of what happens during mealtimes. The black box of children's mealtimes can be unpacked in ways that do not reduce them to individual behaviours or extrapolate to social or cultural norms. This section recaps on the core analytical contributions of interactional approaches to children's mealtimes and eating practices that have been discussed throughout this book: on eating as a collaborative activity, and on the importance of situated, social actions.

Children's eating as a collaborative activity

The first contribution of the analyses in this book is to demonstrate that children's eating practices in social settings are collaborative activities involving the interplay between language, bodies, and food. Interactional approaches focus on social actions – that is, the things that happen when people interact with one another. Social actions are built up through language and gestures as people interact with one another, meaning that talk is analysed in terms of how it is part of interaction rather than an individual behaviour. Concepts such as participation frameworks enable researchers to identify the moments in which people shift from being co-present in a physical space to interacting with one another. In Chapter 4, for example, it was shown how establishing a participation framework was an essential step in sequences of assisted eating. The subtle movements of eye gaze and body alongside the talk unfolded sequentially in ways that were mutually dependent on each other. Similarly, the food offers seen in Chapter 5 were not a fixed set of behaviours but could be produced in several ways and at various points within a meal, each with different implications,

Researching children's eating in terms of social interaction and social actions provides a way to unpack the sociality of mealtimes and examine 'eating together' as moments of participation together, in which various actions and activities are undertaken. The social bonding of commensality, the psychological benefits of family mealtimes, and the influences of peers and parents can all be rendered analytically available through this approach. Mealtimes can be understood as a series of discrete moments of participation in children's eating practices – by caregivers or peers – and it is through these moments that processes otherwise known as 'social influence' or 'parental strategies' take place. The negotiations involving requests to eat two more beans (Chapter 7) or the last bits of sausage (Chapter 8) can be analysed as sequences of turn-taking in which parent and child might be involved in very different action trajectories: to leave the table or to remain seated and eat. These kinds of participatory sequences might even be called 'co-eating' (Wiggins, 2026), in which eating is at times understood as a joint venture: a collaborative activity in which one or more persons participate in the eating practices of another. Analysis of interactional sequences through which participation occurs as part of social actions provides a rigorous tool for understanding what happens when children eat with other people.

Situated, social actions

The second core contribution of the book has been to demonstrate the importance of the passage of time, in the form of sequentiality (that the order of things matters), temporality (that the temporal position of social actions within a mealtime matters), and progressivity (that the transition from one activity to another matters). In many of the extracts presented throughout the book, all three of these issues were incorporated together. Establishing readiness to eat and determining hunger, for instance, involved parental interpretation of infant eye gaze, body movements, and vocalisations within turn-taking sequences. An infant's vocalisations might indicate hunger (as with Eleanor in Chapter 4) or satiety (as with Jessie in Chapter 8), depending on how they are coordinated alongside other features of the interaction and their location within the trajectory of the meal. Jessie's hand movements to grab the food in Extract 8.1, for instance, were treated not as interest in the food but rather the opposite, and the meal ended soon after.

In some instances, the exact timing of the coordinated actions was particularly important. In creating moments of food enjoyment, the precise synchronisation of gustatory *mmms* with food in the mouth was essential in how pleasure was expressed on behalf of an infant (Chapter 6). Sounds of disgust – another form of non-lexical vocalisation – were notable not only for their sequential position following a food offer (e.g. Emma's '*bleughh*' at the pepper in Chapter 2 and 7), but also for their position in relation to a transitional place in the progressivity, as food moved ever closer to the point of ingestion (Chapter 7). Temporality and progressivity were important for food remaining on a child's plate and how it became managed as an accountable issue. For instance, food on the plate was interpreted as Sarah having an 'aversion to eggs' in Chapter 6; as 'not [having] done well in the green beans stakes' for Samuel in Chapter 7; and as an offer of having more fish or having 'had enough' for Magnus in Chapter 8. The same set of behaviours and situations might arise, therefore, at different moments in a mealtime with entirely different consequences. Examining social actions within their specific, situated, interactional context is an integral part of analyses. It enables research to unpack the black box of children's mealtimes and reveal its contents as organised and structured practices that can be analytically interrogated using robust methods. It enables research to capture eating as it happens and examine how children *really* eat.

BOX 9.1 ON WORKING IN A MULTIDISCIPLINARY LANDSCAPE

Much of this book has discussed a multidisciplinary landscape as if it were a straightforward place to navigate; as if researchers can work in a multi-, inter-, or cross-disciplinary manner as easily as they might within a single discipline. In practice, this is not usually so simple. Conducting research that stretches across disciplines, breaks convention, blurs boundaries or challenges paradigms brings with it both benefits and challenges. The benefits are numerous: research can ask very different kinds of questions and draw on a wider range of literature than might be possible within the constraints of disciplinary boundaries. The challenges of working across disciplines, however, can be substantial and at times insurmountable. Academic structures mean that being situated within a discipline has implications for employment and funding opportunities, journal submissions, and the kinds of assessment, ranking, and regulatory procedures that impact on education as well as research opportunities.

For those who do not fit neatly into a disciplinary box, these are serious implications that not only impact on the individual but have a ripple effect through research and its development. The increasingly narrow scope of journals, for instance, can mean that research on children's eating in interaction may be treated as being not sufficiently about children, or eating, or language. As Clift et al (2024: 896) note in relation to the publication of conversation analytic research, 'methods are distinct from – and sometimes at odds with – the conventions of our varied home domains.' Being inter- or multidisciplinary can often mean adjusting to fit the spaces of others. Perhaps it is time for new spaces to be created. As a worldwide community of researchers who contribute to knowledge on children's eating practices, it is our responsibility to ensure that research in a plurality of forms is nourished and given space to grow.

Beyond the mealtime

Video recordings of mealtimes cannot, of course, capture everything. There are vast domains of research concerned with children's eating practices that are not analysable through a camera lens. There is also much that might have been examined within the mealtime examples used in this book, but which was not addressed explicitly. As noted in Chapter 1, the analyses begin with social actions rather than topic areas, so issues such as the consumption of fruit and vegetables, peer influences, or health problems were not directly addressed. The omission of an explicit focus on these topics was not deliberate but rather a byproduct of focusing on children's eating practices in terms of their interactional organisation rather than on isolated topics, behaviours, or concepts. It is for the same reason that discussions of satiety at times overlap with those of hunger and sensory issues: eating is a complex matter that cannot easily be separated into neat categories or topics. Instead, the book has endeavoured to navigate readers through the interactional projects that are particularly common and consequential for children's mealtimes.

There is, of course, more that can be done. In casting the analytical gaze beyond the mealtime, this section considers four broad research areas within which interactional approaches on eating could provide valuable input. Many of these might also be studied within mealtime settings, though the focus here is on how matters that occur beyond the mealtime might be incorporated into interactional research. The aim here is not to be exhaustive but rather to encourage a wider diversity of research that might engage researchers across disciplines and find points of potential collaboration.

Nutrition and health

The field of human nutrition has developed significantly in recent decades, including the emergence of concepts such as the gut microbiome and ultra-processed foods (e.g. Mehta et al, 2021; Mescoloto et al, 2024). There are also related fields such as dentistry, in which eating practices play an essential role in children's oral health; and sports nutrition, in which young athletes have tailored nutritional needs to accommodate demanding training routines. Issues related to children's nutrition and health are thus scattered across numerous research areas, each of which can inform understandings of what, how, and how much children should eat. Understanding the role of talk and social interaction across these various domains is important for considerations of how they become topicalised and negotiated in settings that have real-life consequences. The nutritional needs of a budding athlete may clash with family circumstances or the competing food preferences or needs of other family members, for instance. As the multidisciplinary landscape of research on nutrition and health continues to expand, interactional research could be used to explicate the various ways in which these issues are embedded within social interaction and how they unfold along different trajectories of action. The discursive construction of categories of children, eating practices, and health requirements could be interrogated for their interactional consequences. The ways in which children are socialised into culturally normative health practices around food could be investigated across various settings.

Technologies

There are very few foods that do not rely on some kind of technology, from the basic tools to prepare, transform, or preserve food to a wider range of technologies found at mealtimes that do not necessarily involve food. A fork is a technological advancement. Technology is therefore a very broad and ever-expanding domain, not only about whatever current development is in focus (e.g. the presence of digital mobile screens while eating, e.g. Rusiene, 2019). Interactional research has begun to explore digital interaction around eating, including commensal eating across screens (Gan et al, 2023) and mukbang (Choe, 2019), and this field will continue to expand in line with technological developments. The flexibility of interactional approaches to record life (and eating) as it happens makes them the perfect combination for research that seeks to understand how technology is embedded within children's (and adults) everyday eating practices. Interactional research could investigate the ways in which various forms of technology – from eating utensils to cooking apps – are integrated within sequences of social interaction and their consequences for children's eating practices. Children's own engagement with different technologies could be examined in ways that might expand understandings of sensoriality, for instance. Interactional approaches provide a range of analytical resources that can be used to investigate the ways in which language, food, bodies, and technologies are intertwined to structure and organised everyday eating practices.

Human variation

While this book has illustrated some common eating practices during mealtimes, one size does not fit all. Particular eating challenges can arise for those whose bodies (in the broadest sense of the term) diverge from what is assumed by the situations in which they find themselves. These include an enormous range of children and situations, including those in which there are difficulties related to oral-motor control (e.g. dysphagia), movement coordination of the hands and arms, or the ability to hold the body still enough to consume and ingest food; as well as neurological diversities that can impact on issues related to sensory input, repetition and familiarity with food, changing routines, bodily conduct, and interaction with other people (e.g. those with autism or attention deficit hyperactivity disorder). Variation must also be considered not just in the children but also in the caregivers and peers with whom they share mealtimes. Mainstream eating research typically assumes able-bodied and neurotypical children as well as parents; but life is much more complex than that. Given the focus of interactional approaches on the multimodal details of social interaction and the way in which language, bodies, and food are intertwined, they provide the perfect tool to examine how human diversity is occasioned and becomes consequential prior to or during eating practices, for all involved.

Environment and resources

Not everyone has equal access to food, or to the economic, technological, or knowledge resources required to prepare food adequately for consumption on a regular basis. The foods available in different geographical or environmental situations have a significant impact on what can be eaten and how this is achieved. Examples might include living in areas where there is limited access to resources or which are affected by manmade or natural disasters: children fleeing conflict or floods, for instance, do not face the same food issues as those living free from stress or shortage. It is hard to think about gustatory pleasure when there is not enough food to eat. Food insecurity (e.g. Evans et al, 2025), including that associated with migration (e.g. Dondi et al, 2020), is a major challenge even for so-called 'affluent' societies, with health inequalities affecting eating practices as much as other health issues. There is an increasing need to eat more sustainably to reduce the environmental impact of eating practices, from cutting food miles to reducing food waste. Interactional research could be used to explicate the details of how environmental and resource issues play out in ways that are consequential for how children eat. For example, interactional approaches could unpack the multimodal resources through which food is treated as 'waste' in situations of food purchase or consumption or how children might be encouraged to alter their choice of foods while navigating established food likes and disgust reactions.

Better mealtimes

As illustrated throughout this book, interactional research on children's mealtimes has done much to expand our understanding of how children eat within the home and institutions, across several countries. There is, however, tremendous potential to expand the diversity of eating research not only in terms of topics (see the previous section), but also in terms of how research is conducted. The benefits of working in an interdisciplinary space mean that there is room to expand and to include a broader variety of understandings of how children eat. This final section considers how research could build on what has already been achieved and do better: increasing diversity in people, languages, and eating practices.

Diversity in people

Towards the end of the last century, it was stated that 'nearly all the research with humans on food preferences and food selection has been conducted among affluent, white, middle-class US and Western European populations, where inexpensive, energy-dense food is readily available' (Birch, 1999: 44). This situation has unfortunately changed little in the intervening years. Participants from what have been called 'WEIRD' populations (Western, educated, industrialised, rich, and democratic) (Henrich et al, 2010) are still the predominant participant group in research into children's eating practices in everyday settings (i.e. that included in the 'multidisciplinary landscape' discussed in Chapter 1). People from lower socio-economic backgrounds, for example, are distinctly under-represented in research and yet they are over-represented in terms of poor health outcomes and reduced access to resources (Van der Heijden et al, 2022). Scholarly knowledge of how children eat is too often skewed in favour of Euro-American cultures and privileged groups. Being able to choose one food over another or having access to sufficient food to meet satiety and nutritional needs, for instance, is a luxury that not everyone can afford.

The data examples used in this book – from settings in the UK and Sweden, in which food was not scarce and most participants were white and middle-class – are, of course, a case in point. Both the research contexts and the author of this book represent the privileged majority. The extracts presented were those in which children's rights as autonomous eaters were, to a greater or lesser extent, upheld. There may have been examples in which children were required to eat a certain food or where their food preference was challenged, but there were no examples of force-feeding or other coercive methods. One might also note how gender imbalances can be traced throughout the eating research, on the sides of both the researchers and the participants. Too often, eating (or feeding) is treated as primarily a female concern. The book and its contents therefore represent voices that can be heard in many other spaces, though the aim is that these concrete examples will inspire others to conduct research into children's practices that go beyond the WEIRD minority.

Diversity in languages

Interactional research has long provided evidence that language is the key to how children are socialised into eating practices, and that language shapes relationships and routines around food. Given the importance of language, it is perhaps surprising that so little attention has been given to its use in various research methods that rely on language to define concepts and discuss research. Self-report rating scales have language and categories at their core, for instance. Terminology is also central to the concepts used throughout children's eating. Language plays a crucial role in how breastfeeding is portrayed, for instance, such as talk about 'prolonged breastfeeding rather than premature weaning' (Van Esterik, 2002: 259; see also Chapter 4) or breastfeeding being a 'natural' skill (Locke, 2009). The variability in definitions of terminology was noted in several chapters (e.g. on defining 'picky eating' in Chapter 7) and misunderstandings are inevitable. In Chapter 5, for example, it was noted that even within the same discipline (sensory science), the terms 'flavour' and 'taste' can be used interchangeably. 'Taste' can also mean something very different to a sensory scientist than it does a philosopher or education researcher. Language is both the tool for research and the medium through which the world of eating practices is understood. It underpins all research.

Research is, moreover, limited by the need to use English as the common language through which research is presented (including this book). Other languages must be translated in order to disseminate their findings and in doing so, some of the meaning of the eating practices is lost. In Chapter 8, for instance, the example of the Swedish verb '*orka*' as roughly meaning having the energy or capacity to undertake an activity (including finishing up food) was discussed as being not only a translation issue but also an analytical one. Important understandings about eating are lost in translation. The way forward may be to incorporate a greater range of languages in our research and to avoid simplifying or trying to fit them into an Anglocentric framework. As Mol (2024: 9) argues, 'The art is to avoid naturalising English without simply giving up on it.' Anthropologists are well aware of these kinds of issues, in terms of preserving the integrity of a culture or communication system in an authentic manner. Ethnomethodologists, too, are keen to illustrate the complexity of local practices while making the 'unfamiliar, familiar'. Research into children's eating practices – particularly that interested in language and social interaction – would be well advised to increase the diversity in languages included.

Diversity in eating practices

In an increasingly shifting global climate, there is an even greater urgency to study the future of eating, since the eating practices of children are those of the next generation. As environmental and political factors impact on food production and availability, there have been cultural shifts towards examining how to eat in more sustainable ways, such as reducing food miles or food waste. This includes increasing the diversity in food choice, and research has begun to examine children's responsiveness to foods that may be unfamiliar to them, such as eating insects for those in European contexts (e.g. Erhard et al, 2023). Increasing the diversity in what children eat need not necessarily mean introducing entirely new foods but rather examining those interactional practices that support acceptance of changing habits. As noted in Chapter 6, for instance, children's food likes might be established as 'knowledge' about the child – a sticky category that becomes difficult to shift (Wiggins, 2025). An examination of the interactional practices through which these changes are made could be used to support more sustainable and adaptable eating practices for future generations.

Diversity in eating practices also relates to the ways in which food is treated as different kinds of resources: food can be fuel but also a source of comfort, celebration, sorrow, and pain. There is no single way to understand eating, even for individuals themselves. One eating event may be purely focused on satisfying hunger while another is embedded within the rituals of a group celebration. How children eat is not only about family dinners and preschool lunches but also layered with multiple interpretations and meanings that go beyond nutritional requirements. Knowledge of children's eating practices in many ways lags far behind the diversity of what is studied in adults. This is not just about methods or the challenges of interviewing a five-year-old as to whether they ate a pancake as 'comfort food' or because they felt peer pressure to do so. It is about reframing work on how children eat to accommodate a broader variety of understandings of what it means to 'eat'. Eating research might draw inspiration from other fields, such as studies on emotion regulation development in young children (e.g. Cole et al. 2010) or teaching children language to address mental health issues. There is much scope to understand how children (and adults) might talk about issues such as appetite, hunger, food likes, pleasures, disgust, and satiety in ways that open up rather than close down avenues for eating.

Closing remarks

Researching how children eat is probably the most important, engaging, and intellectually rewarding area of study in which one could wish to be involved. No other research area encompasses such a diverse range of topics and issues and addresses them in a way that can have an immediate impact on people's lives. This book has aimed to expand and draw connections across a research landscape that at times has been hampered by disciplinary fragmentation and methodological prejudice. It has demonstrated the potential of looking across research domains to consider what might be adapted from other fields or where areas of collaboration might be developed. It has emphasised the benefits of interactional research in being able to illuminate some of the most exquisite details of eating in social interaction, using robust and transparent methods. The liminal status of mealtimes, as being considered at once both morally idyllic and domestically mundane, can be used to our advantage. Interactional research can make the ordinary extraordinary. This book is a practical guide to researchers seeking to make their way through this landscape and to conduct their own interactional analyses of children's eating practices in everyday settings. This closing chapter is thus not really an ending; it is merely a transition to the next step in research.

APPENDIX 1

Glossary

Appetite The desire or urge to eat, whether a physiological or psychological craving. Can also be attributed to individual desires or cultural norms.

Approach A set of principles or way of doing research, including underlying principles (sometimes theory) and/or methods for conducting the research. Sometimes used interchangeably with 'perspective', though the latter can be a broader conceptualisation of research.

Avoidant restrictive food intake disorder (ARFID) A clinically registered eating disorder since 2013 (*Diagnostic and Statistical Manual of Mental Disorders*, 5th edition), described as a lack of interest in eating or avoidance of food to an extent which leads to an inability to meet energy or nutritional needs, and which is not accounted for by other eating disorders or mental health illnesses.

Aversion A strong dislike or avoidance of something, such as those related to food.

Avid eaters A term used within some psychological literature to refer to people with eating patterns that are characterised as involving high levels of food responsiveness or a strong desire to eat.

Baby-led weaning A method of introducing infants to solid food in which they are encouraged to 'self-feed' using small pieces of food. Typically used as an alternative to, or complementary method to, spoon-feeding, in which pureed food is offered to infants on a spoon or other utensil.

Cataloguing The process of making notes about video recordings and associated research data in a way that enables researchers to search a data corpus and identify examples for analysis.

Commensality The term used to refer to eating together, which may also incorporate elements that involve distinguishing between the social relationships between dining partners and/or the enjoyment (i.e. conviviality) of eating together.

Communication A term used in some psychological literature to refer to talk and gesture as a means of transmitting or exchanging messages or information between individuals, sometimes referred to as the 'sender-receiver model'. Contrasts with *Discourse* below.

Complementary feeding The stage in which infants transition from a purely liquid (milk) diet to one that includes solid foods (which 'complement' the milk). It is considered to begin at approximately four to six months of age and to last until up to 18 months or two years, though there are cultural and geographical variations that impact on this span.

Conversation analysis (CA) An approach that examines the organisation of talk-in-interaction in everyday settings.

Deviant case A data example that deviates from an identified pattern within a data corpus but which might subsequently be used to validate the analysis. Similar to what some research approaches might refer to as 'outliers'.

Discourse All forms of spoken or written language in use (talk or text). The term 'discourse' or 'discursive' is used to emphasise the focus on talk-in-interaction rather than on linguistic features (i.e. language as theory) or on communication as the transfer of messages or information from one person to another. Contrasts with *Communication*, above.

Discursive psychology (DP) An approach that examines how psychological matters are constructed discursively within everyday social interaction.

Early childhood education and care (ECEC) Primarily institutional settings in which young children receive education and care outside of the home, such as kindergarten, nursery, and preschool.

Eating difficulties A term used to refer to a wide range of challenges that are associated with the ingestion of food, whether due to motor or cognitive impairments or psychological issues.

Eating disorder (or 'feeding disorder') A clinically diagnosed condition characterised by disruptions to, or disturbance of, typical eating routines and practices. The term 'feeding disorder' might also be used but this is often restricted to infants who are unable to eat without assistance from caregivers.

Embodiment The state of being in, and moving as, a body. An alternative to 'bodily movements' that blurs the distinction between gestures of certain body parts (e.g. hand movements or eye gaze) and more gestalt positions of the body or of bodily features that impact on individual action (e.g. breathing, swallowing food).

Ethnomethodology An approach that examines how social order is produced within everyday social interaction, referred to throughout this book by the collective term 'ethnomethodology and conversation analysis' (EMCA).

Food preference The choice or increased liking of one food over another in situations where there is the option of more than one food. May be confused with, or used interchangeably with, the term 'food likes'.

Gustatory *mmm* An extended '*mmm*' sound accompanying the consumption of food or drink and which orients to a positive assessment of the consumed item. Typically has a notable up-down pitch contour and can be exaggerated or extended.

Language socialisation approach An approach to research that examines how novices to a language are socialised into language use and cultural practices through talk and interaction. Originally developed within anthropology.

Lip-smacks A sound made by pressing the lips together then releasing them with a short plosive sound. Often produced in short bursts as a chain of sounds. Can include the tongue or vocal elements.

Multimodal A term used to refer to the combination or involvement of different modalities or modes of expression. Within EMCA research, it is used to refer to the combination of talk, sound, gesture, and other objects within social interaction.

Naturally occurring data (or 'naturalistic data') Data collected from situations that are not contrived by the researcher and that would have taken place regardless of researcher intervention, such as family mealtimes, school lunches, or other settings in which children eat during their regular routines. The term is often used to distinguish from researcher-generated data such as interviews, surveys, or experiments.

Neophobia An avoidance of, or fear of, new or unfamiliar items – that is, food, in the case of eating practices. Can relate specifically to flavour or texture and may include foods that have previously been accepted.

Non-lexical vocalisation A sound that is produced by the voice (i.e. caused by air flow passing over the vocal chords) but is not in the lexicon for that language – that is, sounds which are not words. The term 'vocalisation' is sometimes used to refer to the sounds of babies and infants who are learning to talk (also called 'pre-linguistic sounds', 'cooing', or 'babbling').

Orthographic transcript A transcript that captures what is spoken but no other features of speech such as intonation or emphases. Sometimes referred to as a 'words-only transcript', 'play script', or 'basic transcript'.

Picky eating Also known as 'fussy' eating. A term that is used to describe a range of situations in which there is an inadequate consumption of variety (or quantity) of foods.

Prosody The features of talk that relate to sounds and their production, such as intonation (variations in pitch), volume, timing, and voice quality. Prosody can sometimes be used to refer to the rhythmic features of talk or sound objects (e.g. gustatory *mmms*).

Research question A specific question to guide the analytical focus of a piece of research or project. Used instead of a hypothesis for research that aims to examine data without using a causal approach.

Satiety The psychological or bodily state in which there is a reduced or lack of motivation to eat following the ingestion of food. It is closely related to 'satiation', which describes the processes leading up to satiety.

Social action A term that is commonly used in interactional research to refer to the things that happen when people interact with one another, or collaborative human activity.

Table manners The social or cultural customs or practices for how individuals might be expected to behave while dining at a table; sometimes referred to as 'dining etiquette'.

Weaning An alternative term for complementary feeding used in the UK and other settings; see *Complementary feeding*.

APPENDIX 2

Example consent form

The following is a modified version of an information and consent form used for a preschool lunch project, which can be used as an example for other projects and adapted as required. As various technologies develop, it will become even more relevant to include reassurances about what will (or will not) happen with the video recordings. In the interests of open science and the longevity of data recordings, it would be advisable to include a statement about whether you have permission to make the video recordings available for other researchers with similar research projects. This could include, for instance, a statement in which you specify the conditions under which data would be shared (e.g. if other researchers need to sign an agreement to ensure that the confidentiality of the data will be preserved); participants can then select whether they agree (or not) to this additional use of the data.

Information for parents/guardians

We would like your permission to allow your child/children to take part in a research project. This document provides information about the project and what is involved in participation.

What are the project aims and why is my child/children being asked to participate?

Mealtimes in preschool are an important setting for socialisation, where even very young children learn about food and nutrition as well as how to eat with other people. In this research project, we want to study how children and staff members eat together during lunch periods, to understand whether and how learning takes place. In order to conduct this project, we need to video-record some of the lunchtimes at different preschools and your child/children's preschool is one of the preschools taking part in this project. We are therefore contacting you to request your permission to video-record the lunchtimes during which your child is present.

What will happen in the project?

The interaction between children and staff members at one or two tables will be filmed during the preschool lunchtimes. The lunches will be filmed once or twice a week for part of the autumn term, then again in the spring term. At least two preschools will be involved in the project, since the aim is to see how lunches work in different settings. We are interested in things such as talking and bodily gestures that are used by young children during mealtimes, so the analysis will focus on these features of the video recordings. Small parts of the video recordings will be transcribed (written down as text), and at that point all names (including the name and location of the preschool) will be replaced with pseudonyms so that participants' identities are protected. Before any publication of results, any images or short video clips will be anonymised so that faces cannot be recognised. Exceptions can be made for those participants who give consent to have their image visible without anonymisation. The video recordings will be stored securely (offline) on password-protected hard disks that will be kept in locked cabinets. The recordings will only be used for research purposes and no one other than the research team members will have access to the data.

What will happen with my information?

The project will collect some information about your child, such as their name, age, and any possible food preferences or allergies that might be discussed or shown during the lunchtimes. Since we will use video cameras, your child's face is also likely to be visible in the filming. The person responsible for collecting and securely storing such information is [PROJECT LEADER'S NAME]. According to EU data protection regulations, you have the right to know what information will be kept about your child/children.

How do I get information about the results of the study?

Since the study is focused on social interaction during preschool lunches, the recordings will show at least two children at any time – often more, seated around a table – and members of staff. The study will therefore not generate any results about individuals, but rather focus on the communication that takes place between children and adults in the lunchroom. It is the preschool lunch as a social and pedagogical setting that is the focus of the study and not how an individual child or staff member eats their food. If you are interested in finding out about the results of the study, you are welcome to contact the project leader (see details below).

Participation is voluntary

Your child/children's participation is voluntary and either you or your child/children can, at any point, decide to withdraw from the study. No reason is needed for withdrawing and this will not affect your child's care at the preschool in any way. If you wish to withdraw, please contact either the project leader or one of the staff members at the preschool.

Project leader/person responsible for the study

The researcher who is project leader and responsible for the study is [*insert project leader's name and contact details here*].

Consent to participate in the study [PROJECT NAME]

I have received verbal and written information about the study and have had the opportunity to ask any questions. I understand that participation is voluntary and that we can withdraw from the study up until the recordings have been collected by the researcher.

☐ I consent to my child/children taking part in the study.
☐ I consent to the information about my child/children being handled as described.

If you consent to your child taking part in the study, please choose one of the following alternatives:

☐ I consent that images from the video recordings can be used for scientific publications and presentations in paper or electronic form, without anonymisation of images.
☐ I consent that images from the video recordings can be used for scientific publications and presentations in paper or electronic form, with anonymisation of images.

Parent/guardian name(s) and signature(s) . . . .
Child/children's name(s) and date of birth(s) . . . .
[Insert contact details for project leader here]

APPENDIX 3

Transcription notations

The following transcription symbols are used within the Jeffersonian transcription system (Jefferson, 2008; Sacks, Schegloff, & Jefferson, 1974), with some additions noted by Hepburn and Bolden (2017). The transcripts used in this book frequently use parental titles ('Mum', 'Dad') or roles ('Tea' for teacher) to indicate adults and 'Inf' to indicate infant or the first three letters of the child's name. Multimodal transcripts also make use of other symbols (e.g. &, %, €, ^) to indicate the start and end of participant eye gaze or gestures, as these correspond to specific positions in the verbal turns.

(0.2)	Elapsed time (i.e. of silence) in tenths of seconds
(.)	A brief interval within or between utterances, less than two-tenths of a second
?	A question mark indicates strongly rising intonation
,	A comma indicates continuing intonation
.	A period or full-stop indicates closing intonation
↑ ↓	Upward and downward arrows indicate markedly high or low pitch
[yes]	Square brackets indicate the start and end of overlapping talk
£	The British pound sign indicates smiley voice or suppressed laughter
.hh	A period or full-stop followed by an h indicates an inbreath or audible inhalation; without the dot, this is an outbreath or audible exhalation
wh(h)at's	h in parentheses within words indicates interpolated laughter or plosive sounds within words (e.g. laughing while talking)
heh/hih	Laughter sounds with voiced vocals

::	A lengthening or stretching of the preceding sound. More colons indicate a longer sound, each colon corresponding to one beat of silence
=	Latched talk with no gap between words or speakers
sit down	Emphasised or stressed words or parts of words are underscored
no-	A dash indicates a cut-off at the end of a sound or word
NO	Noticeably increased volume is denoted by upper case or capital letters
°okay°	Degree signs enclose words or sounds that are quieter or softer than surrounding talk
°°oh°°	Double degree signs indicate whispering or barely audible talk
(unclear)	Words in parentheses (or empty parentheses) are unclear or inaudible
((Move))	Gestures and embodied movements are added in double parentheses, sometimes italicised
>quick<	Words spoken quicker than surrounding talk
<slow>	Words spoken slower than surrounding talk
.mpt or .pt	A lip-smack sound
#	A hashtag symbol indicates a 'creaky' voice (similar to vocal fry). Note that in multimodal transcripts, this can also be used to refer to the position of a figure

REFERENCES

Acebo, C. & Thoman, E. B. (1995). Role of infant crying in the early mother-infant dialogue. *Physiology & Behavior*, *57*(3), 541–547.

Addessi, E., Galloway, A. T., Visalberghi, E., & Birch, L. L. (2005). Specific social influences on the acceptance of novel foods in 2–5-year-old children. *Appetite*, *45*, 264–271.

Ahern, S. M., Caton, S. J., Blundell, P., & Hetherington, M. M. (2014). The root of the problem: Increasing root vegetable intake in preschool children by repeated exposure and flavour flavour learning. *Appetite*, *80*, 154–160.

Ahern, S. M., Caton, S. J., Blundell-Birtill, P., & Hetherington, M. M. (2019). The effects of repeated exposure and variety on vegetable intake in pre-school children. *Appetite*, *132*, 37–43.

Aijmer, K. (2004). Interjections in a contrastive perspective. *Emotion in dialogic interaction*, 99–120.

Albert, S., Hoey, E. M., & Raymond, C. W. (2025). The case for open conversation analysis data. *Research on Language and Social Interaction*, *58*(2), 156–164.

Albert, S., Albury, C., Alexander, M., Harris, M. T., Hofstetter, E., Holmes, E. J., & Stokoe, E. (2018). The conversational rollercoaster: Conversation analysis and the public science of talk. *Discourse Studies*, *20*(3), 397–424.

Albert, S. & Hofstetter, E. (2024). Working with data I: Field recordings. In J. Robinson, R. Clift, K. H. Kendrick, & C. W. Raymond (eds.), *The Cambridge handbook of methods in conversation analysis*. (pp. 81–96). Cambridge University Press.

Antaki, C. (ed.) (2011). *Applied conversation analysis: Intervention and change in institutional talk*. Springer.

Antaki, C., Billig, M., Edwards, D., & Potter, J. (2003). Discourse analysis means doing analysis: A critique of six analytic shortcomings. *Discourse Analysis Online*.

Antaki, C., Keevallik, L., & De Stefani, E. (2025). The ethics of collecting, curating, and sharing data in conversation analysis. *Research on Language and Social Interaction*, *58*(2), 109–112.

Antaki, C. & Kent, A. (2012). Telling people what to do (and, sometimes, why): Contingency, entitlement and explanation in staff requests to adults with intellectual impairments. *Journal of Pragmatics*, *44*(6–7), 876–889.

Arcidiacono, F. & Bova, A. (2015). Activity-bound and activity-unbound arguments in response to parental eat-directives at mealtimes: Differences and similarities in children of 3–5 and 6–9 years old. *Learning, Culture and Social Interaction*, *6*, 40–55.
Arcidiacono, F., Pontecorvo, C., & Bova, A. (2022). 'But the vanilla is healthy!' Children's expression of arguments to justify their non-compliances in family conversation. *Learning, Culture and Social Interaction*, *34*, 100630.
Aronsson, K. & Gottzén, L. (2011). Generational positions at a family dinner: Food morality and social order. *Language in Society*, *40*, 405–426.
Aukrust, V. G. & Snow, C. E. (1998). Narratives and explanations during mealtime conversations in Norway and the U.S. *Language in Society*, *27*, 221–246.
Austin, J. L. (1975). *How to do things with words*. Harvard University Press.
Auvray, M. & Spence, C. (2008). The multisensory perception of flavor. *Consciousness and Cognition*, *17*, 1016–1031.
Avena, N. (2015). *Hedonic eating: How the pleasure of food affects our brains and behavior*. Oxford University Press.
Barnes, R. (2024). Methods for 'applying' conversation analysis. In J. Robinson, R. Clift, K. H. Kendrick, & C. W. Raymond (eds.). *The Cambridge handbook of methods in conversation analysis* (pp. 841–860). Cambridge University Press.
Barthomeuf, L., Droit-Volet, S., & Rousset, S. (2012). How emotions expressed by adults' faces affect the desire to eat liked and disliked foods in children compared to adults. *British Journal of Developmental Psychology*, *30*, 253–266.
Barthomeuf, L., Rousset, S., & Droit-Volet, S. (2009). Emotion and food. Do the emotions expressed on other people's faces affect the desire to eat liked and disliked food products? *Appetite*, *52*, 27–33.
Bartoshuk, L. M. (1991). Sensory factors in eating behavior. *Bulletin of the Psychonomic Society*, *29*(2), 250–255.
Bartoshuk, L. M., Duffy, V. B., & Miller, I. J. (1994). PTC/PROP tasting: Anatomy, psychophysics, and sex effects. *Physiology & Behavior*, *56*(6), 1165–1171.
Barwich, A. S. (2017). Up the nose of the beholder? Aesthetic perception in olfaction as a decision-making process. *New Ideas in Psychology*, *47*, 157–165.
Bateman, A. (2015). *Conversation analysis and early childhood education: The co-production of knowledge and relationships*. Routledge.
Bateman, A. (2018). Ventriloquism as early literacy practice: Making meaning in pretend play. *Early Years*, *38*(1), 68–85.
Bateman, A. (2024). Infant embodied requests and teacher-practitioner offers during early childhood education mealtimes. *Appetite*, *200*, 107539.
Bateman, A., Katila, J., & Hofstetter, E. (2025). Exploring nurse responses to spontaneous breastfeeding episodes during routine infant health checks in Finland: A multimodal conversation analytic approach. *Health Communication*, 1–14.
Beals, D. E. (1997). Sources of support for learning words in conversation: Evidence from mealtimes. *Journal of Child Language*, *24*, 673–694.
Beals, D. E. & Snow, C. E. (1994). 'Thunder is when the angels are upstairs bowling': Narratives and explanations at the dinner table. *Journal of Narrative and Life History*, *4*(4), 331–352.
Beauchamp, G. K. & Mennella, J. A. (2009). Early flavor learning and its impact on later feeding behavior. *Journal of Pediatric Gastroenterology and Nutrition*, *48*.
Bennett, C., & Blissett, J. (2014). Measuring hunger and satiety in primary school children. Validation of a new picture rating scale. Appetite, 78, 40–48.
Bennett, W. G. (2014). Some differences between clicks and labio-velars. *South African Journal of International Languages*, *34*(2), 115–126.
Bergmeier, H., Aksan, N., McPhie, S., Fuller-Tyszkiewicz, M., Baur, L., Milgrom, J., Campbell, K., Demir, D., & Skouteris, H. (2016). Mutually responsive orientation: A novel observational assessment of mother-child mealtime interactions. *Appetite*, *105*, 400–409.

Berridge, K. C. (2009). 'Liking' and 'wanting' food rewards: Brain substrates and roles in eating disorders. *Physiology & Behavior*, *97*(5), 537–550.
Betz, E. (2024). Data sessions. In J. Robinson, R. Clift, K. H. Kendrick, & C. W. Raymond (eds.) *The Cambridge handbook of methods in conversation analysis* (pp. 172–188). Cambridge University Press.
Białek-Dratwa, A., Szczepańska, E., Szymańska, D., Grajek, M., Krupa-Kotara, K., & Kowalski, O. (2022). Neophobia—a natural developmental stage or feeding difficulties for children? *Nutrients*, *14*(7), 1521.
Birch, L. L. (1979). Preschool children's food preferences and consumption patterns. *Journal of Nutrition Education*, *11*(4), 189–192.
Birch, L. L. (1980). Effects of peer models' food choices and eating behaviors on preschoolers' food preferences. *Child Development*, *51*, 489–496.
Birch, L. L. (1999). Development of food preferences. *Annual Review of Nutrition*, *19*, 41–62.
Birch, L. L. & Deysher, M. (1986). Calorie compensation and sensory specific satiety: Evidence for self-regulation of food intake by young children. *Appetite*, *7*(4), 323–331.
Birch, L. L., & Fisher, J. O. (1998). Development of eating behaviors among children and adolescents. *Pediatrics*, *101*(2), 539–549.
Birch, L. L., Fisher, J. O., Grimm-Thomas, K., Markey, C. N., Sawyer, R., & Johnson, S. L. (2001). Confirmatory factor analysis of the Child Feeding Questionnaire: a measure of parental attitudes, beliefs and practices about child feeding and obesity proneness. *Appetite*, 36(3), 201–210.
Birch, L. L. & Marlin, D. W. (1982). I don't like it, I never tried it: Effects of exposure on two-year-old children's food preferences. *Appetite*, *3*(4), 353–360.
Black, M. M. & Aboud, F. E. (2011). Responsive feeding is embedded in a theoretical framework of responsive parenting. *The Journal of Nutrition*, *141*(3), 490–494.
Blissett, J. (2011). Relationships between parenting style, feeding style and feeding practices and fruit and vegetable consumption in early childhood. *Appetite*, *57*, 826–831.
Blissett, J. (2018). Effects of modeling on children's eating behavior. *Pediatric Food Preferences and Eating Behaviors*, 53–72.
Blissett, J. & Farrow, C. (2007). Predictors of maternal control of feeding at 1 and 2 years of age. *International Journal of Obesity (2005)*, *31*, 1520–1526.
Bloch, M. (2020). Commensality and poisoning. In M. Bloch (ed.) *Essays on cultural transmission* (pp. 45–59). Routledge.
Blum-Kulka, S. (1990). You don't touch lettuce with your fingers: Parental politeness in family discourse. *Journal of Pragmatics*, *14*, 259–288.
Blum-Kulka, S. (2008). Language socialization and family dinnertime discourse. In: N. H. Hornberger & P. Corson (eds.) *Encyclopedia of Language and Education*. Springer.
Blum-Kulka, S. (2012). *Dinner talk: Cultural patterns of sociability and socialization in family discourse*. Lawrence Erlbaum Associates, Inc.
Blundell, J., De Graaf, C., Hulshof, T., Jebb, S., Livingstone, B., Lluch, A., . . . & Westerterp, M. (2010). Appetite control: Methodological aspects of the evaluation of foods. *Obesity Reviews*, *11*(3), 251–270.
Bolles, R. C. (2014). *Hedonics of taste*. Psychology Press.
Booth, D. A. (2016). 'I like it!' Preference actions separated from hedonic reactions. *Journal of Sensory Studies*, *31*(3), 213–232.
Borrero, C. S. W., Woods, J. N., Borrero, J. C., Masler, E. A., & Lesser, A. D. (2010). Descriptive analyses of pediatric food refusal and acceptance. *Journal of Applied Behavior Analysis*, *43*, 71–88.
Bourdieu, P. (1984). *A social critique of the judgement of taste*. Harvard University Press.

Bova, A. (2021). Co-construction of argumentative discussions between parents and children during mealtime conversations. A pragma-dialectical analysis. *Learning, Culture and Social Interaction*, *29*, 100519.
Bova, A. & Arcidiacono, F. (2014). 'You must eat the salad because it is nutritious'. Argumentative strategies adopted by parents and children in food-related discussions at mealtimes. *Appetite*, *73*, 81–94.
Brannen, J., O'Connell, R., & Mooney, A. (2013). Families, meals and synchronicity: Eating together in British dual earner families. *Community, Work & Family*, *16*(4), 417–434.
Breathnach, H., Danby, S., & O'Gorman, L. (2018). 'We're doing a wedding': Producing peer cultures in pretend play. *International Journal of Play*, *7*(3), 290–307.
Bretherton, I. & Beeghly, M. (1982). Talking about internal states: The acquisition of an explicit theory of mind. *Developmental Psychology*, *18*(6), 906.
Broth, M., Laurier, E., & Mondada, L. (eds.). (2014). *Studies of video practices: Video at work*. Routledge.
Broth, M. & Mondada, L. (2013). Walking away: The embodied achievement of activity closings in mobile interaction. *Journal of Pragmatics*, *47*(1), 41–58.
Brown, A. & Arnott, B. (2014). Breastfeeding duration and early parenting behaviour: The importance of an infant-led, responsive style. *PLOS ONE*, *9*(2), e83893.
Brumark, Å. (2006). Regulatory talk and politeness at the family dinner table. *Pragmatics*, *16*(2–3), 171–211.
Brumark, Å. (2008). 'Eat your hamburger!' 'No, I don't want to!' Argumentation and argumentative development in the context of dinner conversation in twenty Swedish families. *Argumentation*, *22*(2), 251–271.
Brown, A., Jones, S. W., & Rowan, H. (2017). Baby-led weaning: The evidence to date. *Current Nutrition Reports*, *6*(2), 148–156.
Bryant-Waugh, R. (2019). *ARFID avoidant restrictive food intake disorder: A guide for parents and carers*. Routledge.
Bugge, A. B. & Almås, R. (2006). Domestic dinner: Representations and practices of a proper meal among young suburban mothers. *Journal of Consumer Culture*, *6*, 203–228.
Burdelski, M. (2014). Early experiences with food. In P. E. Szatrowski (ed.). *Language and food: Verbal and nonverbal experiences*, (pp. 233–256). John Benjamins.
Burdelski, M. (2025). Interactional and cultural shaping of appetite: Children's talk about food taste during meal and snack time in Japanese preschool. *Appetite*, *211*, 107930.
Burns, E., Schmied, V., Fenwick, J., & Sheehan, A. (2012). Liquid gold from the milk bar: Constructions of breastmilk and breastfeeding women in the language and practices of midwives. *Social Science & Medicine*, *75*(10), 1737–1745.
Burton, M., Wood, J. M., Booth, A. O., Worsley, A., Larsson, C., & Margerison, C. (2022). Enough time for lunch? The duration and governance of lunch eating times in Australian primary schools: a mixed-methods study. *Appetite*, *169*, 105817.
Callaghan, J. E. & Lazard, L. (2012). 'Please don't put the whole dang thing out there!': A discursive analysis of internet discussions around infant feeding. *Psychology & Health*, *27*(8), 938–955.
Campbell, K. & Peebles, R. (2014). Eating disorders in children and adolescents: State of the art review. *Pediatrics*, *134*(3), 582–592.
Cannon, W. B. (1934). Hunger and thirst. In C. Murchison (ed.) *A handbook of general experimental psychology* (pp. 247–263). Clark University Press.
Cannon, W. B. & Washburn, A. L. (1912). An explanation of hunger. *American Journal of Physiology-Legacy Content*, *29*(5), 441–454.
Cappellini, B. & Parsons, E. (2012). Practising thrift at dinnertime: Mealtime leftovers, sacrifice and family membership. *The Sociological Review*, *60*, 121–134.

Cardona Cano, S., Tiemeier, H., Van Hoeken, D., Tharner, A., Jaddoe, V. W., Hofman, A., . . . & Hoek, H. W. (2015). Trajectories of picky eating during childhood: A general population study. *International Journal of Eating Disorders*, *48*(6), 570–579.

Carlin, A.P., Dennis, A., Jenkings, K.N., Lindwall, O. & Mair, M. (eds.) (2025). *The Routledge international handbook of ethnomethodology*. Routledge.

Caronia, L. & Colla, V. (2024). Shaping a moral body in family dinner talk: Children's socialization to good manners concerning bodily conduct. *Appetite*, *199*, 107502.

Carruth, B. R., Skinner, J., Houck, K., Moran III, J., Coletta, F., & Ott, D. (1998). The phenomenon of 'picky eater': A behavioral marker in eating patterns of toddlers. *Journal of the American College of Nutrition*, *17*(2), 180–186.

Cartner, H. (2023). *'A Taste of My Life' . . . Altered Eating and Sjögren's Syndrome: A Participant-Led Exploration of Eating Experience Using Application of a Novel Methodology, 'Food Play'*. Doctoral dissertation, University of Northumbria at Newcastle, UK.

Cashdan, E. (1994). A sensitive period for learning about food. *Human Nature*, *5*(3), 279–291.

Caton, S. J., Blundell, P., Ahern, S. M., Nekitsing, C., Olsen, A., Møller, P., Hausner, H., Remy, E., Nicklaus, S., & Chabanet, C. (2014). Learning to eat vegetables in early life: The role of timing, age and individual eating traits. *PLOS ONE*, *9*(5), e97609.

Cavanaugh, J. R. & Riley, K. C. (2017). Introduction to linguistic anthropology food research methods. *Food Culture: Anthropology, Linguistics and Food Studies*, *2*, 131–142.

Cavanaugh, J. R. & Riley, K. C. (2023). Language and food. In A. Duranti, R. George, & R. Conley Riner (eds.) *A new companion to linguistic anthropology* (pp. 461–476). John Wiley & Sons.

Cavanaugh, J. R., Riley, K. C., Jaffe, A., Karrebæk, M., & Paugh, A. (2014). What words bring to the table: The linguistics anthropological toolkit as applied to the study of food. *Journal of Linguistic Anthropology*, *24*, 84–97.

Cekaite, A. & Holm Kvist, M. (2017). The comforting touch: Tactile intimacy and talk in managing children's distress. *Research on Language and Social Interaction*, *50*(2), 109–127.

Cekaite, A. & Mondada, L. (eds.) (2020). *Touch in social interaction: Touch, language, and body*. Routledge.

Chaffee, L. & da Silva, S. (2022). *A guide to the psychology of eating*. Bloomsbury Academic.

Charles, N. & Kerr, M. (1986). Food for feminist thought. *Sociological Review*, *34*, 537–572.

Chen, C.-H. & Monroy, C.D. (2026). Moving, seeing, hearing, smelling and tasting: How sensory–motor experiences shape early cognitive development. *Behavioral Sciences*, *16*(2), 255.

Chen, A. W., Resurreccion, A. V. A., & Paguio, L. P. (1996). Age-appropriate hedonic scales to measure food preferences of young children. *Journal of Sensory Studies*, *11*(2), 141–163.

Childs, C. (2012). 'I'm not X, I just want Y': Formulating 'wants' in interaction. *Discourse Studies*, *14*, 181–196.

Chistol, L. T., Bandini, L. G., Must, A., Phillips, S., Cermak, S. A., & Curtin, C. (2018). Sensory sensitivity and food selectivity in children with autism spectrum disorder. *Journal of Autism and Developmental Disorders*, *48*(2), 583–591.

Choe, H. (2019). Eating together multimodally: Collaborative eating in mukbang, a Korean livestream of eating. *Language in Society*, *48*(2), 171–208

Choi, B. C. & Pak, A. W. (2006). Multidisciplinarity, interdisciplinarity and transdisciplinarity in health research, services, education and policy: 1. Definitions, objectives, and evidence of effectiveness. *Clinical & Investigative Medicine*, *29*(6).

Chow, C. Y., Skouw, S., Bech, A. C., Olsen, A., & Bredie, W. L. (2024). A review on children's oral texture perception and preferences in foods. *Critical Reviews in Food Science and Nutrition*, *64*(12), 3861–3879.
Classen, C., Howes, D., & Synnott, A. (2002). *Aroma: The cultural history of smell.* Routledge.
Clayman, S. E. (2024). Working with collections in conversation analysis. In J. Robinson, R. Clift, K. H. Kendrick, & C. W. Raymond (eds.) *The Cambridge handbook of methods in conversation analysis* (pp. 191–216). Cambridge University Press.
Clift, R., Gardner, R., McCabe, R., Peräkylä, A., & Potter, J. (2024). Conversation analysis across disciplines: Connecting and engaging through publishing. In J. Robinson, R. Clift, K. H. Kendrick, & C. W. Raymond (eds.) *The Cambridge handbook of methods in conversation analysis* (pp. 895–921). Cambridge University Press.
Clift, R. & Mandelbaum, J. (2024). Discovering a candidate phenomenon. In J. Robinson, R. Clift, K. H. Kendrick, & C. W. Raymond (eds.) *The Cambridge handbook of methods in conversation analysis* (pp. 143–171). Cambridge University Press.
Cole, P. M., Armstrong, L. M., & Pemberton, C. K. (2010). The role of language in the development of emotion regulation. In S. D. Calkins & M. A. Bell (eds.) Child development at the intersection of emotion and cognition (pp. 59–77). American Psychological Association.
Cooke, L. & Fildes, A. (2011). The impact of flavour exposure in utero and during milk feeding on food acceptance at weaning and beyond. *Appetite*, *57*, 808–811.
Cooke, L. J., Haworth, C. M., & Wardle, J. (2007). Genetic and environmental influences on children's food neophobia. *The American Journal of Clinical Nutrition*, *86*(2), 428–433.
Cooke, L. J., Wardle, J., Gibson, E. L., Sapochnik, M., Sheiham, A., & Lawson, M. (2003). Demographic, familial and trait predictors of fruit and vegetable consumption by pre-school children. *Public Health Nutrition*, *7*, 295–302.
Corsaro, W. A. (2011). *The sociology of childhood.* Sage.
Corti, L., Woollard, M., Bishop, L., & Van den Eynden, V. (2019). *Managing and sharing research data: A guide to good practice.* Sage.
Costantini, C., Akehurst, L., Reddy, V., & Fasulo, A. (2018). Synchrony, co-eating and communication during complementary feeding in early infancy. *Infancy*, *23*, 288–304.
Coulthard, H., Abdullahi, N., Bell, K., & Noon, E. (2022). Understanding disgust-based food rejection in picky and non-picky eaters: Willingness to touch and taste familiar foods with changes. *Food Quality and Preference*, *97*, 104442.
Counihan, C. & Højlund, S. (eds.) (2018). *Making taste public: Ethnographies of food and the senses.* Bloomsbury Publishing.
Counihan, C. & Van Esterik, P. (1997). *Food and culture* (Vol 367). Routledge.
Coveney, J. (2006). *Food, morals and meaning: The pleasure and anxiety of eating.* Routledge.
Coveney, J. & Bunton, R. (2003). In pursuit of the study of pleasure: Implications for health research and practice. *Health*, *7*, 161–179.
Craven, A. & Potter, J. (2010). Directives: Entitlement and contingency in action. *Discourse Studies*, *12*, 419–442.
Cruwys, T., Bevelander, K. E., & Hermans, R. C. (2015). Social modeling of eating: A review of when and why social influence affects food intake and choice. *Appetite*, *86*, 3–18.
Cunningham, P. M., Meehan, C. T., Keller, K. L., & Rolls, B. J. (2026). Sensory-specific satiety and the influence of variety on snack intake in school-aged children. *Appetite*, 108451.

Danby, S. & Baker, C. (1998). What's the problem? Restoring social order in the preschool classroom. In I. Hutchby & J. Moran-Ellis (eds.), *Children and social competence: Arenas of action* (pp. 157–186). Falmer Press.

Davis, C. M. (1939). Results of the self-selection of diets by young children. *Canadian Medical Association Journal, 41*(3), 257.

De Castro, J. M. (1991). Social facilitation of the spontaneous meal size of humans occurs on both weekdays and weekends. *Physiology & Behavior, 49*(6), 1289–1291.

De Castro, J. M. (1997). Socio-cultural determinants of meal size and frequency. *British Journal of Nutrition, 77*(S1), S39–S55.

De Geer, B. (2004). 'Don't say it's disgusting!' Comments on socio-moral behavior in Swedish families. *Journal of Pragmatics, 36*, 1705–1725.

De Geer, B., Tulviste, T., Mizera, L., & Tryggvason, M.-T. (2002). Socialization in communication: Pragmatic socialization during dinnertime in Estonian, Finnish and Swedish families. *Journal of Pragmatics, 34*(12), 1757–1786.

de León, L. (2021). The soothing nursing niche: Affective touch, talk, and pragmatic responses to Mayan infants' crying. *Journal of Pragmatics, 185*, 146–160.

Delphy, C. (1980). Sharing the same table: Consumption and the family. *The Sociological Review, 28*(1), 214–231.

Demuth, C. (2013). Socializing infants toward a cultural understanding of expressing negative affect: A Bakhtinian informed discursive psychology approach. *Mind, Culture, and Activity, 20*(1), 39–61.

Desor, J. A. & Beauchamp, G. K. (1987). Longitudinal changes in sweet preferences in humans. *Physiology & Behavior, 39*(5), 639–641.

Dettwyler, K. A. (2017). Beauty and the breast: The cultural context of breastfeeding in the United States. In P. Stuart-Macadam & K. A. Dettwyler (eds.) *Breastfeeding: Biocultural perspectives* (pp. 167–216). Routledge.

Dev, D. A., McBride, B. A., Speirs, K. E., Blitch, K. A., & Williams, N. A. (2016). 'Great job cleaning your plate today!' Determinants of child-care providers' use of controlling feeding practices: An exploratory examination. *Journal of the Academy of Nutrition and Dietetics, 116*(11), 1803–1809.

De Vault, M. L. (1991). *Feeding the family: The social organization of caring as gendered work.* University of Chicago Press.

Dingemanse, M. (2020). Between sound and speech: Liminal signs in interaction. *Research on Language and Social Interaction, 53*(1), 188–196.

Di Prete, A., Del Grosso, D., Focaroli, V., Paoletti, M., Pecora, G., Hodges, E. A., . . . & Addessi, E. (2023). Complementary feeding approach and maternal responsiveness in 8-and 12-month-old Italian infants: A longitudinal study. *Appetite, 190*, 107028.

DiSantis, K. I., Hodges, E. A., Johnson, S. L., & Fisher, J. O. (2011). The role of responsive feeding in overweight during infancy and toddlerhood: A systematic review. *International Journal of Obesity, 35*(4), 480–492.

Dondi, A., Piccinno, V., Morigi, F., Sureshkumar, S., Gori, D., & Lanari, M. (2020). Food insecurity and major diet-related morbidities in migrating children: a systematic review. *Nutrients, 12*(2), 379.

Douglas, M. (1966) *Purity and danger.* Routledge.

Douglas, M. (1972). Deciphering a Meal. *Daedalus, 101*, 61–81.

Douglas, M. & Nicod, M. (1974). Taking the biscuit: The structure of British meals. *New Society, 19*, 744–747.

Dovey, T. M., Staples, P. A., Gibson, E. L., & Halford, J. C. G. (2008). Food neophobia and 'picky/fussy' eating in children: A review. *Appetite, 50*, 181–193.

Duncker, K. (1938). Experimental modification of children's food preferences through social suggestion. *Journal of Abnormal and Social Psychology, 33*(4), 489–507.

Duranti, A., Ochs, E., & Schieffelin, B. B. (eds.) (2011). *The handbook of language socialization*. John Wiley & Sons.

Eccleston, C. (2016). *Embodied: The psychology of physical sensation*. Oxford University Press.

Edwards, D. (1991). Categories are for talking: On the cognitive and discursive bases of categorization. *Theory & Psychology*, *1*(4), 515–542.

Edwards, D. (1999). Emotion discourse. *Culture & Psychology*, *5*(3), 271–291.

Edwards, D. (2006). Discourse, cognition and social practices: The rich surface of language and social interaction. *Discourse Studies*, *8*, 41–49.

Edwards, D. (2012). Discursive and scientific psychology. *British Journal of Social Psychology*, *51*, 425–435.

Edwards, D. & Potter, J. (1992). *Discursive psychology*. Sage.

Edwards, D. & Potter, J. (2017). Some uses of subject-side assessments. *Discourse Studies*, *19*, 497–514.

Edwards, D. & Potter, J. (2020). A word is worth a thousand pictures: Language, interaction, and embodiment. In S. Wiggins & K. Osvaldsson Cromdal (eds.) *Discursive Psychology and Embodiment: Beyond Subject-Object Binaries* (pp. 275–301). Palgrave.

Edwards, K. L., Thomas, J. M., Higgs, S., & Blissett, J. (2022). Exposure to models' positive facial expressions whilst eating a raw vegetable increases children's acceptance and consumption of the modelled vegetable. *Appetite*, *168*, 105779.

Edwards, K. L., Pickard, A., Farrow, C., & Blissett, J. (2025). Validation of the Teddy the Bear hunger and satiety rating scale in 3–5-year-old children. *Appetite*, *211*, 108016.

Egbert, M., Yufu, M., & Hirataka, F. (2016). An investigation of how 100 articles in the Journal of Pragmatics treat transcripts of English and non-English languages. *Journal of Pragmatics*, *94*, 98–111.

Eli, K. (2018). Striving for liminality: Eating disorders and social suffering. *Transcultural Psychiatry*, *55*(4), 475–494.

Enfield, N. J. (2007). Encoding three-participant events in the Lao clause. *Linguistics*, *45*(3), 509–538.

Evans, R., Christiansen, P., Bateson, M., Nettle, D., Keenan, G. S., & Hardman, C. A. (2025). Understanding the association between household food insecurity and diet quality: The role of psychological distress, food choice motives and meal patterning. *Appetite*, *212*, 108007.

Falconer, F. (2021) (ed.). *Space, taste and affect: Atmospheres that shape the way we eat*. Routledge.

Farrow, C. & Blissett, J. (2006). Breast-feeding, maternal feeding practices and mealtime negativity at one year. *Appetite*, *46*, 49–56.

Farrow, C., Blissett, J., Islam, S., Batchelor, R., Norman, R., Webber, C., Addessi, E., Bellagamba, F., Galloway, A. T., & Shapiro, L. (2025). Approach to complementary feeding and infant language use: An observational study. *Maternal & Child Nutrition*, *21*(1), e13762.

Farrow, C., Galloway, A. T., & Fraser, K. (2011). Sibling eating behaviours and differential child feeding practices reported by parents. *Appetite*, *52*(2), 307–312.

Farrow, C. V. & Coulthard, H. (2012). Relationships between sensory sensitivity, anxiety and selective eating in children. *Appetite*, *58*, 842–846.

Fele, G. (2016). Il paradosso del gusto. Forme visibili dell'apprezzamento estetico. *SocietàMutamentoPolitica*, *7*(14), 151–174.

Fele, G. (2019). Olfactory objects: Recognizing, describing and assessing smells during professional tasting sessions. *Objects, bodies and work practices*, 250–284.

Fele, G. & Giglioli, P. P. (2020). Performing taste: The sommelier ceremony. In E. Falconer (ed.), *Space, Taste and Affect* (pp. 44–58). Routledge.

Fele, G. & Liberman, K. (2021). Some discovered practices of lay coffee drinkers. *Symbolic Interaction*, *44*(1), 40–62.

Fildes, A., van Jaarsveld, C. H. M., Llewellyn, C., Wardle, J., & Fisher, A. (2015). Parental control over feeding in infancy. Influence of infant weight, appetite and feeding method. *Appetite*, *91*, 101106.

Finkelstein, J. (1989). *Dining out: A sociology of modern manners*. Polity Press.

Fischler, C. (1980). Food habits, social change and the nature/culture dilemma. *Social Science Information*, *19*, 937–953.

Fischler, C. (2011). Commensality, society and culture. *Social Science Information*, *50*(3–4), 528–548.

Fischler, C. (2013). Introduction. Is sharing meals a thing of the past? In C. Fischler (ed.) *Selective eating: The rise, the meaning and sense of 'personal dietary requirements'* (pp. 15–35). Odile Jacob.

Fisher, J. O., Liu, Y., Birch, L. L., & Rolls, B. J. (2007). Effects of portion size and energy density on young children's intake at a meal. *The American Journal of Clinical Nutrition*, *86*(1), 174–179.

Flint, N. & Rhys, C. S. (2023). Teenage resistance to a parental threat: Intercepting an action-in-progress as a form of resistance. *Journal of Language and Social Psychology*, *42*(5–6), 610–629.

Forde, C. G. (2018). Measuring satiation and satiety. *Methods in Consumer Research*, *2*, 151–182.

Forestell, C. A. (2024). Does maternal diet influence future infant taste and odor preferences? A critical analysis. *Annual Review of Nutrition*, *44*.

Forestell, C. A. & Mennella, J. A. (2007). Early determinants of fruit and vegetable Acceptance. *Pediatrics*, *120*(6), 1247–1254.

Forestell, C. A. & Mennella, J. A. (2012). More than just a pretty face: The relationship between infant's temperament, food acceptance, and mothers' perceptions of their enjoyment of food. *Appetite*, *58*, 1136–1142.

Forestell, C. A. & Mennella, J. A. (2017). The relationship between infant facial expressions and food acceptance. *Current Nutrition Reports*, *6*, 141–147.

Forrester, M. A. (2008). The emergence of self-repair: A case study of one child during the early preschool years. *Research on Language and Social Interaction*, *41*(1), 99–128.

Galatolo, R. & Caronia, L. (2018). Morality at dinnertime: The sense of the other as a practical accomplishment in family interaction. *Discourse & Society*, *29*, 43–62.

Galloway, A., Fiorito, L., Francis, L., & Birch, L. L. (2006). 'Finish your soup': Counterproductive effects of pressuring children to eat on intake and affect. *Appetite*, *46*, 318–323.

Gan, Y., Greiffenhagen, C., & Kendrick, K. H. (2023). Sequence facilitation: Grandparents engineering parent–child interactions in video calls. *Research on Language and Social Interaction*, *56*(1), 65–88.

Gardner, H. & Forrester, M. (eds.) (2009). *Analysing interactions in childhood: Insights from conversation analysis*. John Wiley & Sons

Gardner, R. (1997). The conversation object mm: A weak and variable acknowledging token. *Research on Language and Social Interaction*, *30*, 131–156.

Garfinkel, H. (1967). *Studies in ethnomethodology*. Prentice-Hall.

Gerhardt, C., Frobenius, M., & Ley, S. (2013). *Culinary linguistics: The chef's special*. John Benjamins Publishing Company.

Germov, J. & Williams, L. (2017). *A sociology of food & nutrition: The social appetite*. Oxford University Press.

Gilbert, G. N. & Mulkay, M. (1984). *Opening Pandora's box: A sociological analysis of scientists' discourse*. CUP Archive.

Gilbert, H. R. & Robb, M. P. (1996). Vocal fundamental frequency characteristics of infant hunger cries: Birth to 12 months. *International Journal of Pediatric Otorhinolaryngology*, *34*(3), 237–243.

Gleason, J. B., Perlmann, R. Y., & Greif, E. B. (1984). What's the magic word: Learning language through politeness routines. *Discourse Processes*, *7*(4), 493–502.

Goffman, E. (1961). *Encounters: Two studies in the sociology of interaction.* Ravenio Books.
Goffman, E. (1963). *Behavior in public places: Notes on the social organization of gatherings.* The Free Press.
Goffman, E. (1981). *Forms of talk.* University of Pennsylvania Press.
Goico, S., Gan, Y., Katila, J., & Harness Goodwin, M. (2021). Capturing multisensoriality: Introduction to a special issue on sensoriality in video-based fieldwork. *Social Interaction. Video-Based Studies of Human Sociality, 4*(3).
Golen, R. P. & Ventura, A. K. (2015). What are mothers doing while bottle-feeding their infants? Exploring the prevalence of maternal distraction during bottle-feeding interactions. *Early Human Development, 91,* 787–791.
Goodwin, C. (1979). The interactive construction of a sentence in natural conversation. In G. Psathas (ed.) *Everyday language: Studies in ethnomethodology* (pp. 97–121). Irvington Publishers.
Goodwin, C. (1981). *Conversational organisation: Interaction beteen speakers and hearers.* Academic Press.
Goodwin, C. (2000). Action and embodiment within situated human interaction. *Journal of Pragmatics, 32,* 1489–1522.
Goodwin, M. H. (1980). He-said-she-said: Formal cultural procedures for the construction of a gossip dispute activity. *American Ethnologist, 7*(4), 674–695.
Goodwin, M. H. (1990). *He-said-she-said: Talk as social organization among black children.* Indiana University Press.
Goodwin, M. H., Cekaite, A., Goodwin, C., & Tulbert, E. (2012). Emotion as stance. In A.Peräkylä & M.L.Sorjonen (2012). *Emotion in interaction.* (p. 16-41). Oxford University Press.
Goodwin, M. & Cekaite, A. (2018). *Embodied family choreography: Practices of control, care, and mundane creativity.* Routledge.
Graf, M. D., Lutenbacher, M., Wasser, H., Dietrich, M. S., & Karp, S. M. (2022). Choking, allergic reactions, and pickiness: A qualitative study of maternal perceived threats and risk avoidance strategies during complementary feeding. *Appetite, 171,* 105914.
Grieshaber, S. (1997). Mealtime rituals: Power and resistance in the construction of mealtime rules. *British Journal of Sociology, 48,* 649–666.
Grignon, C. (2001). Commensality and social morphology: An essay of typology. In P. Scholliers (ed.) *Food, drink and identity: Cooking, eating and drinking in Europe since the Middle Ages* (pp. 23–36). Berg.
Gumperz, J. J. (1962). Types of linguistic communities. *Anthropological linguistics,* 28–40.
Haddington, P., Eilittä, T., Kamunen, A., Kohonen-Aho, L., Rautiainen, I., & Vatanen, A. (eds.) (2023). *Complexity of interaction: Studies in multimodal conversation analysis.* Springer Nature.
Halcrow, S. E., Miller, M. J., Pechenkina, K., Dong, Y., & Fan, W. (2021). The bioarchaeology of infant feeding. In S. Han & C. Tomori (eds.) *The Routledge handbook of anthropology and reproduction* (pp. 541–558). Routledge.
Hammons, A. J. & Fiese, B. H. (2011). Is frequency of shared family meals related to the nutritional health of children and adolescents? *Pediatrics, 127*(6), e1565–e1574.
Hänggi, P. & Mondada, L. (2025). 'What is this?': Multisensorial explorations of food with and without sight. *Appetite, 205,* 107530.
Hansen, A. R., Alfonso, M. L., Hackney, A. A., & Luque, J. S. (2015). Preschool children's self-reports of fruit and vegetable knowledge, preference, and messages encouraging consumption. *Journal of School Health, 85,* 355–364.
Harbron, J., Booley, S., Najaar, B., & Day, C. E. (2013). Responsive feeding: Establishing healthy eating behaviour early on in life. *South African Journal of Clinical Nutrition, 26.*

Harris, G. & Mason, S. (2017). Are there sensitive periods for food acceptance in infancy? *Current Nutrition Reports*, *6*(2), 190–196.
Havermans, R. C. (2011). 'You say it's liking, I say it's wanting . . .'. On the difficulty of disentangling food reward in man. *Appetite*, *57*, 286–294.
Haycraft, E. & Blissett, J. (2012). Predictors of paternal and maternal controlling feeding practices with 2- to 5-year-old Children. *Journal of Nutrition Education and Behavior*, *44*, 390–397.
Haycraft, E. L. & Blissett, J. M. (2008). Maternal and paternal controlling feeding practices: Reliability and relationships with BMI. *Obesity*, *16*(7), 1552–1558.
Heath, C. (1986). *Body movement and speech in medical interaction*. Cambridge University Press.
Heath, C., Luff, P., & Hindmarsh, J. (2009). *Video in qualitative research: Analysing social interaction in everyday life*. Sage.
Heath, C. & Luff, P. (2014). Embodied action in organizational activity. In J. Sidnell & T. Stivers (eds.) *The handbook of conversation analysis* (pp. 283–307). Wiley Blackwell.
Helland, S. H., Bere, E., & Øverby, N. C. (2016). Study protocol for a multi-component kindergarten-based intervention to promote healthy diets in toddlers: A cluster randomized trial. *BMC Public Health*, *16*(1), 273.
Helton, J. J., Ju, S., Iwinski, S. J., & Zhang, L. (2023). The effect of adverse childhood experiences on family mealtime frequency: Examining racial and ethnic differences *Journal of Family Psychology*, *37* (6), 796–805.
Hennion, A. (2007). Those things that hold us together: Taste and sociology. *Cultural Sociology*, *1*, 97–114.
Henrich, J., Heine, S. J., & Norenzayan, A. (2010). The weirdest people in the world? *Behavioral and Brain Sciences*, *33*(2–3), 61–83.
Hepburn, A. (2004). Crying: Notes on description, transcription, and interaction. *Research on Language & Social Interaction*, *37*, 251–290.
Hepburn, A. (2020a). Managing embodied misconduct: Burping and spitting in family mealtime interactions. In S. Wiggins & K. Osvaldsson Cromdal (eds.) *Discursive psychology and embodiment: Beyond subject-object binaries* (pp. 57–80). Palgrave.
Hepburn, A. (2020b). The preference for self-direction as a resource for parents' socialisation practices. *Qualitative Research in Psychology*, *17*(3), 450–468.
Hepburn, A. & Bolden, G. (2017). *Transcribing for social research*. Sage.
Hepburn, A. & Mandelbaum, J. (2018). Analysing burp sequences. *The Psychologist*, *31*(12), 40–41.
Hepburn, A. & Potter, J. (2007). Crying receipts: Time, empathy, and institutional practice. *Research on Language & Social Interaction*, *40*, 89–116.
Hepburn, A, & Potter, J. (2011). Threats: Power, family mealtimes, and social influence. *British Journal of Social Psychology*, *50*(1), 99–120.
Hepburn, A. & Potter, J. (2012). Crying and crying responses. In A. Peräkylä & M.-L. Sorjonen (eds.) *Emotion in interaction* (pp. 195–211). Oxford University Press.
Hepburn, A., Wilkinson, S., & Butler, C. W. (2014). Intervening with conversation analysis in telephone helpline services: Strategies to improve effectiveness. *Research on Language and Social Interaction*, *47*(3), 239–254.
Heritage, J. (1984). *Garfinkel and ethnomethodology*. Polity Press.
Heritage, J. & Raymond, G. (2005). The terms of agreement: Indexing epistemic authority and subordination in talk-in-interaction. *Social Psychology Quarterly*, *68*, 15–38.
Herman, C. P., Roth, D. A., & Polivy, J. (2003). Effects of the presence of others on food intake: a normative interpretation. *Psychological Bulletin*, *129*(6), 873.
Hetherington, M. M. (2017). Understanding infant eating behaviour: Lessons learned from observation. *Physiology and Behavior*, *176*, 117–124.

Hetherington, M. M. (2020). Infant appetite: From cries to cues and responsive feeding. In H. Meiselman (ed.) *Handbook of eating and drinking: Interdisciplinary perspectives* (pp. 373–389). Springer.

Hetherington, M. M. & Chawner, L. R. (2022). From food preference development to responsive feeding – Selective studies to commemorate the life and work of Dr Leann Birch. *Appetite*, *175*, 106051.

Hetherington, M. M., Madrelle, J., Nekitsing, C., Barends, C., De Graaff, E., Morgan, S., Parrott, H., & Weenen, H. (2016). Developing a novel tool to assess liking and wanting in infants at the time of complementary feeding: The Feeding Infants: Behaviour and Facial Expression Coding System. *Food Quality and Preference*, *48*, 238–250.

Hetherington, M. M. & McNally, J. (2019). Reading appetite cues in infancy: A role for nutrition education. *Nestlé Nutrition Institute Workshop Series*, *92*, 41–51.

Higgs, S. & Ruddock, H. (2020). Social influences on eating. In H. Meiselman (ed.) *Handbook of eating and drinking: Interdisciplinary perspectives* (pp. 277–291). Springer.

Hodges, E. A., Johnson, S. L., Hughes, S. O., Hopkinson, J. M., Butte, N. F., & Fisher, J. O. (2013). Development of the responsiveness to child feeding cues scale. *Appetite*, *65*, 210–219.

Hoey, E. M. (2018). Drinking for speaking: The multimodal organization of drinking in conversation. *Social Interaction. Video-Based Studies of Human Sociality*, *1*(1), 10.7146.

Hoey, E. M. & Webb, J. (2024). Conversation-analytic methods of data collection. In J. Robinson, R. Clift, K. H. Kendrick, & C. W. Raymond (eds.) *The Cambridge handbook of methods in conversation analysis* (pp. 51–80). Cambridge University Press.

Hofstetter, E. & Albert, S. (2024). Working with data II: Clips and collections. In J. Robinson, R. Clift, K. H. Kendrick, & C. W. Raymond (eds.) *The Cambridge handbook of methods in conversation analysis* (pp. 217–233). Cambridge University Press.

Houldcroft, L., Haycraft, E., & Farrow, C. (2014). Peer and friend influences on children's eating. *Social Development*, *23*(1), 19–40.

Højlund, S. (2015). Taste as a social sense: Rethinking taste as a cultural activity. *Flavour*, *4*, 4–7.

Holm, L. & Lund, T. B. (2019). Are family meals declining? The example of Denmark. In H. L. Meiselman (ed.) *Context* (pp. 227–240). Woodhead Publishing.

Humă, B. & Joyce, J. B. (2023). 'One size doesn't fit all': Lessons from interaction analysis on tailoring Open Science practices to qualitative research. *British Journal of Social Psychology*, *62*(4), 1590–1604.

Humă, B., Joyce, J. B., & Raymond, G. (2023). What does 'resistance' actually look like? The respecification of resistance as an interactional accomplishment. *Journal of Language and Social Psychology*, *42*(5–6), 497–522.

Humă, B. & Potter, J. (2023). Discursive psychology. In M. Handford & J. P. Gee (eds.) *The Routledge handbook of discourse analysis* (pp. 53–66). Routledge.

Humă, B. & Stokoe, E. (2023). Resistance in business-to-business "cold" sales calls. *Journal of Language and Social Psychology*, *42*(5–6), 630–652.

Humă, B., Stokoe, E., & Sikveland, R. O. (2021). Vocabularies of social influence: Managing the moral accountability of influencing another. *British Journal of Social Psychology*, *60*, 319–339.

Hymes, D. (1964). Introduction: Toward ethnographies of communication 1. *American Anthropologist*, *66*(6_Part2), 1–34.

Icbay, M. A. (2026). Exploring the EMCA community: Strengths, challenges, and opportunities. *Symbolic Interaction*, *49*(1), 134–175.

James, A., Curtis, P., & Ellis, K. (2009). Negotiating family, negotiating food: Children as family participants? In A. James, A. T. Kjørholt & V. Tingstad (eds.) *Children, Food, and Identity in Everyday Life* (pp. 35–51). Palgrave Macmillan.

James, A., Kjørholt, A. T. & Tingstad.V. (2009) (eds.). *Children, food, and identity in everyday life*. Palgrave Macmillan.

Jarrett, R. L., Bahar, O. S., & Kersh, R. T. (2016). 'When we do sit down together': Family meal times in low-income African American families with preschoolers. *Journal of Family Issues*, *37*, 1483–1513

Jefferson, G. (2008). Glossary of transcript symbols with an introduction. In G. Lerner (ed.) *Conversation analysis: Studies from the first generation* (pp. 13–31). John Benjamins Publishing Company.

Jenkings, K. N., Lindwall, O., Carlin, A., Mair, M., & Dennis, A. (2025). Ethnomethodology and ethnomethodological conversation analysis: An orientation to studies. In A. P. Carlin, A. Dennis, K. N. Jenkings, O. Lindwall, & M. Mair (eds.) *The Routledge international handbook of ethnomethodology* (pp. 1–20). Routledge.

Jenkins, L. & Hepburn, A. (2015). Children's sensations as interactional phenomena: A conversation analysis of children's expressions of pain and discomfort. *Qualitative Research in Psychology*, *12*(4), 472–491.

Jepson, M., Salisbury, C., Ridd, M. J., Metcalfe, C., Garside, L., & Barnes, R. K. (2017). The 'One in a Million' study: Creating a database of UK primary care consultations. *British Journal of General Practice*. *67*, e345–351.

Jönsson, H., Michaud, M., & Neuman, N. (2021). What is commensality? A critical discussion of an expanding research field. *International Journal of Environmental Research and Public Health*, *18*(12), 6235.

Kalindjian, N., Hirot, F., Stona, A. C., Huas, C., & Godart, N. (2022). Early detection of eating disorders: A scoping review. *Eating and Weight Disorders – Studies on Anorexia, Bulimia and Obesity*, *27*(1), 21–68.

Karaburun, I. E. G. & Yalçın, S. S. (2024). Breast refusal: An analysis of frequency, onset timing, recovery status, and their interplay with breastfeeding self-efficacy and maternal depression. *BMC Public Health*, *24*(1), 3568.

Karrabæk, M. S. (2012). 'What's in your lunch box today?': Health, respectability, and ethnicity in the primary classroom. *Journal of Linguistic Anthropology*, *22*, 1–22.

Karrabæk, M. S. (2013). Lasagna for breakfast: The respectable child and cultural norms of eating practices in a Danish kindergarten classroom. *Food, Culture & Society*, *16*(1), 85–106.

Katila, J. (2018). Touch between child and mother as an affective practice: (Re)producing bodies in haptic negotiations of intimate space. In T. Juvonen & M. Kolehmainen (eds.) *Affective Inequalities in Intimate Relationships* (pp. 201–217). Routledge.

Katila, J. & Cekaite, A. (2023). Trajectories of love: Affective reciprocity during kissing in the everyday life of romantic couples. *Journal of Pragmatics*, *214*, 38–53.

Keller, K. L., Assur, S. A., Torres, M., Lofink, H. E., Thornton, J. C., Faith, M. S., & Kissileff, H. R. (2006). Potential of an analog scaling device for measuring fullness in children: development and preliminary testing. *Appetite*, *47*(2), 233–243.

Keller, K. L., Shehan, C., Cravener, T., Schlechter, H., & Hayes, J. E. (2022). Do children really eat what they like? Relationships between liking and intake across laboratory test-meals. *Appetite*, *172*, 105946.

Keller, K. L., Pearce, A. L., Fuchs, B., Rolls, B. J., Wilson, S. J., Geier, C. F., . . . & Garavan, H. (2024). PACE: A novel eating behavior phenotype to assess risk for obesity in middle childhood. *The Journal of Nutrition*, *154*(7), 2176–2187.

Kent, A. (2012). Compliance, resistance and incipient compliance when responding to directives. *Discourse Studies*, *14*, 711–730.

Kent, A., Meredith, J., & Budds, K. (2025). 'Surely a little discretion isn't too difficult'? The discursive construction of discretion in users' comments on UK newspaper articles about public breastfeeding. *Psychology & Health, 40*(3), 358–376.

Kerzner, B., Milano, K., MacLean Jr, W. C., Berall, G., Stuart, S., & Chatoor, I. (2015). A practical approach to classifying and managing feeding difficulties. *Pediatrics, 135*(2), 344–353.

Kidwell, M. (2005). Gaze as social control: How very young children differentiate 'the look' from a 'mere look' by their adult caregivers. *Research on Language & Social Interaction, 38,* 417–449.

Kidwell, M. (2009). Gaze shift as an interactional resource for very young children. *Discourse Processes, 46*(2–3), 145–160.

Kidwell, M. (2011). Epistemics and embodiment in the interactions of very young children. *The Morality of Knowledge in Conversation, 29,* 257.

Kidwell, M. (2013). Interaction among children. In J. Sidnell & T. Stivers (eds.) *The handbook of conversation analysis* (pp. 511–532). Wiley Blackwell.

Kidwell, M. & Zimmerman, D. H. (2007). Joint attention as action. *Journal of Pragmatics, 39*(3), 592–611.

Korsmeyer, C. (1999). *Making sense of taste: Food and philosophy.* Cornell University Press.

Korsmeyer, C. (2017). Taste and other senses: Reconsidering the foundations of aesthetics. *Nordic Journal of Aesthetics, 26*(54), 20–34.

Korsmeyer, C. & Sutton, D. (2011). The sensory experience of food. *Food, Culture and Society, 14,* 461–475.

Köster, E. P. (2003). The psychology of food choice: Some often encountered fallacies. *Food Quality and Preference, 14,* 359–373.

Köster, E. P. (2009). Diversity in the determinants of food choice: A psychological perspective. *Food Quality and Preference, 20,* 70–82.

Kramer, L., Nettlau, A., Merz, A. K., Martin, A., Hilbert, A., & Schmidt, R. (2025). Sensory sensitivity and food disgust in avoidant/restrictive food intake disorder presentations across ages. *Appetite,* 108329.

Kremer-Sadlik, T. & Morgenstern, A. (2022). The reflective eater: Socializing French children to eating fruits and vegetables. *Appetite, 172,* 105954.

Kremer-Sadlik, T., Morgenstern, A., Peters, C., Beaupoil, P., Caët, S., Debras, C., & Le Mené, M. (2015). Eating fruits and vegetables. An ethnographic study of American and French family dinners. *Appetite, 89,* 84–92.

Kringelbach, M. L. (2015). The pleasure of food: Underlying brain mechanisms of eating and other pleasures. *Flavour, 4*(1), 20.

Krugman, S. D. & Dubowitz, H. (2003). Failure to thrive. *American Family Physician, 68*(5), 879–884.

Kultti, A. (2014). Mealtimes in Swedish preschools: Pedagogical opportunities for toddlers learning a new language. *Early Years, 34*(1), 18–31.

Kurihara, K. (2015). Umami the fifth basic taste: History of studies on receptor mechanisms and role as a food flavor. *BioMed Research International, 2015*(1), 189402

Küttner, U.-A., Vatanen, A., & Zinken, J. (2022). Invoking rules in everyday family interactions: A method for appealing to practical reason. *Human Studies, 45*(4), 793–823.

Lafraire, J., Rioux, C., Giboreau, A., & Picard, D. (2016). Food rejections in children: Cognitive and social/environmental factors involved in food neophobia and picky/fussy eating behavior. *Appetite, 96,* 347–357.

Lahne, J., Trubek, A. B., & Pelchat, M. L. (2014). Consumer sensory perception of cheese depends on context: A study using comment analysis and linear mixed models. *Food Quality and Preference, 32,* 184–197.

Lalli, G. (2017). An investigation into commensality in the 'school restaurant'. *Educational Futures, 8*(2), 69–88.
Lamb, M. W. & Ling, B. C. (1946). An analysis of food consumption and preferences of nursery school children. *Child Development, 17*(4), 187–217.
Laurier, E. (2008). Drinking up endings: Conversational resources of the café. *Language and Communication, 28*, 165–181.
Laurier, E. (2014). The graphic transcript: Poaching comic book grammar for inscribing the visual, spatial and temporal aspects of action. *Geography Compass, 8*(4), 235–248.
Laurier, E. & Philo, C. (2006). Cold shoulders and napkins handed: Gestures of responsibility. *Transactions of the Institute of British Geographers, 31*, 193–207.
Laurier, E. & Wiggins, S. (2011). Finishing the family meal. The interactional organisation of satiety. *Appetite, 56*, 53–64.
Lester, J. N. & O'Reilly, M. (2018). *Applied conversation analysis: Social interaction in institutional settings.* Sage.
Le Moal, F., Michaud, M., & Coveney, J. (2024). Exploring unequal class logics of mealtime food socialisation. An ethnography of family meals in France and Australia. *Appetite, 195*, 107195.
Leer, J. & Wistoft, K. (2018). Taste in food education: A critical review essay. *Food and Foodways, 26*(4), 329–349.
Lerner, G. H., Zimmerman, D. H., & Kidwell, M. (2011). Formal structures of practical tasks: A resource for action in the social life of very young children. In J. Streeck, C. Goodwin & L. LeBaron (eds.) *Embodied interaction: Language and body in the material world* (pp. 44–58). Cambridge University Press.
Lestar, T., Pilato, M., & Séraphin, H. (eds.) (2024). *Eating together in the twenty-first century: Social challenges, community values, and individual wellbeing.* Routledge.
Levinson, S. C. (2014). Action formation as ascription. In J. Sidnell & T. Stivers (eds.) *The handbook of conversation analysis* (pp. 103–130). Wiley Blackwell.
Lévi-Strauss, C. (2012). The culinary triangle. In C. Counihan & P. Van Esterik (eds.) *Food and culture: A reader* (pp. 54–61). Routledge.
Liberman, K. (2022). *Tasting coffee: An inquiry into objectivity.* SUNY Press.
Lim, J. (2011). Hedonic scaling: A review of methods and theory. *Food Quality and Preference, 22*(8), 733–747.
Linell, P. (2009). *Rethinking language, mind, and world dialogically: Interactional and contextual theories of human sense-making.* Emerald Publishing Limited.
Llewellyn, C. H., Van Jaarsveld, C. H., Boniface, D., Carnell, S., & Wardle, J. (2008). Eating rate is a heritable phenotype related to weight in children. *The American Journal of Clinical Nutrition, 88*(6), 1560–1566.
Locke, A. (2009). 'Natural versus taught' competing discourses in antenatal breastfeeding workshops. *Journal of Health Psychology, 14*, 435–446.
Loewen, R., & Pliner, P. (2000). The food situations questionnaire: A measure of children's willingness to try novel foods in stimulating and non-stimulating situations. *Appetite, 35*(3), 239–250.
Lumeng, J. C. & Fisher, J. O. (eds.) (2018). *Pediatric food preferences and eating behaviors.* Academic Press.
Lumeng, J. C., Ozbeki, T. N, Appugliese, D. P., Kaciroti, N., Corwyn, R. F., & Bradley, R. H. (2012). Observed assertive and intrusive maternal feeding behaviors increase child adiposity. *American Journal of Clinical Nutrition, 95*, 640–647.
Lupton, D. (1996). *Food, the body and the self.* Sage.
Lycett, K., Miller, A., Knox, A., Dunn, S., Kerr, J. A., Sung, V., & Wake, M. (2017). 'Nudge' interventions for improving children's dietary behaviors in the home: A systematic review. *Obesity Medicine, 7*, 21–33.

Madrelle, J., Lange, C., Boutrolle, I., Valade, O., Weenen, H., Monnery-Patris, S., Issanchou, S., & Nicklaus, S. (2017). Development of a new in-home testing method to assess infant food liking. *Appetite, 113*, 274–283.

Maher, V. (ed.) (2024). *Anthropology of breast-feeding: Natural law or social construct.* Taylor & Francis.

Mameli, C., Cattaneo, C., Panelli, S., Comandatore, F., Sangiorgio, A., Bedogni, G., . . . & Pagliarini, E. (2019). Taste perception and oral microbiota are associated with obesity in children and adolescents. *PLOS ONE, 14*(9), e0221656.

Mann, A. & Mol, A. (2019). Talking pleasures, writing dialects: Outlining research on Schmecka. *Ethnos, 84*(5), 772–788.

Mann, A., Mol, A., Satalkar, P., Savirani, A., Selim, N., Sur, M., & Yates-Doerr, E. (2011). Mixing methods, tasting fingers Notes on an ethnographic experiment. *Journal of Ethnographic Theory, 1*, 221–243.

Manno, C. J., Fox, C., Eicher, P. S., & Kerwin, M. E. (2005). Early oral-motor interventions for pediatric feeding problems: What, when and how. *Journal of Early and Intensive Behavior Intervention, 2*(3), 145.

Martins, Y. & Pliner, P. (2006). 'Ugh! That's disgusting!': Identification of the characteristics of foods underlying rejections based on disgust. *Appetite, 46*, 75–85.

Marty, L., Chambaron, S., Nicklaus, S., & Monnery-Patris, S. (2018). Learned pleasure from eating: An opportunity to promote healthy eating in children? *Appetite, 120*, 265–274.

Maxwell, C., Fleming, V., & Porcellato, L. (2023). Why have a bottle when you can have draught? Exploring bottle refusal by breastfed babies. *Maternal & Child Nutrition, 19*(2), e13481.

Maynard, D. W. & Gill, V. T. (2024). In J. Robinson, R. Clift, K. H. Kendrick, & C. W. Raymond (eds.) *The Cambridge handbook of methods in conversation analysis* (pp. 512–540). Cambridge University Press.

McIlvenny, P. (Producer), Davidsen, J. G. (Producer), Kovács, A. B. (Developer), & Stein, A. (Developer). (2022). *DOTE: Distributed Open Transcription Environment.* Computer programme, Github. https://github.com/BigSoftVideo/DOTE/

McNally, J., Hugh-Jones, S., Caton, S., Vereijken, C., Weenen, H., & Hetherington, M. (2016). Communicating hunger and satiation in the first 2 years of life: A systematic review. *Maternal and Child Nutrition, 12*, 205–228.

McNally, J., Hugh-Jones, S., Caton, S., Vereijken, C., Weenen, H., & Hetherington, M. M. (2019). The eyes have it: Infant gaze as an indicator of hunger and satiation. *Appetite, 133*, 353–361.

McNally, J., Hugh-Jones, S., & Hetherington, M. M. (2020). 'An invisible map': Maternal perceptions of hunger, satiation and 'enough' in the context of baby led and traditional complementary feeding practices. *Appetite, 148*, 104608.

McQuaid, J. (2016). *Tasty: The art and science of what we eat.* Scribner.

Mead, M. (1961). Anthropology Among the Sciences. *American Anthropologist, 63*: 475–482.

Mead, M. & Bateson, G. (1977). On the use of the camera in anthropology. *Studies in the Anthropology of Visual Communication, 4*(2), 78–80

Meiselman, H. (1992). Methodology and theory in human eating research. *Appetite, 19*, 49–55.

Meiselman, H. L. (2008). Dimensions of the meal. *Journal of Foodservice, 19*(1), 13–21.

Meiselman, H. L. (2020). *Handbook of eating and drinking: Interdisciplinary perspectives.* Springer.

Meiselmaan, H. L., Jaeger, S. R., Carr, B. T., & Churchill, A. (2022). Approaching 100 years of sensory and consumer science: Developments and ongoing issues. *Food Quality and Preference, 100*, 104614.

Meiselman, H. L., Johnson, J. L., Reeve, W., & Crouch, J. E. (2000). Demonstrations of the influence of the eating environment on food acceptance. *Appetite, 35*, 231–237.

Meiselman, H. L. & Schutz, H. G. (2003). History of food acceptance research in the US Army. *Appetite*, *40*(3), 199–216.

Mela, D. J. (2006). Eating for pleasure or just wanting to eat? Reconsidering sensory hedonic responses as a driver of obesity. *Appetite*, *47*(1), 10–17.

Mennell, S. (1996). *All manners of food: Eating and taste in England and France from the Middle Ages to the present*. University of Illinois Press.

Mennella, J. A. & Bobowski, N. K. (2015). The sweetness and bitterness of childhood: Insights from basic research on taste preferences. *Physiology & Behavior*, *152*, 502–507.

Mennella, J. A. & Castor, S. M. (2012). Sensitive period in flavor learning: Effects of duration of exposure to formula flavors on food likes during infancy. *Clinical Nutrition*, *31*(6), 1022–1025.

Mennella, J. A., Daniels, L. M., & Reiter, A. R. (2017). Learning to like vegetables during breastfeeding: A randomized clinical trial of lactating mothers and infants. *The American Journal of Clinical Nutrition*, *106*(1), 67–76.

Mennella, J. A., Forestell, C. A., Morgan, L. K., & Beauchamp, G. K. (2009). Early milk feeding influences taste acceptance and liking during infancy. *The American Journal of Clinical Nutrition*, *90*(3), 780S–788S.

Mennella, J. A., Nolden, A. A., & Bobowski, N. (2018). Measuring sweet and bitter taste in children: Individual variation due to age and taste genetics. In J. C. Lumeng & J. O. Fisher (eds.) *Pediatric Food Preferences and Eating Behaviors* (pp. 1–34). Academic Press.

Middleton, G., Golley, R. K., Patterson, K. A., & Coveney, J. (2022). The Family Meal Framework: A grounded theory study conceptualising the work that underpins the family meal. *Appetite*, *175*, 106071.

Miller, W. I. (1997). *The anatomy of disgust*. Harvard University Press.

Mita, S. C., Gray, S. A., & Goodell, L. S. (2015). An explanatory framework of teachers' perceptions of a positive mealtime environment in a preschool setting. *Appetite*, *90*, 37–44.

Mitchell, G. L., Farrow, C., Haycraft, E., & Meyer, C. (2013). Parental influences on children's eating behaviour and characteristics of successful parent-focussed interventions. *Appetite*, *60*, 85–94.

Moerman, M. (1988). *Talking culture: Ethnography and conversation analysis*. University of Pennsylvania Press.

Mol, A. (2021). *Eating in theory*. Duke University Press.

Mol, A. (2024). *Eating is an English word*. Duke University Press.

Momin, S. R., Hughes, S. O., Elias, C., Papaioannou, M. A., Phan, M., Vides, D., & Wood, A. C. (2018). Observations of toddlers' sensory-based exploratory behaviors with a novel food. *Appetite*, *131*, 108–116.

Mondada, L. (2009). The methodical organization of talking and eating: Assessments in dinner conversations. *Food Quality and Preference*, *20*, 558–571.

Mondada, L. (2011). Understanding as an embodied, situated and sequential achievement in interaction. *Journal of Pragmatics*, *43*, 542–552.

Mondada, L. (2013). Interactional space and the study of embodied talk-in-interaction. *Space in language and linguistics: Geographical, interactional and cognitive perspectives*, 247–275.

Mondada, L. (2014a). Ethics in action: Anonymization as a participant's concern and a participant's practice. *Human Studies*, *37*, 179–209.

Mondada, L. (2014b). The conversation analytic approach to data collection. In J. Sidnell & T. Stivers (eds.) *The handbook of conversation analysis* (pp. 32–56). Wiley.

Mondada, L. (2018). The multimodal interactional organization of tasting: Practices of tasting cheese in gourmet shops. *Discourse Studies*, *20*, 743–769.

Mondada, L. (2020a). Audible sniffs: Smelling-in-interaction. *Research on Language and Social Interaction*, *53*, 140–163.

Mondada, L. (2020b). Orchestrating multi-sensoriality in tasting sessions: Sensing bodies, normativity, and language. *Symbolic Interaction*.
Mondada, L. (2021). *Sensing in social interaction: The taste for cheese in gourmet shops*. Cambridge University Press.
Mondada, L. (2023). Tasting vs. eating: The methodic and situated differentiation of embodied multisensorial activities in social interaction. In P. Haddington, T. Eilittä, A. Kamunen, L. Kohonen-Aho, I. Rautiainen, & A. Vatanen (eds.) *Complexity of interaction: Studies in multimodal conversation analysis* (pp. 29–64). Springer Nature.
Mondada, L. (2025). The normative order of sensing: Enacting the tasting sheet in tasting training sessions. *Text & Talk*, *45*(1), 79–113.
Mondada, L. & Peräkylä, A. (2023). *New perspectives on Goffman in language and interaction*. Taylor & Francis.
Mescoloto, S. B., Pongiluppi, G., & Domene, S. M. Á. (2024). Ultra-processed food consumption and children and adolescents' health. *Jornal de pediatria*, *100*, S18–S30.
Mura Paroche, M., Caton, S. J., Vereijken, C. M., Weenen, H., & Houston-Price, C. (2017). How infants and young children learn about food: A systematic review. *Frontiers in Psychology*, *8*, 1046.
Murcott, A. (1982). On the social significance of the 'cooked dinner' in South Wales. *Social Science Information*, *21*(4–5), 677–696.
Murcott, A. (1997). 'The nation's diet': An overview of early results. *British Food Journal*, *99*(3), 89–96.
Murcott, A. (2012). Lamenting the 'decline of the family meal' as a moral panic? Methodological reflections. *Recherches sociologiques et anthropologiques*, *43*(43–1), 97–118.
Murcott, A. (2013). Family meals: A thing of the past? In P. Caplan (ed.) *Food, health and identity* (pp. 32–49). Routledge.
Murcott, A. (2019). *Introducing the sociology of food and eating*. Bloomsbury Publishing.
Nederkoorn, C., Jansen, A., & Havermans, R. C. (2015). Feel your food. The influence of tactile sensitivity on picky eating in children. *Appetite*, *84*, 7–10.
Nederkoorn, C., Theißen, J., Tummers, M., & Roefs, A. (2018). Taste the feeling or feel the tasting: Tactile exposure to food texture promotes food acceptance. *Appetite*, *120*, 297–301.
Negayama, K. (1993). Weaning in Japan: A longitudinal study of mother and child. *Early Development and Parenting*, *2*, 29–37.
Neuman, N. (2024). Commensal attraction: Eating together as a social tool. *Journal for the Theory of Social Behaviour*, *54*(4), 556–570.
Neuman, N. & Jönsson, H. (2024). Beyond conviviality: Facets of eating together. In T. Lestar, M. Pilato & E. Séraphin (eds.). *Eating together in the twenty-first century: Social challenges, community values, and individual wellbeing* (pp. 180–190). Routledge.
Neumark-Sztainer, D., Wall, M., Fulkerson, J. A., & Larson, N. (2013). Changes in the frequency of family meals from 1999 to 2010 in the homes of adolescents: Trends by sociodemographic characteristics. *Journal of Adolescent Health*, *52*(2), 201–206.
Nicklaus, S. (2016a). The role of food experiences during early childhood in food pleasure learning. *Appetite*, *104*, 3–9.
Nicklaus, S. (2016b). Complementary feeding strategies to facilitate acceptance of fruits and vegetables: A narrative review of the literature. *International Journal of Environmental Research and Public Health*, *13*(11), 1160.
Nicklaus, S. (2017). The role of dietary experience in the development of eating behavior during the first years of life. *Annals of Nutrition and Metabolism*, *70*, 241–245.

Nicklaus, S. & Schwartz, C. (2019). Early influencing factors on the development of sensory and food preferences. *Current Opening in Clinical Nutrition and Metabolic Care, 22*, 230–235.

Nicolas, L., Marquilly, C., & O'Mahony, M. (2010). The 9-point hedonic scale: Are words and numbers compatible? *Food Quality and Preference. 21*(8), 1008–1015.

Nishizaka, A. (2024) Single-case analysis. In J. Robinson, R. Clift, K. H. Kendrick, & C. W. Raymond (eds.) *The Cambridge handbook of methods in conversation analysis* (pp. 487–511). Cambridge University Press.

O'Leary, S. (2022). *Mealtime in Finnish kindergarten: Teachers' understanding of their role during mealtime.* Doctoral dissertation, Tamper University, Finland.

Ochs, E. (1982). Talking to children in Western Samoa. *Language in Society, 11*(1), 77–104.

Ochs, E. (1988). *Culture and language development: Language acquisition and language socialization in a Samoan village* (No. 6). CUP Archive.

Ochs, E., Pontecorvo, C., & Fasulo, A. (1996). Socializing taste. *Ethnos, 61*, 7–46

Ochs, E. & Shohet, M. (2006). The cultural structuring of mealtime socialization. *New Directions for Child and Adolescent Development, 111*, 83–97.

Ochs, E. & Schieffelin, B. B. (1979) (eds.) *Developmental pragmatics.* Academic Press.

Ogden, R. & Keevallik, L. (2020). Sounds on the margins of language at the heart of interaction. *Research on Language and Social Interaction, 53.* 1–18.

Orrell-Valente, J. K., Hill, L. G., Brechwald, W. A., Dodge, K. A., Pettit, G. S., & Bates, J. E. (2007). 'Just three more bites': An observational analysis of parents' socialization of children's eating at mealtime. *Appetite, 48*(1), 37–45.

Palfreyman, Z., Haycraft, E., & Meyer, C. (2014). Development of the Parental Modelling of Eating Behaviours Scale: Links with food intake among children and their mothers. *Maternal and Child Nutrition, 10*, 617–629.

Palfreyman, Z., Haycraft, E., & Meyer, C. (2015). Parental modelling of eating behaviours: Observational validation of the Parental Modelling of Eating Behaviours scale (PARM). *Appetite, 86*, 31–37.

Pan, B. A., Perlmann, R. Y., & Snow, C. E. (1999). Food for thought: Dinner table as a context for observing parent-child discourse. In L. Menn & H. Bernstein Rather (eds.) *Methods for studying language production* (pp. 205–224). Lawrence Erlbaum.

Paugh, A. & Izquierdo, C. (2009). Why is this a battle every night?: Negotiating food and eating in American dinnertime interaction. *Journal of Linguistic Anthropology, 19*, 185–204.

Paugh, A. & Riley, K. (forthcoming). *Food talk.* Routledge.

Pelchat, M. L. & Pliner, P. (1995). 'Try it. You'll like it.' Effects of information on willingness to try novel foods. *Appetite, 24*, 153–165.

Pérez-Escamilla, R., Curry, L., Minhas, D., Taylor, L., & Bradley, E. (2012). Scaling up of breastfeeding promotion programs in low-and middle-income countries: The 'breastfeeding gear' model. *Advances in Nutrition, 3*(6), 790–800.

Persson Osowski, C. & Mattsson Sydner, Y. (2019). The family meal as an ideal: Children's perceptions of foodwork and commensality in everyday life and feasts. *International Journal of Consumer Studies, 43*(2), 178–186.

Peryam, D. R. & Haynes, J. G. (1957). Prediction of soldiers' food preferences by laboratory methods. *Journal of Applied Psychology, 41*(1), 2–6.

Peryam, D. R. & Pilgrim, F. J. (1957). Hedonic scale method of measuring food preferences. *Food technology, 11*(S1), 9–14.

Pickard, A., Edwards, K. L., Farrow, C., Haycraft, E., Herle, M., Llewellyn, C., . . . & Blissett, J. (2025). Parents' use of coercive and indulgent feeding practices for children with avid eating behaviour: An Ecological Momentary Assessment study. *International Journal of Behavioral Nutrition and Physical Activity, 22*(1), 16.

Pliner, P. (1994). Development of measures of food neophobia in children. *Appetite*, *23*(2), 147–163.

Pliner, P. & Hobden, K. (1992). Development of a scale to measure the trait of food neophobia in humans. *Appetite*, *19*(2), 105–120.

Pliner, P. & Mann, N. (2004). Influence of social norms and palatability on amount consumed and food choice. *Appetite*, *42*, 227–237.

Podanovitch, H., Campbell, J. E., Rossiter, M. D., Whitfield, K. C., & McIsaac, J. L. D. (2025). 'A few more bites?': Manifestation of pressure-to-eat in child care. *Nutrition & Dietetics*, 1–11.

Pomerantz, A. (1980). Telling my side: 'Limited access' as a 'Fishing' device. *Sociological Inquiry*, *50*, 186–198.

Pomerantz, A. (1984a). Agreeing and disagreeing with assessments: Some features of preferred/dispreferred turn shapes. In J. M. Atkinson & J. Heritage (eds.) *Structures of Social Action* (pp. 57–101). Cambridge University Press.

Pomerantz, A. (1984b). Pursuing a response. In J. M. Atkinson & J. Heritage (eds.), *Structures of social action: Studies in conversation analysis* (pp152–163). Cambridge University Press.

Pomerantz, A. (2024). Evidence for claims about interactants' sense-making practices. In J. Robinson, R. Clift, K. H. Kendrick, & C. W. Raymond (eds.) *The Cambridge handbook of methods in conversation analysis* (pp. 356–385). Cambridge University Press.

Pontecorvo, C. & Fasulo, A. (1999). Planning a typical Italian meal: A family reflection on culture. *Culture & Psychology*, *5*, 313–335.

Pontecorvo, C., Fasulo, A., & Sterponi, L. (2001). Mutual apprentices: The making of parenthood and childhood in family dinner conversations. *Human Development*, *44*, 340–361.

Potter, J. (1996). *Representing reality: Discourse, rhetoric and social construction.* Sage.

Potter, J. (1998). Discursive social psychology: From attitudes to evaluative practices. *European Review of Social Psychology*, *9*(1), 233–266.

Potter, J. & Edwards, D. (2014). Sociolinguistics, cognitivism, and discursive psychology. In N. Coupland, S. Sarangi, & C.N. Candlin (eds.) *Sociolinguistics and social theory* (pp. 88–103). Routledge.

Potter, J. & Hepburn, A. (2020). Shaming interrogatives: Admonishments, the social psychology of emotion, and discursive practices of behaviour modification in family mealtimes. *British Journal of Social Psychology*, *59*(2), 347–364.

Potter, J. & Shaw, C. (2018). The virtues of naturalistic data. In U. Flick (ed.) *The SAGE handbook of qualitative data collection* (pp. 182–199). Sage.

Potter, J. & Wetherell, M. (1987). *Discourse and social psychology.* Sage.

Prout, A. & James, A. (2015). A new paradigm for the sociology of childhood? Provenance, promise and problems. In *Constructing and reconstructing childhood* (pp. 6–28). Routledge.

Pursi, A., Lipponen, L., & Sajaniemi, N. K. (2018). Emotional and playful stance taking in joint play between adults and very young children. *Learning, Culture and Social Interaction*, *18*, 28–45.

Qu, F., Chen, Y., Song, X., Wei, X., Wu, R., Wang, J., . . . & Zhu, D. (2025). Bidirectional association between parental pressure to eat and children's satiety responsiveness: The moderating effect of children's temperament. *Maternal & Child Nutrition*, *21*(2), e13766.

Quay, S. (2008). Dinner conversations with a trilingual two-year-old: Language socialization in a multilingual context. *First Language*, *28*(1), 5–33.

Ragelienė, T. & Grønhøj, A. (2020). The influence of peers' and siblings' on children's and adolescents' healthy eating behavior. A systematic literature review. *Appetite*, *148*, 104592.

Ramsay, S. A., Branen, L. J., Fletcher, J., Price, E., Johnson, S. L., & Sigman-Grant, M. (2010). 'Are you done?' Child care providers' verbal communication at mealtimes that reinforce or hinder children's internal cues of hunger and satiation. *Journal of Nutrition Education and Behavior*, *42*, 265–270.

Raymond, C.W., Clift, R., Kendrick, K.H. & Robinson, J.D. (2024). Methods of conversation analysis. In Robinson, J. D., Clift, R., Kendrick, K. H., & Raymond, C. W. (eds.). (2024). *The Cambridge handbook of methods in conversation analysis.* (p. 3–48). Cambridge University Press.

Raymond, C. W. & Robinson, J. D. (2024) Evidencing conversation analytic claims: How participants orient to social action. In J. Robinson, R. Clift, K. H. Kendrick, & C. W. Raymond (eds.) (2024) *The Cambridge handbook of methods in conversation analysis* (pp. 315–355). Cambridge University Press

Razuri, E. B., Hiles Howard, A. R., Purvis, K. B., & Cross, D. R. (2017). Mental state language development: The longitudinal roles of attachment and maternal language. *Infant Mental Health Journal*, *38*(3), 329–342.

Reber, E. (2012). *Affectivity in interaction: Sound objects in English.* John Benjamins.

Redsell, S. A., Slater, V., Rose, J., Olander, E. K., & Matvienko-Sikar, K. (2021). Barriers and enablers to caregivers' responsive feeding behaviour: A systematic review to inform childhood obesity prevention. *Obesity Reviews*, *22*(7), e13228.

Reverdy, C. (2011). Sensory education: French perspectives. In V. R. Preedy, R. R. Watson, & C. R. Martin (eds.) *Handbook of behavior, food and nutrition* (pp. 143–157). Springer New York.

Reverdy, C., Schlich, P., Köster, E. P., Ginon, E., & Lange, C. (2010). Effect of sensory education on food preferences in children. *Food Quality and Preference*, *21*(7), 794–804.

Reynolds, E. (2021). Respecifying dualities: The case of 'feel enquiries' used in sports coaching. In S. Wiggins & K. Osvaldsson Cromdal (eds.) *Discursive psychology and embodiment: Beyond subject-object binaries* (pp. 139–167). Palgrave.

Richards, K. & Seedhouse, P. (eds.) (2016). *Applying conversation analysis.* Springer.

Riley, K. C. & Paugh, A. L. (2018). *Food and language: Discourses and foodways across cultures.* Routledge.

Rioux, C., Lafraire, J., Picard, D., & Blissett, J. (2019). Food rejection in young children: Validation of the Child Food Rejection Scale in English and cross-cultural examination in the UK and France. *Food Quality and Preference*, *73*, 19–24.

Ritzer, G. (2000). *The McDonaldization of Society.* Thousand Oaks.

Robinson, J. D. (2007). The role of numbers and statistics within conversation analysis. *Communication Methods and Measures*, *1*(1), 65–75.

Robinson, J. D., Clift, R., Kendrick, K. H., & Raymond, C. W. (eds.) (2024). *The Cambridge handbook of methods in conversation analysis.* Cambridge University Press.

Rossano, F. (2014). Gaze in conversation. In J. Sidnell & T. Stivers (eds.) *The handbook of conversation analysis* (pp. 308–329). Wiley Blackwell.

Rozin, P., Lowery, L., & Ebert, R. (1994). Varieties of disgust faces and the structure of disgust. *Journal of Personality and Social Psychology*, *66*, 870–881.

Rozin, P., Haidt, J. & McCauley, C. (2000). Disgust. In M. Lewis & J. Haviland-Jones (eds.) *Handbook of emotions* (pp. 637–653). Guilford Press.

Rudolph, C. D. & Link, D. T. (2002). Feeding disorders in infants and children. *Pediatric Clinics*, *49*(1), 97–112.

Rüdiger, S. & Mühleisen, S. (eds.) (2020). *Talking about food: The social and the global in eating communities* (Vol 47). John Benjamins Publishing Company.

Sacks, H. (1992). *Lectures on conversation.* Blackwell.

Sacks, H., Schegloff, E. A., & Jefferson, G. (1974). A simplest systematics for the organization of turn-taking for conversation. *Language*, *50*, 696–735.

Schegloff, E. A. (2007). *Sequence organization in interaction: A primer in conversation analysis I.* Cambridge University Press.
Schegloff, E. A., & Sacks, H. (1973). Opening up closings. *Semiotica, 8*(4).
Schegloff, E. A., Jefferson, G., & Sacks, H. (1977). The preference for self-correction in the organization of repair in conversation. *Language, 53*(2), 361–382.
Schieffelin, B. B. (1990). *The give and take of everyday life: Language, socialization of Kaluli children* (No. 9). CUP Archive.
Schieffelin, B. B. & Ochs, E. (1986). Language socialization. *Annual Review of Anthropology, 15*, 163–191.
Schratz, L. M., Larkin, O., Dos Santos, N., & Martin, C. (2023). Caregiver influences on eating behaviors in children: An opportunity for preventing obesity. *Current Atherosclerosis Reports, 25*(12), 1035–1045.
Sepp, H. & Höijer, K. (2016). Food as a tool for learning in everyday activities at preschool – an exploratory study from Sweden. *Food & Nutrition Research, 60*(1), 32603.
Seymour-Smith, S., Gough, B., Matthews, C. R., & Rutherford, Z. (2020). Food assessment: A discursive analysis of diet talk in interviews with older men who are obese. *Psychology & Health, 35*(8), 946–967.
Shaw, C. (2024). Communicating findings to non-CA professionals. In J. D. Robinson, R. Clift, K. H. Kendrick, & C. W. Raymond (eds.) (2024). *The Cambridge handbook of methods in conversation analysis* (pp. 928–940). Cambridge University Press.
Shepherd, G. M. (2012). *Neurogastronomy: How the brain creates flavor and why it matters.* Columbia.
Shloim, N., Edelson, L. R., Martin, N., & Hetherington, M. M. (2015a). Parenting styles, feeding styles, feeding practices, and weight status in 4–12 year-old children: A systematic review of the literature. *Frontiers in Psychology, 6.*
Shloim, N., Rudolf, M., Feltbower, R., Mohebati, L., & Hetherington, M. (2015b). Breast is best: Positive mealtime interactions in breastfeeding mothers from Israel and the United Kingdom. *Health Psychology Open, 2.*
Shloim, N., Shafiq, I., Blundell-Birtill, P., & Hetherington, M. M. (2018). Infant hunger and satiety cues during the first two years of life: Developmental changes of within meal signalling. *Appetite, 128*, 303–310.
Shloim, N., Vereijken, C., Blundell, P., & Hetherington, M. (2017). Looking for cues: Infant communication of hunger and satiation during milk feeding. *Appetite, 108*, 74–82.
Shohet, M. (2018). Beyond the clinic? Eluding a medical diagnosis of anorexia through narrative. *Transcultural Psychiatry, 55*(4), 495–515.
Sidnell, J. (2011). The epistemics of make-believe. In T. Stivers, L. Mondada, & J. Steensig (eds.) *The morality of knowledge in conversation* (pp. 131–156). Cambridge University Press
Sidnell, J. (2014). Basic conversation analytic methods. In J. Sidnell & T. Stivers (eds.) *The handbook of conversation analysis* (pp. 77–99). Wiley Blackwell.
Sidnell, J. (2016). A conversation analytic approach to research on early childhood. In A. Farrell, S. L. Kagan, & E. K. M. Tisdall (eds.) *The SAGE handbook of early childhood research* (pp. 255–276). Sage Publications
Sidnell, J. & Stivers, T. (2014) (eds.) *The handbook of conversation analysis.* Wiley Blackwell.
Silkenbeumer, J., Lüken, L. M., Holodynski, M., & Kärtner, J. (2024). Emotion socialization in early childhood education and care: How preschool teachers support children's emotion regulation. *Social and Emotional Learning: Research, Practice, and Policy, 4*, 100057.
Simmel, G. (1910). *The sociology of the meal.*
Skafida, V. (2013). The family meal panacea: Exploring how different aspects of family meal occurrence, meal habits and meal enjoyment relate to young children' s diets. *Sociology of Health and Illness, 35*, 906–923.

Smith, B., Rogers, S. L., Blissett, J., & Ludlow, A. K. (2020). The relationship between sensory sensitivity, food fussiness and food preferences in children with neurodevelopmental disorders. *Appetite*, *150*, 104643.

Sneijder, P. & te Molder, H. F. M. (2004). 'Health should not have to be a problem': Talking health and accountability in an internet forum on veganism. *Journal of Health Psychology*, *9*, 599–616.

Sneijder, P. & te Molder, H. F. M. (2006). Disputing taste: Food pleasure as an achievement in interaction. *Appetite*, *46*, 107–116.

Sneijder, P. & te Molder, H. (2009). Normalizing ideological food choice and eating practices: Identity work in online discussions on veganism. *Appetite, 52*, 621–630.

Snow, C. & Beals, D. E. (2006). Mealtime talk that supports literacy development. *New directions for child and adolescent development*, *111*, 83–97.

Snuggs, S. & Harvey, K. (2023). Family mealtimes: A systematic umbrella review of characteristics, correlates, outcomes and interventions. *Nutrients*, *15*(13), 2841.

Sobal, J. & Nelson, M. K. (2003). Commensal eating patterns: A community study. *Appetite*, *41*(2), 181–190.

Splane, E. C., Rowland, N. E., & Mitra, A. (2024). *Psychology of eating: From biology to culture to policy*. Routledge.

Spence, C. (2017). *Gastrophysics: The new science of eating*. Penguin UK.

Steiner, J. E. (1979). Human facial expressions in response to taste and smell stimulation *Advances in Child Development and Behavior*, *13*(C), 257–295.

Sterponi, L. (2009). Accountability in family discourse: Socialization into norms and standards and negotiation of responsibility in Italian dinner conversations. *Childhood*, *16*, 441–459.

Stevanovic, M. & Weiste, E. (2017). Conversation analytic data session as a pedagogical institution. *Learning, Culture & Social Interaction, 15*, 1–17.

Stevenson, R. J., Oaten, M. J., Case, T. I., Repacholi, B. M., & Wagland, P. (2010). Children's response to adult disgust elicitors: Development and acquisition. *Developmental Psychology*, *46*, 165–177.

Stevenson, R. J., Serebro, J., Mruk, A., Martin-Rivera, D., Wyver, S., & Francis, H. M. (2024). Caregivers' attention toward, and response to, their child's interoceptive hunger and thirst cues. *Developmental Psychobiology*, *66*(6), e22531.

Stokoe, E. (2014). The Conversation Analytic Role-play Method (CARM): A method for training communication skills as an alternative to simulated role-play. *Research on language and social interaction, 47*(3), 255–265.

Stokoe, E., Antaki, C., Chrisostomou, L., Hendersen, E., Stewart, S. (2026). The softness of hard data: Discursive psychology, conversation analysis, and psychological science. *Qualitative Psychology*.

Stone, S. & Murakami, K. (2023). 'I like it when I can sit with my best friends': Exploration of children's agency to achieve commensality in school mealtimes. In G. Singh Lalli, A. Turner, & M. Rutland (eds.) *Food Futures in Education and Society* (pp. 207–216). Routledge.

Streeck, J., Goodwin, C. & Le Baron, C. (2011) (eds.) *Embodied interaction: Language and body in the material world*. Cambridge University Press.

Street, S., Simoncini, K., & Byrne, R. (2024). Peer influence on eating behaviour in early childhood: A scoping review. *Appetite*, *203*, 107708.

Sutton, D. E. (2010). Food and the senses. *Annual Review of Anthropology*, *39*, 209–223.

Svensson, H. (2024). Requesting another to taste: Passing food and the distribution of agency in the organization of bodily trajectories. *Discourse Studies*, 14614456241242945.

Svensson, H. (2025). Claiming and attributing (dis)taste: Issues of sharing a meal as a competent member. *Appetite*, *205*, 107546.

Swindle, T., Rutledge, J. M., Dix, B., & Whiteside-Mansell, L. (2017). Table Talk: development of an observational tool to assess verbal feeding communications in early care and education settings. *Public Health Nutrition*, *20*(16), 2869–2877.

Symons, M. (1994/2010). Simmel's gastronomic sociology: An overlooked essay. *Food and Foodways, 5*, 333–351.
Szatrowski, P. E. (2014). *Language and food: Verbal and nonverbal experiences.* John Benjamins.
Takeda, W. & Melby, M. K. (2017). Spatial, temporal, and health associations of eating alone: A cross-cultural analysis of young adults in urban Australia and Japan. *Appetite, 118*, 149–160.
Tan, C. C., Riley, H. O., Sturza, J., Lumeng, J. C., & Miller, A. L. (2021). Observed behavioral indicators of child satiation at mealtime: Associations with child characteristics and parent-reported child eating behaviors. *Appetite, 166*, 105480.
Taormina, P., McVittie, C., & McKinlay, A. (2021). 'This is not what it's supposed to be like': Avoiding unwelcome identifications associated with public breastfeeding. *American Journal of Qualitative Research, 5*(1), 30–43.
Taquet, J., Verbeken, S., & Goossens, L. (2024). Examining the whole plate: The role of the family context in the understanding of children's food refusal behaviors. *Eating Behaviors, 52*, 101828.
Taylor, C. M. & Emmett, P. M. (2019). Picky eating in children: Causes and consequences. *Proceedings of the Nutrition Society, 78*(2), 161–169.
Thompson, K. L., Romeo, C., Estrem, H. H. *et al.* (2025). Preparedness of speech language pathologists and occupational therapists to treat pediatric feeding disorder: A cross-sectional survey. *Dysphagia, 40*, 187–199.
Thomson, J. L., McCabe-Sellers, B. J., Strickland, E., Lovera, D., Nuss, H. J., Yadrick, K., Duke, S., & Bogle, M. L. (2010). Development and evaluation of WillTry. An instrument for measuring children's willingness to try fruits and vegetables. *Appetite, 54*(3), 465–472.
Tomara, E., Dagla, M., Antoniou, E., & Iatrakis, G. (2023). Ankyloglossia as a barrier to breastfeeding: A literature review. *Children, 10*(12), 1902.
Toyama, N. (2013). Japanese mother–infant collaborative adjustment in solid feeding. *Infant Behavior and Development, 36*(2), 268–278.
Toyama, N. (2014). The development of Japanese mother–infant feeding interactions during the weaning period. *Infant Behavior and Development, 37*(2), 203–215.
Treckel, P. A. (1989). Breastfeeding and maternal sexuality in colonial America. *The Journal of Interdisciplinary History, 20*(1), 25–51.
Trevarthen, C. & Aitken, K. J. (2001). Infant intersubjectivity: Research, theory, and clinical applications. *The Journal of Child Psychology and Psychiatry and Allied Disciplines, 42*(1), 3–48.
Tuomainen, H. (2014). Eating alone or together? Commensality among Ghanaians in London. *Anthropology of Food* (S10).
Udagawa, T. (2022). Rethinking family commensality: Through Japanese cases and Italian ones. In A. Nobayashi (ed.) *Making food in local and global contexts: Anthropological perspectives* (pp. 101–118). Springer.
Ustun, B., Reissland, N., Covey, J., Schaal, B., & Blissett, J. (2022). Flavor sensing in utero and emerging discriminative behaviors in the human fetus. *Psychological Science, 33*(10), 1651–1663.
Vacaru, S. V., Ma, S., van Schie, H. T., & Hunnius, S. (2022). Eating in synch: An investigation of parent-infant behaviour coordination during feeding interactions. *Infant Behavior and Development, 66*, 101669.
van den Brand, A. J. P., Hendriks-Hartensveld, A. E. M., Havermans, R. C., & Nederkoorn, C. (2023). Child characteristic correlates of food rejection in preschool children: A narrative review. *Appetite, 190*, 107044.
Van der Heijden, A., te Molder, H., Huma, B., & Jager, G. (2022). To like or not to like: Negotiating food assessments of children from families with a low socioeconomic position. *Appetite, 105853.*

Van der Horst, K. (2012). Overcoming picky eating. Eating enjoyment as a central aspect of children's eating behaviors. *Appetite, 58,* 567–574.

Van Dijk, M., Bruinsma, E., & Hauser, M. P. (2016). The relation between child feeding problems as measured by parental report and mealtime behavior observation: A pilot study. *Appetite, 99,* 262–267.

Van Dijk, M., Hunnius, S., & Van Geert, P. (2012). The dynamics of feeding during the introduction to solid food. *Infant Behavior and Development, 35,* 226–239.

van Dijk, M., Leonardi, G., Pérez, D. L., & Rączaszek-Leonardi, J. (2022). Co-regulation of movements during infant feeding. *Infant Behavior and Development, 69,* 101755.

van Dijk, M., van Voorthuizen, B., & Cox, R. F. A. (2018). Synchronization of mother-infant feeding behavior. *Infant Behavior and Development, 52,* 97–103.

Van Esterik, P. (2002). Contemporary trends in infant feeding research. *Annual Review of Anthropology, 31*(1), 257–278.

Van Esterik, P. & O'Connor, R. A. (2017). *The dance of nurture: Negotiating infant feeding* (Vol 6). Berghahn Books.

Vannini, P., Ahluwalia-Lopez, G., Waskul, D., & Gottschalk, S. (2010). Performing taste at wine festivals: A somatic layered account of material culture. *Qualitative Inquiry, 16*(5), 378–396.

Vannini, P., Waskul, D. & Gottschalk, S. (2014). *The senses in self, society, and culture: A sociology of the senses.* Routledge.

Ventura, A. (2022). *Promoting responsive feeding during breastfeeding, bottle-feeding, and the introduction to solid foods.* Academic Press.

Ventura, A., Hupp, M., & Lavond, J. (2021). Mother–infant interactions and infant intake during breastfeeding versus bottle-feeding expressed breast milk. *Maternal & Child Nutrition, 17*(4), e13185.

Ventura, A. K. & Birch, L. L. (2008). Does parenting affect children's eating and weight status? *International Journal of Behavioral Nutrition and Physical Activity, 5*(1), 15.

Videon, T. M. & Manning, C. K. (2003). Influences on adolescent eating patterns: the importance of family meals. *Journal of Adolescent Health, 32*(5), 365–373.

Visser, M. (2015). *The rituals of dinner: The origins, evolution, eccentricities, and meaning of table manners.* Open Road Media.

Vogel, E. & Mol, A. (2014). Enjoy your food: On losing weight and taking pleasure. *From Health Behaviours to Health Practices,* 145–157.

Walton, K., Kuczynski, L., Haycraft, E., Breen, A., & Haines, J. (2017). Time to re-think picky eating? A relational approach to understanding picky eating. *International Journal of Behavioral Nutrition and Physical Activity, 14*(1), 62.

Wang, L., Yang, Y., & Wang, G. (2022). The clean your plate campaign: Resisting table food waste in an unstable world. *Sustainability, 14*(8), 4699.

Warde, A. (1997). *Consumption, food and taste.* Sage.

Warde, A. & Martens, L. (2000). *Eating out: Social differentiation, consumption and pleasure.* Cambridge University Press.

Wardle, J., Guthrie, C. A., Sanderson, S., & Rapoport, L. (2001). Development of the children's eating behaviour questionnaire. *The Journal of Child Psychology and Psychiatry and Allied Disciplines, 42*(7), 963–970.

Wardle, J., Sanderson, S., Guthrie, C. A., Rapoport, L., & Plomin, R. (2002). Parental feeding style and the inter-generational transmission of obesity risk. *Obesity Research, 10*(6), 453–462.

Waring, H. Z. (2025). Invoking (dis)likes at the dinner table. *Symbolic Interaction, 49*(2), 421–447.

Waring, H. Z. & Yu, D. (2017). Crying as a child resource for renegotiating a 'done deal'. Research on Children and Social Interaction, *1*(2), 116–140.

Weiser, H., Waling, M., & Bohm, I. (2026). Food-related sensory activities for children in educational settings: A scoping review. *Appetite, 216*, 108259.

Wergedahl, H. (2024). Eating together: Staff members' perceptions of a social lunch meal in kindergarten. In T, Lestar, M. M. Pilato, & H. Séraphin (eds.), *Eating together in the twenty-first century* (pp. 88–98). Routledge.

Wetherill, M. S., Williams, M. B., Reese, J., Taniguchi, T., Sisson, S. B., Malek-Lasater, A. D., Love, C. V., & Jernigan, V. B. B. (2021). Methods for assessing willingness to try and vegetable consumption among children in indigenous early childcare settings: The fresh study. *Nutrients, 14*(1), Article 58.

Whitfield, K. C. & Ventura, A. K. (2019). Exploration of responsive feeding during breastfeeding versus bottle feeding of human milk: a within-subject pilot study. *Breastfeeding Medicine, 14*(7), 482–486.

World Health Organization & United Nations Children's Fund. (2023). *Nurturing young children through responsive feeding: Thematic brief.* https://iris.who.int/handle/10665/367886

Wichchukit, S. & O'Mahony, M. (2015). The 9-point hedonic scale and hedonic ranking in food science: Some reappraisals and alternatives. *Journal of the Science of Food and Agriculture, 95*(11), 2167–2178.

Widen, S. C. & Russell, J. A. (2010). The 'disgust face' conveys anger to children. *Emotion, 10*, 455–466.

Widen, S. C. & Russell, J. A. (2011). In building a script for an emotion, do preschoolers add its cause before its behavior consequence? *Social Development, 20*, 471–485.

Wiggins, S. (2002). Talking with your mouth full: Gustatory mmms and the embodiment of pleasure. *Research on Language & Social Interaction, 35*, 311–336.

Wiggins, S. (2004). Good for 'you': Generic and individual healthy eating advice in family mealtimes. *Journal of Health Psychology, 9*, 535–548.

Wiggins, S. (2013). The social life of 'eugh': Disgust as assessment in family mealtimes. *British Journal of Social Psychology, 52*, 489–509.

Wiggins, S. (2014a). Adult and child use of love, like, don't like and hate during family mealtimes. Subjective category assessments as food preference talk. *Appetite, 80*, 7–15.

Wiggins, S. (2014b). Family mealtimes, yuckiness, and the socialisation of disgust responses by preschool children. In P. Szatrowski (ed.) *Language and food: Verbal and nonverbal experiences* (pp. 211–232). John Benjamins Publishing Company.

Wiggins, S. (2017). Discursive psychology: Theory, method, and applications. London: Sage.

Wiggins, S. (2019). Moments of pleasure: A preliminary classification of gustatory mmms and the enactment of enjoyment during infant mealtimes. *Frontiers in Psychology, 10*, 1404.

Wiggins, S. (2023). How infant food likes become established as knowledge: Parental food assessments during infant mealtimes in the home. *Appetite, 184*, 106489.

Wiggins, S. (2025). Sticky categories, discursive practices, and the potential for change: The case of children's food 'likes'. *Journal of Language and Social Psychology, 44*(3–4), 319–342.

Wiggins, S. (2026). When eating becomes collaborative: Co-eating examples from children's mealtimes. *Research on Language and Social Interaction.*

Wiggins, S., Cromdal, J., & Willemsen, A. (2024). Daring to taste: The organisation of children's tasting practices during preschool lunches. *Appetite, 198*, 107378.

Wiggins, S. & Humă, B. (2026a). Resisting eating during a family mealtime: The moral and identity work of food refusal. *British Journal of Social Psychology, 65*(1), e70029.

Wiggins, S. & Humă, B. (2026b). How to do discursive psychology. *Qualitative Psychology*, (January).

Wiggins, S. & Keevallik, L. (2021a). Enacting gustatory pleasure on behalf of another: The multimodal coordination of infant tasting practices. *Symbolic Interaction*, *44*(1), 87–111.
Wiggins, S. & Keevallik, L. (2021b). Parental lip-smacks during infant mealtimes: Multimodal features and social functions. *Interactional Linguistics*, *1*(2), 241–272.
Wiggins, S. & Keevallik, L. (2023). Transformations of disgust in interaction: The intertwinement of face, sound, and the body. *Social Interaction. Video-Based Studies of Human Sociality*, *6*(2).
Wiggins, S. & Keevallik, L. (2026) Disgust at the table: The sequential location and production of young children's food disgust expressions in the home and preschool. *Research on Children and Social Interaction, 9*(2).
Wiggins, S. & Laurier, E. (2020). Our daily bread and onions: Negotiating tastes in family mealtime interaction. In E. Falconer (ed.) *Space, taste and affect* (pp. 115–128). Routledge.
Wiggins, S., Majlesi, A. R., Ekström, A., Hydén, L.-C., & Cekaite, A. (2024). How assisted eating becomes a caring practice in institutional settings: Embodied gestures and stages of assisted eating. *Appetite*, *200.*
Wiggins, S. & Osvaldsson Cromdal, K. (2020). Multimodal konstruktion av psykologiska fenomen. In M.Broth & L.Keevallik (Eds.), Multimodal interaktionsanalys. (p.217-234). Studentlitteratur.
Wiggins, S. & Potter, J. (2003). Attitudes and evaluative practices: Category vs. item and subjective vs. objective constructions in everyday food assessments. *British Journal of Social Psychology*, *42*, 513–531.
Wiggins, S., Potter, J., & Wildsmith, A. (2001). Eating your words: Discursive psychology and the reconstruction of eating practices. *Journal of Health Psychology*, *6*.
Wiggins, S., Willemsen, A., & Cromdal, J. (2023). Eating prickly peas: Sharing play worlds during preschool meals. *International Journal of Early Childhood*, *56*, 1–18.
Wiggins, S., Cromdal, J., Willemsen, A. & Nyberg-Akremi, S. (2026, in press). Pedagogical appetites: Negotiating how much food children can eat during preschool lunches. In K. Eriksson Barajas & A. Rydén Gramner (eds.) *Discursive Psychology and Education*. Palgrave.
Wilhite, M. (1983). Children's acquisition of language routines: The end-of-meal routine in Cakchiquel. *Language in Society*, *12*(1), 47–64.
Wilk, R. (2010). Power at the table: Food fights and happy meals. *Cultural Studies? Critical Methodologies*, *10*(6), 428–436.
Wilkinson, N. M., Hetherington, M. M., Kannan, S., Ganguri, H., & Evans, C. E. L. (2025). High willingness-to-taste in UK children aged 4–7 years was driven by contextual facilitation, not intervention, in a randomized controlled trial of sensory food education. *Appetite*, *204*, 107756.
Williamson, F. A., Layton, D., & Lester, J. N. (2025). Producing trustworthiness: Locating the adequacy of findings in interactional research. *Qualitative Inquiry*, *32*(6), 11–18.
Wittgenstein, L. (1953). *Philosophical investigations.* Blackwells.
Wolstenholme, H., Kelly, C., & Heary, C. (2022). 'Fussy eating' and feeding dynamics: School children's perceptions, experiences, and strategies. *Appetite*, *173*, 106000.
Wootton, A. J. (1994). Object transfer, intersubjectivity and third position repair: Early developmental observations of one child. *Journal of Child Language*, *21*(3), 543–564.
Yates, L. & Warde, A. (2017). Eating together and eating alone: Meal arrangements in British households. *The British Journal of Sociology*, *68*(1), 97–118.

Yeomans, M. R. (2020). Satiety. In H. L. Meiselman (ed.) *Handbook of eating and drinking: Interdisciplinary perspectives* (pp. 1–22). Springer International Publishing.

Yu, S., Birtill, P., Fildes, A., Tang, T., & Hetherington, M. M. (2025a). Towards developing a 'baby translator': An exploration of how infant appetite cues are understood. *Appetite*, *206*, 107850.

Yu, S., Fildes, A., Birtill, P., Tang, T., & Hetherington, M. M. (2025b). Tuning into affect and appetite in caregivers, and its association with recognising and responding to infant appetite cues. *Maternal & Child Nutrition*, e70099.

Zeskind, P. S., Sale, J., Maio, M. L., Huntington, L., & Weiseman, J. R. (1985). Adult perceptions of pain and hunger cries: A synchrony of arousal. *Child Development*, *56*(3), 549–554.

Zotevska, E. & Martín-Bylund, A. (2022). How to do things with food: The rules and roles of mealtime 'things' in everyday family dinners. *Children & Society*, *36*(5), 857–876.

INDEX